"Behold, He Cometh!"

"Behold, He Cometh!"

A Verse-by-Verse Commentary on
the Book of Revelation

By
John R. Rice, D.D., Litt. D.

SWORD OF THE LORD PUBLISHERS
Box 1099   Murfreesboro, Tennessee 37130

Printed and bound in the United States of America

Table of Contents

CHAPTER 3

CHAPTER 4

CHAPTER 5

AN INTERLUDE BETWEEN
CHAPTERS 5 AND 6

CHAPTER 6

CHAPTER 7

CHAPTER 19

CHAPTER 20

CHAPTER 21

CHAPTER 22

Introduction

This book is God's *revelation*. It is not His *concealment*. God intended the book to be read and understood by common Christians, so He said, "Blessed is he that readeth" (Rev. 1:3).

So we take it that Christians with humble, believing hearts who simply mean business and give attention to it, as an honest heart ought to seek the truth, can understand the book of Revelation.

First, you should begin where God begins on prophecy, that is, in the Old Testament.

1. God had a covenant with Abraham, repeated many times, that the land of Palestine would be given to Abraham and his descendants but particularly to Abraham and his Seed, Christ (Gal. 3:16). The land of Canaan is to be "an everlasting possession." If I take that as an honest statement of fact, I should expect the millennial reign of Christ and beyond on the new earth, when I come to it in the book of Revelation.

2. God said to David that He would establish, in the future, the throne of His kingdom forever (II Sam. 7:16). And Isaiah 11 tells of that Branch from the root of David who will reign. When the Angel Gabriel spoke to the virgin Mary about the coming birth of Christ, he said, "And the Lord God shall give unto him the throne of his father David: And he shall reign over the house of Jacob for ever; and of his kingdom there shall be no end" (Luke 1:32,33).

3. Then the Saviour foretold the miraculous regathering of His elect, Israel, by angels after the tribulation period (Matt. 24:29-31). Isaiah, Jeremiah, Ezekiel, Zechariah and other prophets have all foretold this marvelous regathering of Israel. Not Zionism, with the rebellious, Christ-rejecting, unbelieving Jews taking by force land from the Arab owners. Not now, but after the tribulation time when Israel will turn to Christ and be cir-

cumcised in heart to serve God. Deuteronomy 30:1-6 tells how they will be regathered and converted. Rebels will be purged out of Israel at the wilderness of wanderings (Ezek. 20:35-38).The remnant will see the return to the Saviour and be saved, a nation in a day. So we approach Revelation knowing God has plans for Palestine and for the remnant of the Jewish nations who will be saved.

But Daniel, also, is the introduction to the book of Revelation. The book of Daniel tells of four great world empires: Babylon, Media-Persia, Greece and Rome. Then it tells how the Roman Empire more or less dissolves into the two legs and then the ten toes of that statue in Daniel 2. Then eventually it will be regathered and the Roman Empire will be revived under a world dictator. So we find him the "Man of Sin" in "the Beast" of Revelation. And there are even hints and types and pictures of him in the Pharaoh of the Exodus, and Antiochus Epiphanes mentioned in Daniel. But Daniel told, too, of that Great Stone—really Christ Himself—cut out of a mountain and falling to grind the great statue of the world empires to powder and then He becomes the King who rules the whole earth.

We must take the Bible literally whenever the context allows it.

Two witnesses are two witnesses. They are real people, foretold back in the Old Testament, but they appear in Revelation again.

The battles described in Revelation are real battles. When God speaks of seventy weeks of years and sixty-nine of those weeks have already been fulfilled, then the honest attitude would be to take the other remaining week of Daniel's prophecy as seven years. And when the Bible speaks of the Antichrist appearing in the middle of the week to commit the abomination of desolation and claim to be Christ and demand to be worshiped, we have a right to believe that the middle of the week leaves 3½ years, or 42 months, or 1,260 days, or "a time and times and the dividing of time," as the Bible variously tells us.

When Christ reigns a thousand years, and the number is named six times in Revelation, chapter 20, an honest heart attitude demands we take it for one thousand years.

When Christ so often said, "But of that day and hour knoweth no man, no, not the angels of heaven, but my Father only" (Matt. 24:36), and such statements in Mark 13:32, in Matthew 25:13, etc., then why should anybody tolerate setting up a schedule of events and ages that must come and be fulfilled before Christ comes? No, we should simply be content not to know when. And when Christ warned the apostles, "And what I say unto you I say unto all, Watch" (Mark 13:37), then an honest reader can take it at face value that Christ might have come during the time of the apostles; He may come now at any time. We are bound to believe that the any-moment rapture is possible, that Christ's coming is imminent, that is, unpredicted as to when, but certain and possible at any moment.

Now I congratulate you that you are starting out to study this marvelous book of Revelation. If we can be of some help to you and make the Word precious and sweet and clear, we will be glad.

John R. Rice

Murfreesboro, Tennessee
September, 1977

"Behold, He Cometh"

A Verse-by-Verse Commentary on the Book of Revelation

Chapter 1

VERSES 1—3:

THE Revelation of Jesus Christ, which God gave unto him, to shew unto his servants things which must shortly come to pass; and he sent and signified *it* by his angel unto his servant John:

2 Who bare record of the word of God, and of the testimony of Jesus Christ, and of all things that he saw.

3 Blessed *is* he that readeth, and they that hear the words of this prophecy, and keep those things which are written therein: for the time *is* at hand.

This book of the Bible is "The Revelation of Jesus Christ," not "The Revelation of St. John the Divine," as it is titled in the King James Version. The writer was quite evidently the Apostle John. He is named in verses 1, 4 and 9 in this first chapter and in 22:8 (the last chapter). The book was inspired and written on the Isle of Patmos (vs. 9), where John was exiled for preaching the Word of God.

The message was given by an angel. Halley's Handbook says:

Angels play a large part in directing the panorama and scenery of the visions, and in the writing of the book. An angel dictated the book to John (1:2; 22:16). Each of the Seven Churches had an angel (1:20; 2:1, etc.) An angel was interested in the Sealed Book (5:2). 100,000,000 angels sang praise to the Lamb (5:11). Four angels were given power to hurt the earth (7:1-4). An angel sealed the Elect (7:1-4). The angels fell down on their faces before God (7:11). An angel was used in answering prayers of the saints (8:3-5). Seven angels sounded the Seven Trumpets (8:6, 7, etc.). An angel of the abyss was king of the locust army (9:11). Four angels loosed 200,000,000 Euphratean horsemen (9:15, 16). An angel had the open book, announcing the end (10:1, 2, 6). Michael and his angels warred with dragon and his angels (12:7). A flying angel proclaimed the Gospel to the nations (14:6). Another flying angel proclaimed the fall of Babylon (14:8). An angel pronounced doom of the beast's followers (14:9, 10). An angel announced the harvest of the earth (14:15). An angel announced the vintage of the earth (14:18, 19). Seven angels had the Seven Last Plagues (15:1). An angel announced judgment on Babylon (17:1, 5). An angel again announced the fall of Babylon (18:2). An angel had part in dealing Babylon its death-blow (18:21). An angel presided over the destruction of the beast (19:17). An angel bound Satan (20:12). An angel showed John the New Jerusalem (21:9). Twelve angels guarded the twelve gates of the New Jerusalem (21:19). An angel forbade John to worship him (22:9).

Thus, here, in the book of Revelation, are twenty-seven different references to the activities of angels.

Walvoord says in his book, *The Revelation of Jesus Christ,* page 13:

> The evidence for John the Apostle hangs largely on the question whether the Apostle John actually was exiled on the Isle of Patmos, as the author of this book claims (1:9). There is good historical evidence in support of this claim. Clement of Alexandria refers to the Apostle John as returning from the Isle of Patmos. Eusebius not only affirms John's return from the isle but dates it immediately following the death of Domitian, which occurred in A.D. 96.
>
> Irenaeus adds his confirming word when he states that John lived in Ephesus after returning from Patmos until the reign of Trajan. Though the Scriptures do not dogmatically confirm that John the Apostle is the author, the existing evidence is heavily in favor of this conclusion.

This John wrote the three letters: I John, II John, III John, and the fourth Gospel—the same John who leaned his head on the bosom of Jesus, and into whose hands Jesus gave His mother at the crucifixion.

Many give this brief outline of the book:

1. Introduction—Chap. 1
2. Seven Churches—Chap. 2 and 3
3. Seven Seals—Chap. 4-7 (including 8:1). Lead to
4. Seven Trumpets—Chap. 8-11. Lead to
5. Seven Bowls—Chap. 12-16

6. Seven Dooms—Chap. 17-20

7. Conclusion—Chap. 21 and 22.

This is "The Revelation of Jesus Christ," and that is the theme of the book. So everything in the book of Revelation looks forward to and clusters around that marvelous time when Christ shall come with clouds, revealed visibly to every human being on earth, and the details that precede and follow His wonderful return.

Dr. H. A. Ironside shows how Revelation completes the circle started in Genesis:

> The Word of God is one absolutely perfect, unbroken and unbreakable circle. A comparison of Genesis and Revelation will readily make this plain, and show how we have the types in Genesis and the completion of the truth in Revelation—in the one book the beginning, in the other the consummation.
>
> Genesis gives us the creation of the heavens and the earth. Revelation presents a new heaven and a new earth.
>
> Genesis shows us the earthly paradise, with the tree of life and the river of blessing, lost through sin. Revelation gives us the Paradise of God with the Tree of Life and the pure river of water of life proceeding out of the throne of God and the Lamb—Paradise regained through Christ's atonement.
>
> In Genesis we see the first man and his wife set over all God's creation. In Revelation we behold the Second Man and His Bride ruling over a redeemed world.
>
> In Genesis we are told of the first typical sacrificial lamb. In Revelation the Lamb once slain is in the midst of the throne.
>
> In Genesis we learn of the beginning of sin, when the serpent first entered the garden of delight to beguile Adam and Eve with his sophistries. In Revelation that old Serpent called the Devil and Satan is cast into the lake of fire.
>
> In Genesis we have the first murderer, the first polygamist, the first rebel, the first drunkard, etc. In Revelation all such, who refuse to accept God's grace in Christ Jesus, are banished from His presence forever.
>
> In Genesis we view the rise of Babel, or Babylon. In Revelation we are called to contemplate its doom.
>
> In Genesis we see man's city; in Revelation the city of God.
>
> Genesis shows us how sorrow, death, pain and tears, the inevitable accompaniments of sin and rebellion, came into the world. Revelation does not close until we have seen God wiping away all tears, and welcoming His redeemed into a home where

sin, death, pain and sorrow never come.

And so we might go on and on contrasting and comparing these two books. . . .

Verse 1 says, *"The Revelation of Jesus Christ, which God gave unto him. . . ."* God gave to Christ revelation about Christ's future coming!

We remember that Mark 13:32 says, "But of that day and that hour knoweth no man, no, not the angels which are in heaven, neither the Son, but the Father." So we understand that when Jesus became a man, He laid aside some of the outward garments and manifestations of His deity. He was God on earth, but He had humbled Himself and taken on Himself the form of a servant, so He gave up some of the things He had a right to as God.

We learn that as a boy He "increased in wisdom and stature, and in favour with God and man" (Luke 2:52). We know that He "learned. . .obedience by the things which he suffered" (Heb. 5:8).

Are we to understand, then, that Christ, who did not while living on earth know the time of the Second Coming, after His resurrection then had all that revealed to Him from the Father? Yes, at His death and resurrection He entered into the glory He had with the Father before the world began. And God revealed to Him whatever He had temporarily laid aside in knowledge. Of course He knew all that God the Father knew before He became Man, and He knows now all that the Father knows. This is "The Revelation of Jesus Christ, which God gave unto him" [His Son].

This is a revelation of *"things which must shortly come to pass. . . ."* Then the book of Revelation is primarily of future events prefaced by letters to seven churches. To us who take the Bible literally and at face value, the book of Revelation is not a symbolic and allegorical presentation of the times in which it was written, but a revelation of the future.

And that theme is expressed very strongly in verse 7: *"Behold, he cometh with clouds; and every eye shall see him. . . ."* So the book is about the revelation of Jesus Christ, particularly about the Second Coming and events surrounding that event.

The things *"which must SHORTLY come to pass. . . ."* The

Greek word is *tachei* and is so used in Acts 25:4; Romans 16:20 and in Revelation 22:6. The word means quickly or speedily. It does not mean immediately; it does not mean *soon*, since it is used about the destruction of Satan in Romans 16:20 and about the Heavenly Jerusalem coming down from Heaven after the millennial reign in Revelation 22:6.

In other words, this refers to the imminence of Christ's coming, that is, it is always impending but not at any set time. Christ might have come at any time, let us say, since Pentecost and may come now at any moment, and the things that are prophesied would follow; but it is obviously an indefinite reference, not setting a date even approximately.

The Basic Truth: Christ's Imminent Coming

The one thing the Lord Jesus most often emphasized about His Second Coming was that no one could possibly know the time. In Matthew 24:36 He said, "But of that day and hour knoweth no man, no, not the angels of heaven, but my Father only."

Mark 13:32-37 says:

"But of that day and that hour knoweth no man, no, not the angels which are in heaven, neither the Son, but the Father. Take ye heed, watch and pray: for ye know not when the time is. For the Son of man is as a man taking a far journey, who left his house, and gave authority to his servants, and to every man his work, and commanded the porter to watch. Watch ye therefore: for ye know not when the master of the house cometh, at even, or at midnight, or at the cockcrowing, or in the morning: Lest coming suddenly he find you sleeping. And what I say unto you I say unto all, Watch."

Any honest interpretation of that passage must mean that a Christian is to watch regularly and pray expectantly, knowing that Christ Jesus may come at any time, at any moment. If the apostles were commanded to watch in their lifetime, then Jesus could have come in their lifetime. And then He gives all of us the same command—to watch.

In Matthew 25:13, after the parable of the ten virgins and the sudden coming of the bridegroom, Jesus says, "Watch therefore, for ye know neither the day nor the hour wherein the Son of man cometh."

Jesus did not say, "Watch for the Antichrist" or, "Watch, for the tribulation events." Jesus must come before them. We are to watch for Christ's coming.

That teaching is so plain that no one has a right to interpret any Scripture to contradict it. Not a single Scripture gives any evidence that Christ's coming for His own waits on any prophesied event. Christ could have come before the rise of the papacy, before the thirty years' war in Europe, before the first World War, before the second World War, before the rise of communism, before the atomic bomb. It is unscholarly and spiritually less than honest to teach that anyone can know when the end of this age approaches or tell when the Saviour is coming.

Paul himself, obeying the plain command of Jesus to watch, expected to be alive at Christ's coming when "the dead in Christ shall rise first: Then we which are alive and remain shall be caught up together with them in the clouds, to meet the Lord in the air" (I Thess. 4:16, 17).

He said again in I Corinthians 15:51, 52, "We shall not all sleep, but we shall all be changed, In a moment, in the twinkling of an eye, at the last trump: for the trumpet shall sound, and the dead shall be raised incorruptible, and we shall be changed." Ah, Paul said, "The dead shall be raised and we shall be changed." He expected to be among the living who would be changed.

New Testament Christians were all taught to continually watch for Christ's coming. In I Thessalonians 1:9, 10 Paul writes, ". . .how ye turned to God from idols to serve the living and true God; And to wait for his Son from heaven." And in Philippians 3:20 the inspired Word says, "For our conversation is in heaven; from whence also we look for the Saviour, the Lord Jesus Christ." The one basic foundation truth about Christ's literal return is clearly stated: *No one can know when.* There are no signs by which one may tell when the time approaches.

We speak of the Second Coming of Christ as a series of events, including two phases. First, when we are called out to meet

Christ in the air at the rapture, and second, when Christ returns with His saints and angels to set up His kingdom and reign. When I speak of the first coming of Christ, I do not simply mean the day He was born in Bethlehem, but the whole matter of His incarnation, His virgin birth, His ministry and death and resurrection.

The time of the first phase of Christ's coming is a secret known only to God. After Christ comes to receive His own, then there is a clear-cut schedule in the Bible of events that will follow.

Therefore No "Signs" by Which Anybody Can Tell When End of Age Approaches

It is an old, sad and carnal business to try to set dates for Christ's return. Though the Lord plainly said to the disciples, "It is not for you to know" (Acts 1:7), in the year 1,000 many, many jumped to the conclusion that at the close of the age Christ would come.

Martin Luther thought the pope was the Antichrist. Farmer Miller in New York State saw some falling stars, read in the book of Daniel, decided that a day meant a year, figured out that the Lord must come in October of 1843. Others listened and got ready. Christ didn't come. Farmer Miller refigured and decided he was a year too early, but a year later, neither did the Lord Jesus come.

Every kind of cult and false teacher tries to set up some particular time to show how wise he is, that he can tell when Christ is coming. All that is utterly unscriptural.

People falsely interpret Scriptures to contradict the plain statement that no one can know about the time of His coming.

"The sign of thy coming, and of the end of the world" in Matthew 24:3 is explained as not an evidence of the first phase of His coming, but simply the miraculous appearance when Christ returns with His saints and angels after the rapture, after the tribulation (Matt. 24:30, 31).

The great "falling away" of II Thessalonians 2:3 is rather "the departure," that is, when Christians are caught up to meet Christ in the air.

"As ye see the day approaching" in Hebrews 10:25 means the destruction of Jerusalem, not the Second Coming.

The "end time" or the "time of the end," mentioned frequently in Daniel, is always the Great Tribulation time for Israel, not the closing days of this age.

The "budding of the fig tree" of Matthew 24:32 is the miraculous regathering of Israel after the rapture, after the tribulation, after Christ returns in glory and sends His angels to gather every Jew together in the world. Infidel Zionists or Christ-rejecting Zionists now could not fulfill that Scripture. There are no signs by which anyone can tell when the coming of Christ is near. It is always imminent but unpredictable. The time is a secret known only to God.

A Blessing in Reading Revelation

"Blessed is he that readeth, and they that hear the words" (vs. 3). It is blessed to read any part of the Bible. The 1st Psalm says, "Blessed is the man. . .his delight is in the law of the Lord; and in his law doth he meditate day and night. And he shall be like a tree planted by the rivers of water, that bringeth forth his fruit in his season; his leaf also shall not wither; and whatsoever he doeth shall prosper." But there is a special blessing in Revelation because the course of the age becomes more clear. We can have courage in affliction and persecution. We can know how God will triumph wonderfully in the future. We will know about Christ's return, His reign, about the Heavenly Jerusalem. What a comfort and blessing in this book of Revelation!

The Second Coming of Christ is "that blessed hope" (Titus 2:13) and so Revelation has special blessing telling about Christ's coming. God meant the book of Revelation, then, to be read, preached and understood. There is a blessing of God on all study of the Scripture, but verse 3 shows that there is a *special* blessing on those that read and hear the words of *this* prophecy. No such special promise of blessing is attached to any other portion of God's Word, although, of course, blessings do follow the reading of all portions of Holy Scripture. Dr. L. W. Munhall once said that he read it once every six weeks, for he wanted the promised blessing.

Postmillennial and amillennial preachers who teach that the book of Revelation is of little importance, hard to understand, that a study of it is largely speculation, and that most of it has already been fulfilled, speak out of their ignorance and indifference toward the Second Coming of Christ. They do very great harm and sin against God and His people.

As God has promised a special blessing to those who study the book of Revelation *"and keep those things which are written therein"* (vs. 3), so the book closes with a special warning to those who add to or take from this book (Rev. 22:18, 19). Study this book, then, expecting to understand it. Pray for the Holy Spirit to guide you. Believe what God has said, that in this book He is showing us the things which must shortly come to pass. Take God's Word at face value. Do not spiritualize it away. Do not make everything symbolical or figurative. When God says *blood,* take it to mean blood, even if it is a river of blood flowing to the bridles of the horses (Rev. 14:20) and for a course of 1,600 furlongs or 200 miles (Rev. 14:20). If God's Word says 42 months, or 1,260 days, or 3½ times (or years), then take it as it was meant to be taken, that is, a revelation to be plainly understood. The days mean days, not years. The time element in Revelation is literal. And where symbolical language is used, the key is always given in the Scripture itself. To understand the Bible does not take a vivid imagination; just a simple, humble, childlike faith, willing to believe what God has said.

The book of Revelation, then, has a very great claim on the Christian as one of the most important books of the Bible. It is the very last inspired Word that God Almighty ever gave; it is a prophecy of the future. God Himself put more emphasis on Revelation than on most other books of the Bible.

Take it seriously, then, and study it long and prayerfully.

————————

VERSE 4:

4 JOHN to the seven churches which are in Asia: Grace *be* unto you, and peace, from him which is, and which was, and which is to come; and from the seven Spirits which are before his throne;

To the Seven Churches of Asia

Asia now, to most, means the whole continent. Sometimes the word refers to Asia Minor, that peninsula which is a large part of the country of Turkey. But in Bible times it referred only to a small part of that peninsula.

Note it is not "seven of the churches of Asia," but "the seven churches." There may have been other churches in that province, but probably not. Or it may be that these seven churches had sent messengers to John in prison on the Isle of Patmos to learn of his state and bring his message.

At any rate, they were literal churches in literal cities. They are named in verse 11, and again they are called "the seven churches which are in Asia," including Ephesus, Smyrna, Pergamos, Thyatira, Sardis, Philadelphia and Laodicea. The messages are the Word of God and so they are inspired for the blessing of everyone but they were addressed to these particular churches.

They do not symbolize the various eras in this age before Christ comes. In the first place, since God has determined that no one can know any evidence of when Christ will return, then He certainly would not lay out a plan where really smart people could figure it out and divide the whole New Testament age into periods so that Christ could not come until these two thousand years were finished. If every Christian were to watch for His coming at any moment—and He might have come at any moment—then there could not intervene a period of seven steps before Christ's return, represented by these seven churches in Asia.

I. To Have Prophecy Outlining the Age Would Contradict Imminency of Christ's Coming

Dr. Scofield says, "It is incredible that in a prophecy covering the church period there should be no such foreview." But the contrary is true. There was no reason why one who understands the nature of prophecy concerning the Second Coming should expect here an outline of say nineteen centuries of church histories for the following reasons.

(a) The Lord Jesus had already established one great scriptural doctrine about Christ's return; that is, the time is kept secret. Jesus might have come at any time after Pentecost. Paul expected Christ's return in his lifetime (see I Thess. 4:15; I Cor. 15:52). There were no prophesied events that needed to happen before Christ could return. Every Christian was to "look for his Son from heaven." New Testament Christians were taught to "watch therefore, for ye know neither the day nor the hour wherein the Son of man cometh" (Matt. 25:13).

Now for the Holy Spirit to ignore that clear Bible principle, that there could be no outline of events and no prophesied events before Christ would return, because He could return at any moment during these years, is unthinkable. That makes it certain that He will not now give an outline of events that contradicts the doctrine so strongly expressed elsewhere. There simply could not be any foreview of the whole church age up until the coming of Christ, giving an outline of events that would happen, if Jesus might have come at any moment and the prophecies thus have been proven untrue and not to be fulfilled. No, there is no reason to expect such a foreview.

(b) Again, here in Revelation the Lord Jesus is not speaking of "the church" in the sense of the Scofield notes, but He is speaking about the local churches. Rome has perverted the Bible meaning of the word *church*. And there is a general idea that Catholics and Protestants and various cults all make up parts of the church, referring to a worldly organization. The term is never so used in the Bible. The word *church* never means a denomination nor a group of denominations. As for that mystical body of Christ which will be caught out at the rapture, including all the saved, it is not made up of human organizations, but of individual souls who have trusted Christ. That body of Christ has no organized entity, and has no discernible history in human affairs.

No, there was no reason to expect an outlined *"spiritual*

history of the church" during this age. And that doubtless is why God gave none.

2. To Claim a "Foreview" of Seven Periods of Church History Is Speculation and Spiritualizes Scripture to Teach What Is Not Stated

Dr. Scofield says, "These messages (to the seven churches of Asia) must contain that foreview if it is in the book at all. . . ." Read that again. What Dr. Scofield is really saying is that the Bible does not profess to give an outline of spiritual history of the church. The Scripture does not say that these seven churches in Asia Minor represent seven periods of church history. There is not even a hint in the Scriptures themselves that any such history is intended. Dr. Scofield concluded that there ought to be such a history, that it was incredible for it to be omitted so he supplied by spiritualizing passages. Note how weak is this argument.

(a) Dr. Scofield does here what he wisely and emphatically decries in others. Postmillennialists and others spiritualize the Scriptures. They make Israel mean the church. They make Mount Zion mean Heaven. They make Jews of Israel mean Christians. They make the throne of David mean the throne of God. I say Dr. Scofield elsewhere very wisely criticizes that misuse of Scripture and that spiritualizing away of explicit statements of the Scriptures. And yet here he does the same thing. Where the Bible says nothing at all about the periods of church history, Dr. Scofield makes the message to each of these seven churches picture a phase of 'spiritual history of the church.'

(b) Again, Dr. Scofield violates one of the rules he elsewhere praises: the rule of good Bible interpretation that we are never to found a doctrine on a type or symbol. A man may be wrong about what he thinks is a type. Doctrines must be founded on clear statements of Scripture. There is not a single such statement in the Bible that the seven churches of Asia represent phases in the spiritual history of the church. That Dr. Scofield admits. Then he ought never to have made such a doctrine which is not even hinted at in the Scriptures. These seven churches were literal congregations in seven cities. Of course, all churches and all individuals can get help from the divine revelation given here. But we ought not add some meaning which the Bible does not give because perhaps we think it would fit some doctrine of ours, that there would be many signs so we would know ahead of time when Jesus is coming.

3. The Messages Distinctly Local, to Specific Local Churches

Dr. Scofield gives another argument for his theory here: "Again, these messages by their very terms go beyond the local assemblies mentioned." Not necessarily so. In the notes on the next page Dr. Scofield says, "There is no ancient authority for a sect of the Nicolaitanes." Why should there be any record of a small group in a local church in one town or two at most (mentioned only in the connection with Ephesus and the nearby town of Pergamos)? But Dr. Scofield tries to make out the term "Nicolaitanes" a worldwide heresy, when there is no such inference in these Scriptures.

In fact, there are many distinctly local references in these seven letters. In Ephesus there were some who said they were apostles but were not. In Smyrna there were some who claimed to be Jews who were not. Pergamos was "where Satan's seat is," evidently a center of idolatry. At Thyatira there was a woman prophetess who established a false cult. She is here called Jezebel. Again, in Philadelphia there were some who claimed to be Jews and were not. But this distinction claimed in two churches would naturally come because of the early Judaizing influence, which churches have never had after the first century.

I am saying that the messages were addressed outright to local churches, and the Bible itself never hints that they had any prophetic significance beyond those local churches, and whatever warnings and admonitions would apply to other Christians in like situations.

4. Actually Seven Churches Do Not Fit Even Dr. Scofield's Outline of Church History

But Dr. Scofield's main argument that these seven churches

mark out events and periods in church history is this: "Most conclusively of all, these messages do present an exact foreview of the *spiritual* history of the church, and in this precise order."

Alas, but careful examination will prove that these churches do not give "an exact foreview. . .in this precise order."

(a) Compare the first message to Ephesus in Revelation 2:1-7, with the third message to Pergamos in Revelation 2:12-17. Dr. Scofield wants the first message to represent apostolic Christianity in the time of John. And the next one to represent the rise of Romanism under Constantine beginning in A.D. 316. But the messages are very much the same.

The Christians at Ephesus are praised for labor and patience and their hatred of evil. And the Christians at Pergamos are likewise praised for their works, for holding fast Christ's name and not denying the faith, even though some were martyrs like Antipas! (Remember Antipas is a person in a definite local touch, not general nor universal, representing an age.)

Again, to the church at Ephesus the Lord said, "Nevertheless I have somewhat against thee, because thou hast left thy first love." And to the church at Pergamos, in the rise and defilement of Romanism, the Lord says, "But I have a few things against thee, because thou hast there them that hold the doctrine of Balaam. . . ." The reproof of Ephesus is stronger than Pergamos.

I say, the messages do not fit the ages which they are assigned.

(b) In fact, Dr. Scofield in his own outline shows that these are not "an exact foreview" and "in this precise order" of church history. The message of Sardis in Revelation 3:1-6 is supposed to represent the period of the Reformation, but there is nothing there about the Reformation. The message could have been applied to any other age of those Dr. Scofield has selected (or Darby). And the message to the church at Philadelphia (3:7-13) is not ascribed to any particular time, by Dr. Scofield and Plymouth Brethren. It is getting down too close to the present and it cannot be divided by speculation, to represent any particular time. So Dr. Scofield simply calls it "the true church and the professing church." When? In what "precise order"? If this is to be an exact foreview of the "precise order" of church history, then there ought to be some hint as to what period the church of Philadelphia would represent. Dr. Scofield does not find it.

(c) Dr. Scofield says the message to Laodicea represents "the final state of apostasy." But actually apostasy is not mentioned in that letter at all. The complaint of Christ here is "that thou art neither cold nor hot," but rather "lukewarm." God knows church members everywhere need to be warned about that ever-recurring sin of lukewarmness, but lukewarmness is not the same as modernism, denial of the Faith. And there is no hint that this is "the final state."

No, this is an artificial arrangement, made to fit a preconceived opinion. But the Bible does not teach that the messages to these seven churches give an outline of church history.

In these messages to the seven churches, there is no picture of Roman Catholicism which took over most of the churches. There is no revealing of the whole disastrous and terrible Dark Ages. Dr. Scofield, following his Reformation theology and the common misuse of the word *church* to represent denominations on earth, has tried to find a preview of these phases "in this precise order." But he has gone beyond the Scripture and it is a mistake in which thousands of others have followed him through the Scofield Reference Bible.

No, Jesus might have come at any moment, before any of the events Dr. Scofield thinks are pictured here occurred. So Paul could write, "We which are alive and remain" till the rapture he expected in his lifetime, by divine inspiration. The events are not foretold because God did not want to foretell them. The Lord Jesus wanted to leave Himself free to come at any moment, and He wanted people to watch for His coming because He had commanded it, not because they had learned of some order of events that must be fulfilled before Christ could come.

So, when we go into chapters 2 and 3 of Revelation and study the messages to the seven churches, you will remember that they were literal cities, literal local congregations of Christians. Antipas (2:13), was a real man, a martyr at Pergamos. "That woman Jezebel" (2:20), was a real woman, a wicked woman in the Thyatira church. The problem of the teaching and practice of the Nicolaitanes which are mentioned, meant the teaching and practice of a particular cult then appearing in two of the churches. All this is the Word of God, but no one has a right to put meaning into it that the Bible does not teach. The seven churches do not represent the church age. The moral and spiritual truth are for all, just as in other epistles to churches at Corinth or Colosse or Philippi.

VERSES 5—8:

5 And from Jesus Christ, *who is* the faithful witness, *and* the first begotten of the dead, and the prince of the kings of the earth. Unto him that loved us, and washed us from our sins in his own blood,

6 And hath made us kings and priests unto God and his Father; to him *be* glory and dominion for ever and ever. Amen.

7 Behold, he cometh with clouds; and every eye shall see him, and they *also* which pierced him: and all kindreds of the earth shall wail because of him. Even so, Amen.

8 I am Alpha and Ō-mĕg-̓ă, the beginning and the ending, saith the Lord, which is, and which was, and which is to come, the Almighty.

Emphasis Now on Christ as Coming King

The Lord Jesus is mentioned here not simply as "the Son of man"—which title He loved so well; not simply as "the only begotten Son"—as the only Person physically begotten of God: He is *"the first begotten of the dead"*—He is raised from the dead. He is *"the prince of the kings of the earth."* This looks forward to His coming to put down all kingdoms and take over the rule of this world.

And about Christians, verse 6 does not simply mention that we are children of God, that we are born again, we are to carry out the Great Commission, but God *"hath made us kings and priests."* Christians kings? Yes. The Scripture says, "If we suffer, we shall also reign with him" (II Tim. 2:12).

In the parable of the pounds which pictures Christ as coming back to set up His kingdom and require a report by His workers, to the man whose pound had gained ten pounds, He said, "Well, thou good servant: because thou has been faithful in a very little, have thou authority over ten cities." To the man whose pound gained five pounds He said, "Be thou also over five cities" (Luke 19:16-19). When Peter asked what rewards they would have, Jesus said that the twelve apostles would "sit upon twelve thrones, judging the twelve tribes of Israel" (Matt. 19:27, 28).

We are made "priests" also. That means we should intercede for sinners and try to get them saved. It may mean that in the millennial age Christians will have some special service as priests. But the emphasis in Revelation is particularly on the return of Christ.

Oh, but remember this message is about "him that loved us, and washed us from our sins in his own blood." Those who are to reign with Christ, those who are to rejoice in His coming are born-again ones whose sins are all blotted out. It is a past tense salvation now continuing. It is not that Christ is little by little washing us and making us fit for Heaven, but by a one-time regeneration Christians become children of God, born in the family, sins all blotted out, and we receive a new heart and the Spirit of God moves into our bodies as temples. There is not a question, *Will* you be saved? The question is, *Are* you saved already? There is a one-time transformation, and one who is a Christian has already been born again, been washed in the blood, with his sins all forgiven.

This emphasis on the Second Coming is stated so clearly in verse 7: *"Behold, he cometh with clouds; and every eye shall see him, and they also which pierced him: and all kindreds of the earth shall wail because of him. Even so, Amen."*

"Every eye shall see him." Then the coming of Christ back to the earth does not mean only that those on earth will see Him. Everybody on earth, in Heaven, and in Hell, will face Him.

Philippians 2:9-11 discusses that glad time:

"Wherefore God also hath highly exalted him, and given him a name which is above every name: That at the name of Jesus every knee should bow, of things in heaven, and things in earth, and things under the earth; And that every tongue should confess that Jesus Christ is Lord, to the glory of God the Father."

"Every knee. . .of things in heaven. . .in earth, and
. . .under the earth"—everybody in Heaven and earth and Hell
will bow the knee to Jesus.

That means that people already in Hell will know about
Christ's glorious return to take over the kingdom of this world
and reign, and *"they also which pierced him"* (vs. 7); so those
who had to do with the crucifixion of Jesus, even if they are in
Hell, will in some miraculous way see Christ return and know it
and bow the knee and confess that He is Lord of all. They may
not love Him but they must honor Him.

When Caiaphas put Jesus on oath, "Tell us whether thou be
the Christ, the Son of God," then "Jesus saith unto him, Thou
hast said: nevertheless I say unto you, Hereafter shall ye see the
Son of man sitting on the right hand of power, and coming in the
clouds of heaven." We have no record that the wicked high priest
Caiaphas was saved. If not, down in Hell he will see Christ coming in the clouds of Heaven.

Pictured Here Is Not Rapture, First Phase of Christ's Coming, but His Later Return in Glory

We have said there are two phases to Christ's Second Coming.
In one phase, when "the Lord himself shall descend from heaven
with a shout, with the voice of the archangel, and with the trump
of God: and the dead in Christ shall rise first: Then we which are
alive and remain shall be caught up together with them in the
clouds, to meet the Lord in the air: and so shall we ever be with
the Lord."

Examine the first phase of Christ's coming, before this return
to reign.

In one phase of His coming He will be like the bridegroom
coming to the wedding and the ten virgins waiting expectantly,
not knowing when the bridegroom will come. Suddenly he comes
and finds them sleeping and some of them with no oil. That pictures the phase of His coming about which Jesus plainly said no
man knows the day nor the hour.

In this first phase of His coming we are told:

"Behold, I shew you a mystery; We shall not all sleep, but we

shall all be changed, In a moment, in the twinkling of an eye, at the last trump: for the trumpet shall sound, and the dead shall be raised incorruptible, and we shall be changed. For this corruptible must put on incorruption, and this mortal must put on immortality."—I Cor. 15:51-53.

Notice the suddenness of Christ's unexpected return: "In a moment, in the twinkling of an eye." This is evidently in that first phase of His coming. Note again I Thessalonians 4:13-17:

"But I would not have you to be ignorant, brethren, concerning them which are asleep, that ye sorrow not, even as others which have no hope. For if we believe that Jesus died and rose again, even so them also which sleep in Jesus will God bring with him. For this we say unto you by the word of the Lord, that we which are alive and remain unto the coming of the Lord shall not prevent them which are asleep. For the Lord himself shall descend from heaven with a shout, with the voice of the archangel, and with the trump of God: and the dead in Christ shall rise first: Then we which are alive and remain shall be caught up together with them in the clouds, to meet the Lord in the air: and so shall we ever be with the Lord."

Note that this coming of Christ is to raise the Christian dead and change the living and together we "shall be caught up together with them in the clouds, to meet the Lord in the air." Away then from this earth to the wedding. Away then with the resurrected Christians to the judgment seat of Christ in Heaven.

There is no room here for the battle of Armageddon. This first phase is not the same phase of *"Behold, he cometh with clouds; and every eye shall see him, and they also which pierced him: and all kindreds of the earth shall wail because of him"* (vs. 7). Not in this first phase is He coming to regather Israel from all the earth, purge out the rebels and set up the Jewish kingdom, and when the whole nation is saved. That waits for the second phase, when Christ will come as King, pictured here in verse 7.

The second phase of Christ's coming is the theme of Revelation.

Enoch, the seventh from Adam, prophesied, saying, "Behold,

the Lord cometh with ten thousands of his saints, To execute judgment upon all, and to convince all that are ungodly among them of all their ungodly deeds which they have ungodly committed, and of all their hard speeches which ungodly sinners have spoken against him."

Saints will go to Heaven with Christ, caught away to meet Him in the clouds. Living Christians will be changed and dead Christians raised and caught away to Heaven. Then at the second phase, mentioned here in Revelation 1:7, Christ will come "with ten thousands of his saints, To execute judgment" (Jude 14, 15). This is pictured further in Revelation 19:11-16:

"And I saw heaven opened, and behold a white horse; and he that sat upon him was called Faithful and True, and in righteousness he doth judge and make war. His eyes were as a flame of fire, and on his head were many crowns; and he had a name written, that no man knew, but he himself. And he was clothed with a vesture dipped in blood: and his name is called The Word of God. And the armies which were in heaven followed him upon white horses, clothed in fine linen, white and clean. And out of his mouth goeth a sharp sword, that with it he should smite the nations: and he shall rule them with a rod of iron: and he treadeth the winepress of the fierceness and wrath of Almighty God. And he hath on his vesture and on his thigh a name written, KING OF KINGS, AND LORD OF LORDS."

Christ, in the first phase of His coming, suddenly, at the rapture, when Christians are changed and caught up to be with Him and meet the Christian dead raised up and then carried away to Heaven, promises comfort and a happy reunion with loved ones.

But in this second phase of His coming, Christ is spoken of as KING OF KINGS, AND LORD OF LORDS. He has a sharp sword with which He will smite the nations. He comes in righteousness to judge and make war. The armies of Heaven follow Him.

Make sure that you get it clear that there are two separate phases of Christ's coming. In the first phase, Christ comes to call His own out to meet Him in the air and He takes us away to a wedding feast and the judgment seat of Christ, along with the redeemed of all ages. But in the second phase of His coming, He returns to earth with the armies of Heaven and with ten thousands of His saints, and at that time He is greatly dreaded by those who will see and meet Him; then every knee shall bow to Him in earth and Heaven and Hell.

"Behold, he cometh with clouds" (vs. 7). When Jesus ascended from the Mount of Olives and clouds received Him out of the sight of the apostles, two angels standing by said, "Ye men of Galilee, why stand ye gazing up into heaven? this same Jesus, which is taken up from you into heaven, shall so come in like manner as ye have seen him go into heaven" (Acts 1:11).

So, when Jesus returns in clouds, it will be as He left that day on the Mount of Olives and was received into the clouds.

Again, on the Mount of Transfiguration, which, we are told, is a picture of Jesus at His glorious Second Coming, a cloud covered Him.

Jesus ascended from the Mount of Olives, but Zechariah 14:4 says about His second coming, "And his feet shall stand in that day upon the mount of Olives." That resurrected Saviour in a physical body is returning as He went away.

"All kindreds of the earth shall wail because of him" (vs. 7). Remember, this is the second phase of Christ's second coming, not the rapture. At the rapture the dead in Christ shall rise first and the living Christians shall be changed and it will happen "in a moment, in the twinkling of an eye" and we will be "caught up together with them in the clouds, to meet the Lord in the air," so the rest of the world may mourn over loved ones gone. That is not the time when every knee shall bow to Him in earth and Heaven and Hell. That is not the time He will come riding a white horse, crowned with many crowns, to fight the battle of Armageddon. That is not the time for nations to mourn so much at the rapture, the first phase of His coming. But this is the second phase of His coming. This is the time of triumph when He comes back for judgment and punishment. He came the first time in loving mercy.

Remember, it is the second phase of His coming when He is

manifested to the whole world, which is most discussed in the
Old Testament. Naturally what Jews were thinking about was
the restoration of Israel. So the apostles asked, "Lord, wilt thou
at this time restore again the kingdom to Israel?" (Acts 1:6). And
He answered that it was not for them to know. It was Christ coming in "the end of the world" literally the end of this age, the end
of the times of the Gentiles, when Christ returned to reign, about
which the disciples asked in Matthew 24:3.

To the Virgin Mary the promise of Christ's coming was, "And
the Lord God shall give unto him the throne of his father David:
And he shall reign over the house of Jacob for ever; and of his
kingdom there shall be no end." You can understand, then, that
the main emphasis with the Jews, as with the apostles, was on
Christ coming to regather Israel to set up His kingdom on earth,
etc. The main promises in all the Old Testament about the Second Coming had to do with the second phase of His coming, the
regathering of Israel, the conversion of Israel as a nation, the
restoration of the throne of David, etc.

It is this second phase of His coming that pictures that stone
cut out of a mountain without hands of Daniel, chapter 2, the
stone that would crush the great image picturing the empires of
the world and grind them to powder and Christ would then reign
in their place. When Jesus said in Matthew 24:33, "So likewise
ye, when ye shall see all these things, know that it is near, even at
the doors." What is near? Note that it is after the tribulation,
after Christ's appearance with the armies of Heaven and ten
thousands of His saints coming back to the earth, after Israel,
His elect, is regathered into Palestine, then, when everybody sees
these things—"it is near." What is near? The reign of Christ on
earth, the setting up of the kingdom.

So this second phase of Christ's return, described in Revelation 1:7, is some way the culmination of a series of events which
we call the Second Coming of Christ.

Christ is *"Alpha and Omega, the beginning and the ending"*
(vs. 8). That means infinity in power, righteousness and deity—
before the world began and into the infinite future. But it seems
also to remind us that the cross and Christ's rejection by a

wicked world are not the end. He is the ending as well as the beginning, and He "which was" is the One "which is to come, the Almighty."

VERSES 9—11:

9 I John, who also am your brother, and companion in tribulation, and in the kingdom and patience of Jesus Christ, was in the isle that is called Patmos, for the word of God, and for the testimony of Jesus Christ.

10 I was in the Spirit on the Lord's day, and heard behind me a great voice, as of a trumpet,

11 Saying, I am Alpha and Ō-mĕg-́ă, the first and the last: and, What thou seest, write in a book, and send *it* unto the seven churches which are in Asia; unto Ephesus, and unto Smyrna, and unto Pĕr-́gă-mŏs, and unto Thȳ-ă-tī-́ră, and unto Sardis, and unto Philadelphia, and unto Lā-ŏd-ĭ-çē-́ă.

Apostle John Exiled to Patmos for His Faith

Patmos is an island in the Aegean Sea about ten miles long, a few miles from the coast of Asiatic Turkey. The Encyclopaedia Britannica says, "As a remote islet it was the place of banishment of St. John the Evangelist under Domitian, in A.D. 95. He was released about 18 months later under Nerva."

Dr. Seiss wrote: "Less than a year ago I passed that island. It is a mere mass of barren rocks; dark in color and cheerless in form. It lies out in the open sea, near the coast of western Asia Minor. It has neither trees nor rivers, nor any land for cultivation, except some little nooks between ledges of rocks. There is still a dingy grotto remaining in which the aged apostle is said to have had his vision. That was John's prison!"

John would have been the last living apostle at this time. And by the Romans he was banished to this prison island *"for the word of God, and for the testimony of Jesus Christ"* (vs. 9). How simple and matter-of-fact is the thrilling viewpoint of the apostle concerning banishment, prison and persecution! *"I John, who also am your brother, and companion in tribulation, and in the kingdom and patience of Jesus Christ"* (vs. 9). No complaint about his persecution! John takes that as the normal part of devoted and Spirit-filled proclamation of the Gospel. He remembers his brother James had been beheaded by Herod (Acts 12:2). Stephen had been stoned to death in Jerusalem. Paul had been beheaded at Rome nearly thirty years before John's imprisonment. We do not believe the unreliable Catholic tradition that Peter was in Rome and was crucified head downward. There is much evidence that Peter was never in Rome. He was an apostle to the circumcision, not to the Gentiles (Gal. 2:7). His later ministry was in Babylon from whence he wrote the I and II Epistles of Peter (I Pet. 5:13). Second Peter is dated probably about the year 66, perhaps the same year Paul was beheaded at Rome. When Paul went to Rome, Acts 28 does not give any indication that Peter was there or that he met Paul. In Paul's letter to Rome, the 16th chapter, greeting some 28 persons or families, does not even mention the Apostle Peter.

In II Peter 1:14 Peter said, "Knowing that shortly I must put off this tabernacle, even as our Lord Jesus Christ hath shewed me." So it is not unlikely that Peter died a martyr's death. Hebrews 10:32-34 tells of the kind of persecution Christians of those days endured:

"But call to remembrance the former days, in which, after ye were illuminated, ye endured a great fight of afflictions; Partly, whilst ye were made a gazingstock both by reproaches and afflictions; and partly, whilst ye became companions of them that were so used. For ye had compassion of me in my bonds, and took joyfully the spoiling of your goods, knowing in yourselves that ye have in heaven a better and an enduring substance."

And Jesus had said to John and the other apostles:

"But beware of men: for they will deliver you up to the councils, and they will scourge you in their synagogues; And ye shall be brought before governors and kings for my sake, for a testimony against them and the Gentiles. But when they deliver you up, take no thought how or what ye shall speak: for it shall be given you in that same hour what ye shall speak. For it is not ye that speak, but the Spirit of your Father which speaketh in you. And the brother shall deliver up the brother to death, and the father the child: and the children shall rise up against their

parents, and cause them to be put to death. And ye shall be hated of all men for my name's sake: but he that endureth to the end shall be saved. But when they persecute you in this city, flee ye into another; for verily I say unto you, Ye shall not have gone over the cities of Israel, till the Son of man be come. The disciple is not above his master, nor the servant above his lord."—Matt. 10:17-24.

Oh, that God would give us a complacent, happy spirit to expect and to deserve some persecution for Jesus' sake. So Paul was comforted in his persecution. In Philippians 1:12-14 he said:

"But I would ye should understand, brethren, that the things which happened unto me have fallen out rather unto the furtherance of the gospel; So that my bonds in Christ are manifest in all the palace, and in all other places; and many of the brethren in the Lord, waxing confident by my bonds, are much more bold to speak the word without fear."

Notice that John is not only a companion in tribulation but in *"patience of Jesus Christ"* (vs. 9). That may be a reference to James 1:2-4: "My brethren, count it all joy when ye fall into divers temptations; Knowing this, that the trying of your faith worketh patience. But let patience have her perfect work, that ye may be perfect and entire, wanting nothing."

The same thought is expressed in Romans 12:12, ". . .patient in tribulation." And Hebrews 12:1 says that we should "run with patience the race that is set before us."

Patience in the presence of affliction, joy in the presence of suffering; yes, and we remember how when James and John were beaten for preaching the Gospel, "they departed from the presence of the council, rejoicing that they were counted worthy to suffer shame for his name. And daily in the temple, and in every house, they ceased not to teach and preach Jesus Christ" (Acts 5:41, 42).

So the aged Apostle John seemed to take in a contented stride the persecution which came upon him for the Word of God.

"I was in the Spirit. . ." (vs. 10). That evidently means more than simply the anointing or fullness of the Spirit as the "endue-

ment of power from on high," spoken of in Luke 24:49; Acts 2:4; Acts 4:31, etc. He was "in the Spirit" in the sense of perfectly controlled by the Holy Spirit. In other words, in the inspiration from above John is inspired not merely to tell but to *"write in a book"* (vs. 11) what God gives him here. So John could say with Paul in I Corinthians 2:13, "Which things also we speak, not in the words which man's wisdom teacheth, but which the Holy Ghost teacheth; comparing spiritual things with spiritual." That is Spirit-given thoughts and Spirit-given words.

In Exodus 24:4 we read, "And Moses wrote all the words of the Lord. . . ." And in Isaiah 51:16 God says, "And I have put my words in thy mouth. . . ." In Jeremiah 1:9 God told Jeremiah, "Behold, I have put my words in thy mouth." God told Ezekiel, "Thou shalt speak my words unto them" (Ezek. 2:7). And in the last words of David he said, "The Spirit of the Lord spake by me, and his word was in my tongue" (II Sam. 23:2). So of the book of Revelation, as of the rest of the Bible, the words of Jesus in Matthew 4:4 are true, "It is written, Man shall not live by bread alone, but by every word that proceedeth out of the mouth of God."

Here John writes the book of Revelation as the very words of God, in the original manuscript.

". . .in the Spirit on the Lord's day" (vs. 10). Many think "the Lord's day" here refers to Sunday, the first day in the week. We know the disciples in New Testament times met on Sunday and in Acts 20:7 we learn that at Troas "upon the first day of the week, when the disciples came together to break bread, Paul preached unto them. . . ." And Paul commanded Christians to lay aside for the Lord's work "upon the first day of the week" (I Cor. 16:2).

Seventh-Day Adventists would like to maintain the Jewish Sabbath, and so they hold that when Jesus said, "The Son of man is Lord also of the sabbath" (Luke 6:5), He was setting aside the Sabbath as the Lord's Day. Jesus was plainly saying that He was Master of all the ceremonial law, and He had a right to interpret it or to change it. He did not recognize the Pharisaical traditions that had been added to the Sabbath.

The simple truth is that the Sabbath was first made known to Israel as part of the law as we see from Nehemiah 9:14, and that no Christian should be judged by the Sabbath (Col. 2:14-17). We take it that Christians honored the first day of the week because that was the day the Lord arose from the dead.

However, Seiss goes into great detail to explain that in Christian writings "the Lord's day" was never used for the first day of the week for the first one hundred years, but that the term means the famous oft-prophesied "day of the Lord" of the Old Testament when Christ should come in judgment to destroy the kingdoms of this world and reign. He thinks that thus in spirit John was carried away into the time when these prophesied events will happen.

Dr. John F. Walvoord agrees, and the arguments of both men are very convincing.

Jesus said, *"I am Alpha and Omega, the first and the last"* (vs. 11)—Alpha and Omega, the first and last letters of the Greek alphabet. At first Jesus was in the beginning with God the Father. At the last He will be with God the Father and all rule is to be put under His feet. The death of Jesus on the cross is not the end of the story. Now He must come to reign. Now He must preside at the judgment of the living Gentiles in Matthew 25:31-46. Now He must preside at the last judgment of the unsaved dead after the thousand years' reign on the earth (Rev. 20).

And what John is to write is to "the seven churches which are in Asia" named here: Ephesus, Smyrna, Pergamos, Thyatira, Sardis, Philadelphia and Laodicea.

And behind John he heard *"a great voice, as of a trumpet."* Get ready, John, to meet the awesome presence of Jesus Christ who is God Almighty.

VERSES 12—18:

12 And I turned to see the voice that spake with me. And being turned, I saw seven golden candlesticks;

13 And in the midst of the seven candlesticks *one* like unto the Son of man, clothed with a garment down to the foot, and girt about the paps with a golden girdle.

14 His head and *his* hairs *were* white like wool, as white as snow; and his eyes *were* as a flame of fire;

15 And his feet like unto fine brass, as if they burned in a furnace; and his voice as the sound of many waters.

16 And he had in his right hand seven stars: and out of his mouth went a sharp twoedged sword: and his countenance *was* as the sun shineth in his strength.

17 And when I saw him, I fell at his feet as dead. And he laid his right hand upon me, saying unto me, Fear not; I am the first and the last:

18 *I am* he that liveth, and was dead; and, behold, I am alive for evermore, Amen; and have the keys of hell and of death.

Awesome Majesty of Resurrected Christ as He Gives to John the Revelation

This is no light matter. There is an impressive setting. There are seven golden lampstands or candlesticks—seven for perfection and deity. No doubt there is a likeness to the golden candlestick in the Tabernacle, the seven lamps burning with oil which pictured Christ, the eternal Light of the world burning in the power of the Holy Spirit. The Person is *"one like unto the Son of man"* (vs. 13). This is the same Jesus who arose from the dead and ascended from the Mount of Olives. Seiss reminds us that He is described in the same way in the Psalms, in the visions of Daniel, and in His own discourses concerning Himself. Even then the disciples, who did not expect His resurrection, did not immediately recognize Him.

John sees the same body, but now it is a glorified body. Christ had poured out His soul unto death and poured out all His blood, but He had been raised from the dead and the body is now a perfect body, to eat and drink. It is the body the disciples have handled (I John 1:1; Luke 24:39).

His hair is white like wool, white as snow; His eyes as a flame of fire (vs. 14)! The Scripture tells us that "the hoary head is a crown of glory." The same appears in Daniel's vision of "the Ancient of Days, whose garment was white as snow, and the hair of his head like pure wool."

"And his eyes were as a flame of fire" (vs. 14). "Here is intelligence; burning, all-penetrating intelligence. Here is power to read secrets, to bring hidden things to light, to warm and search all hearts at a single glance," says Seiss. And remember the Scripture says that "Neither is there any creature that is not

manifest in his sight: but all things are naked and opened unto the eyes of him with whom we have to do."

Even the dear feet of the Saviour, we suppose with the marks of the nails still in them, are like the fine brass burning in a furnace (vs. 15). Make no mistake of it: Jesus here appears in His deity, in His divine perfection and holiness. He appears as a judge *"and out of his mouth went a sharp twoedged sword."* His face is *"as the sun shineth in his strength"* (vs. 16). And the seven stars, picturing the messengers to the seven churches, are His to control as He will. And the churches, represented by the seven candlesticks, are completely His. Here is the all-powerful Saviour, revealed in His power and majesty. We should not be surprised that John says, *"And when I saw him, I fell at his feet as dead"* (vs. 17).

We remember that occasionally in His earthly ministry this august and terrible power shined through the limitations of His humanity. And when the soldiers of the high priest faced Him in the Garden of Gethsemane and heard Him speak, they fell backward. Jesus said well to Pilate, "Thou couldest have no power at all against me, except it were given thee from above" (John 19:11).

Do you think that even Christians, then, will tremble when they come to face Jesus Christ? Yes, we have solemn warning in I John 2:28, "Now, little children, abide in him; that, when he shall appear, we may have confidence, and not be ashamed before him at his coming." Some Christians will be ashamed when they come to face the Saviour. And in II Corinthians 5:9, 10 Paul said, "Wherefore we labour, that, whether present or absent, we may be accepted of him. For we must all appear before the judgment seat of Christ; that every one may receive the things done in his body, according to that he hath done, whether it be good or bad."

Paul was so eager for the dear Lord Jesus to say, "Well done, good and faithful servant!" And in verse 11 he said, "Knowing therefore the terror of the Lord, we persuade men. . . ." Do you mean that even Christians may know some terror when we come to face the Lord Jesus and face our failures and come to the judgment seat of Christ? Yes. The Scripture so teaches.

Revelation 1: 7 above says, ". . .and all kindreds of the earth shall wail because of him." Not only lost people will tremble to face the Saviour but Christians who have failed Him, too, no doubt.

In I Corinthians 3:15 we are told about the judgment seat of Christ, "If any man's work shall be burned, he shall suffer loss: but he himself shall be saved; yet so as by fire." Some Christians will suffer loss at the judgment seat of Christ. And that may be part of the reason why, after Christians are a thousand years and more in resurrection bodies, Revelation 21:4 says, "And God shall wipe away all tears from their eyes." Tears in glorified bodies! Thank God, the time of tears will then be over! And after that there will be no more pain, nor death, nor tears.

Again the Lord Jesus reminds John and us, *"I am he that liveth, and was dead; and, behold, I am alive for evermore"* (vs. 18). Oh, John faced, as all of us must face, the living, resurrected Saviour, God in human form, who has the keys of Hell and death!

VERSES 19, 20:

19 Write the things which thou hast seen, and the things which are, and the things which shall be hereafter; 20 The mystery of the seven stars which thou sawest in my right hand, and the seven golden candlesticks. The seven stars are the angels of the seven churches: and the seven candlesticks which thou sawest are the seven churches.

Things Present, Things Future Here Foretold

If we take literally the plain statement here about the theme of the book of Revelation, we must acknowledge that much of the book is prophetic, telling of future events: ". . .*the things which shall be hereafter"* (vs. 19).

John wrote to the people in the seven churches then existing. He wrote also to all of us the inspired lessons, exhortations and commandments which He gave to the seven churches as is true of all Scripture. It is ours. He was to write the things he had seen, then the seven churches and things related to them then present, and about the things that shall be hereafter—prophecy about the future.

And it is only honest to see that that theme was so clearly stated in verse 7, "Behold, he cometh with clouds; and every eye shall see him, and they also which pierced him: and all kindreds of the earth shall wail because of him. Even so, Amen."

Let us then expect, as we go through chapters 2 and 3, messages to churches that were then present and the exhortations, commandments, warnings and blessings there announced. But beginning with the 4th chapter we start to look into "the things which shall be hereafter."

One Format to Seven Letters in Chapters 2 and 3

Remarkable Same Pattern for All the Seven Letters to Seven Churches

In chapters 2 and 3 there are letters to the seven churches at Ephesus, Smyrna, Pergamos, Thyatira, Sardis, Philadelphia and Laodicea. Let us first notice this uniform outline, and then we can study the seven messages separately.

"Unto the angel of the church in. . .," so each of the seven letters begins. The word "angel" is the Greek word *aggelos.* Young's Analytical Concordance defines the word "messenger or agent." It is translated a good many times "angel," but seven times in the New Testament in the King James it is translated "messenger" and does not mean a heavenly being. It is used once about the *messengers* John the Baptist sent to Jesus (Luke 7:24) and three times about John the Baptist himself (Luke 7:27; Matt. 11:10; Mark 1:2). And once it refers to *messengers* of Jesus sent to a Samaritan village to seek accommodations there (Luke 9:52).

So these angels were messengers from these seven churches. It is possible that they had come to consult with John, the last of the apostles alive, and that he was inspired to write the seven messages and send them to these churches. The messengers may have been elders or pastors. The counsel would certainly fit as addressed to pastors and leaders of churches today.

Each letter continues, "These things saith. . .," and there follows a title or attributes referring to Jesus. The letter was from:

". . .he that holdeth the seven stars in his right hand, who walketh in the midst of the seven golden candlesticks" (2:1).

". . .the first and the last, which was dead, and is alive" (2:8).

". . .he which hath the sharp sword with two edges" (2:12).

". . .the Son of God, who hath his eyes like unto a flame of fire, and his feet are like fine brass" (2:18).

Ephesus, Smyrna, Pergamum, Thyatira, Sardis, Philadelphia, Laodicea.
These Seven Cities, connected on a great triangular highway, are named
in their geographical order beginning with Ephesus, thence north about 100
miles to Pergamum, and thence southeast to Laodicea, which was about 100
miles east of Ephesus.

—From *Halley's Handbook.*

". . .he that hath the seven Spirits of God, and the seven
stars" (3:1).

". . .he that is holy, he that is true, he that hath the key of
David, he that openeth, and no man shutteth; and shutteth, and
no man openeth" (3:7).

". . .the Amen, the faithful and true witness, the beginning of
the creation of God" (3:14).

Summed up, the messages show the omnipotence, the absolute holiness, and the place of Jesus Christ as above all as
Saviour and Lord.

Every letter continues, "I know thy works. . . ," to every

church, and then the praise or warning or correction varies with each church.

Each letter closes with the holy exhortation, "He that hath an ear, let him hear what the Spirit saith unto the churches."

Jesus, in His earthly ministry, said the same thing a number of times (Matt. 11:15; 13:9, 43; Mark 4:9; 7:16; Luke 8:8; 14:35).

Here we come face to face with a solemn truth. If one does not have a disposition to hear, he doesn't hear the Word of God. If one does not have a heart tuned in to understand a Scripture, he will not understand it. The Lord Jesus, on earth, spoke in parables with a deliberate intention that one whose heart was not tuned in to hear would not get the message. God does not want people compelled by mental acceptance of the truth to a position when they have no heart to love and obey the Saviour.

And then each letter closes with a promise, "To him that over-cometh," and the promise varies in wording with each church. I think now the Lord is not here especially offering rewards for overcoming but He is reminding Christians of the great blessing they already have coming, and so they should be encouraged to overcome. Those at Ephesus are promised that they may "eat of the tree of life, which is in the midst of the paradise of God." I do not believe that is for a favorite few. It is not an earned salvation, nor in this case, we think, a reward, but a happy reminder of the blessings that are coming. It may be that some people, by a degree of overcoming more than others, have more joy and reward in Heaven, but that is not the specific promise here, we think.

To the people at Smyrna, "He that overcometh shall not be hurt of the second death." Again, we are not speaking of a salva-tion earned by good works. No child of God will be so hurt at the second death. Christians are simply reminded, oh, because fear-ful things will come to some Christians—persecution and trou-ble. Yet, Christians, do not be afraid. Here is encouragement as people look forward to the great blessing they already have been promised. And so we should overcome because of all God has already done for us and promised for us.

To the church in Pergamos, in verse 17, it is promised, "To him that overcometh will I give to eat of the hidden manna, and will give him a white stone, and in the stone a new name written, which no man knoweth saving he that receiveth it." It is as if the Lord Jesus is naming one by one some of the great blessings that are already stored up for Christians and that should make us love Him more and be faithful all the more.

The overcomers in Thyatira are promised, ". . .to him will I give power over the nations: And he shall rule them with a rod of iron. . .And I will give him the morning star." But the Scripture has already promised, "If we suffer, we shall also reign with him" (II Tim. 2:12). The man whose labor multiplied the one pound to ten pounds is promised that he shall rule over ten cities, and the five-pound man is to rule over five cities. Here, then, is a promise with more meaning to some than to others, for there are more rewards in Heaven for some than for others.

In Revelation 3:5 the overcomers in Sardis are promised to be "clothed in white raiment; and I will not blot out his name out of the book of life." But God doesn't blot anybody's name out of the book of life, so this is a happy reminder of a truth and blessing already promised. John 5:24 says, "Verily, verily, I say unto you, He that heareth my word, and believeth on him that sent me, hath everlasting life, and shall not come into condemnation; but is passed from death unto life." And one saved already has everlasting life. In John 10:28 Jesus says of His sheep, "I give unto them eternal life; and they shall never perish." And Romans 8:38, 39 says, "For I am persuaded, that neither death, nor life, nor angels, nor principalities, nor powers, nor things present, nor things to come, Nor height, nor depth, nor any other creature, shall be able to separate us from the love of God, which is in Christ Jesus our Lord." There is not a threat implied that God will blot out anybody's name out of the book of life, but there is a happy reminder that God is faithful, so we ought to be faithful, too.

To the church in Philadelphia the overcomers are promised: "Him that overcometh will I make a pillar in the temple of my God, and he shall go no more out: and I will write upon him the name of my God, and the name of the city of my God, which is new Jerusalem. . . ."

Summing up these promises to the overcomer give hints and references to the amazing richness of our lives in Heaven. And to the church of the Laodiceans is promised, "To him that overcometh will I grant to sit with me in my throne. . ." and reign with Christ. But we have already been promised that "if we suffer, we shall also reign with him." The twelve apostles have already been promised they shall sit on twelve thrones judging the twelve tribes of Israel.

The promise to reign is not universal; it is part of the earned rewards of faithfulness and persecution which Christians may have.

And now let us take up the messages to the seven churches one by one.

Chapter 2

VERSES 1—7:

UNTO the angel of the church of Ephesus write; These things saith he that holdeth the seven stars in his right hand, who walketh in the midst of the seven golden candlesticks;

2 I know thy works, and thy labour, and thy patience, and how thou canst not bear them which are evil: and thou hast tried them which say they are apostles, and are not, and hast found them liars:

3 And hast borne, and hast patience, and for my name's sake hast laboured, and hast not fainted.

4 Nevertheless I have *somewhat* against thee, because thou hast left thy first love.

5 Remember therefore from whence thou art fallen, and repent, and do the first works; or else I will come unto thee quickly, and will remove thy candlestick out of his place, except thou repent.

6 But this thou hast, that thou hatest the deeds of the Nĭc-ō-lā-ĭ́-tānes, which I also hate.

7 He that hath an ear, let him hear what the Spirit saith unto the churches; To him that overcometh will I give to eat of the tree of life, which is in the midst of the paradise of God.

To the Church at Ephesus

Ephesus was a city of 225,000 population at this time. Its temple of Diana was one of the Seven Wonders of the World.

Dr. Ironside reminds us that "Paul had lived there for two years, working miracles, preaching the Gospel with wonderful effectiveness, turning men from their idols to the living God, witnessing a bonfire of evil books worth, we are told, fifty thousand pieces of silver, and seeing Diana, her favorite goddess, brought into such disrepute. . .John himself had resided there, and ministered to that people. There Apollos had been converted; there Timothy had had his home, and according to tradition, suffered his martyrdom at the hand of a mob. . . ."

Here in verse 1 Jesus is described as *"he that holdeth the seven stars in his right hand."* The stars are the messengers of the churches, godly elders, pastors probably. They are saved and so kept secure in Christ's hands.

In John 10:27-29 Jesus said:

"My sheep hear my voice, and I know them, and they follow me: And I give unto them eternal life; and they shall never perish, neither shall any man pluck them out of my hand. My Father, which gave them me, is greater than all; and no man is able to pluck them out of my Father's hand."

In the hands of Christ and the Father we are secure forever. None can take us from His hand.

Holding them in His hands, as He holds all of us who are saved, they belong to Him. Nothing can come to them but as He chooses or permits. Hence, "all things work together for good to them that love God, to them who are the called according to his purpose" (Rom. 8:28).

Perhaps in the midst of such labor and trials these men needed to be reminded, "There hath no temptation taken you but such as is common to man: but God is faithful, who will not suffer you to be tempted above that ye are able; but will with the temptation also make a way to escape, that ye may be able to bear it" (I Cor. 10:13), and be assured again of the ever-present care of Christ. Every Christian needs such care and assurance. Those chosen for leadership in Christ are chosen for more trials, more persecutions, and some need the care more.

I sat on a plane beside an old and sick Roman Catholic bishop of the Solomon Islands. He was a sacrificial and, I believe, a godly man. His superiors wanted him to retire or take a charge in the States now. But he begged me to pray that he could go back to his beloved work in the rugged, primitive Solomon Islands. I said, "The Lord is just as near in a heathen island as at home." And he replied quickly, "He is nearer! One needs Him so much more there!" God's messengers are in His safe, loving, controlling hands.

"In the midst of the seven golden candlesticks" Christ walks. So Christ is active, walking among the churches. He notes and is concerned for His people as they meet together in the churches.

An All-Seeing God!

He says, *"I know thy works"* (vs. 2). He always does. He notes the fall of every sparrow. He colors every little wild flower. The hairs of every Christian are numbered in His mind.

Commenting on verse 2: Dr. Riley says,

"I know. . ." Beloved, if we keep those two words in mind, they must have their effect in all our work.

When Phidias was working on the statue of Diana for the Acropolis at Athens, he was perfecting her hair, bringing out with the keen edge of his chisel every line and filament, when a passer-by asked, "What is the use of such painstaking with that part of the work? That statue is to go up a hundred feet high, and the back of the head will be toward the wall, and nobody can see it." To this criticism Phidias replied, "The gods will see it," and carved on.

Beloved, when tempted to leave any work deficient, and Satan shall whisper of the deficiency, "Nobody will know," listen and hear the Son of God saying, *"I know"; "I know thy works."* And when, with painstaking you have perfected something; some plan, some project, and the public seems unappreciative, and your heart is tempted to grow sore, listen again and be comforted by the words of the Christ, *"I know thy works."*

God heard the cry of the child Ishmael, laid down by his despairing mother, Hagar, to die of thirst. And God made a well.

God remembered Noah in the tossing ark at the end of a whole world (Gen. 8:1). And God remembered Hannah as she wept for a baby boy, and she conceived (I Sam. 1:19). And we have the

promise, "Let your conversation be without covetousness; and be
content with such things as ye have: for he hath said, I will never
leave thee, nor forsake thee. So that we may boldly say, The Lord
is my helper, and I will not fear what man shall do unto me"
(Heb. 13:5, 6).

Your labor, your loneliness, your sacrifice, may be unnoticed
and thankless among men, but not unnoticed nor left without
reward by the Saviour.

"I know thy works, and thy labour, and thy patience. . . ."
(vs. 2). Yes, the ever-present, always attentive Saviour knows.
Labor? Yes. Not that they attend services, that they said nice
prayers or gave an offering and lived moral lives, though all are
good. All these things He knew and they have their place, but
they are not doing the work the Lord Jesus died for, that is, saving souls! Jesus said in Matthew 9:37, 38, "The harvest truly is
plenteous, but the labourers are few; Pray ye therefore the Lord
of the harvest, that he will send forth labourers into his harvest."

He said again in Luke 10:2, "The harvest truly is great, but the
labourers are few: pray ye therefore the Lord of the harvest, that
he would send forth labourers into his harvest."

Ah, the Lord's work is a labor of plowing, sowing, reaping, win-
nowing, saving the lost, lifting the weak, restoring the fallen.
There are many ministers, pastors, assistant pastors, youth
workers, musicians and deacons but still "the *labourers* are few."
Oh, the Lord's work includes real labor. Labor like that commanded by the Saviour in Mark 16:15, "Go ye into all the world,
and preach the gospel to every creature." Every creature at every
house! Every person within possible reach should be approached
with the Gospel. That work is hard work. Not many ministers
spend hours knocking on doors seeking lost people, staying to
warn, to plead, to woo them to Christ day after day. But is not
that the idea Jesus gave in His Great Commission? Labor? Yes.

Laborers like the Apostle Paul are few. He told the elders in
this same church at Ephesus some thirty years before, in Acts 20,
in effect, "I am pure from the blood of all men," because for three
years he had "not shunned to declare unto you all the counsel of
God" in Ephesus. He said, "I. . .have taught you publickly, and

from house to house" (vs. 20). And, "Therefore watch, and remember, that by the space of three years I ceased not to warn every one night and day with tears" (vs. 31).

I was in the ruins of old Ephesus three or four years ago, and I imagined the Apostle Paul at 11:00 at night going from house to house, weeping as he went, knocking on doors, explaining that though he was a stranger, a Jew, he had a wonderful message to give them. He went "publickly, and from house to house. . . night and day with tears." So the people at Ephesus had labored, too, and that labor pleased God.

The labor the Lord Jesus asks of us is to enter into His concern and labor to get people saved. Paul said, "Wherefore we labour, that, whether present or absent, we may be accepted of him. For we must all appear before the judgment seat of Christ; that every one may receive the things done in his body, according to that he hath done, whether it be good or bad" (II Cor. 5:9,10). And Paul rejoiced that he exceeded, not in wisdom nor in evidence of spiritual power (as was true) but "in labours more abundant" than others (II Cor. 11:23). So the labor of the servant pressing hard to fill the banquet rooms with guests in the parable of Jesus in Luke 14:16-24.

"And how thou canst not bear them which are evil" (vs. 2). It is a grievous wrong when Christians are complacent about sin. The one who pleases Christ will be one who "canst not bear" those who sell liquor or dope, who favor abortion, the adulterers and profane, the homosexuals, the lewd. Happy is the Christian who is distressed and protests the evolution teaching in the schools, the widespread immodesty in dress. Christ's love does not mean a spineless acceptance of sin. We are commanded, "Let love be without dissimulation. Abhor that which is evil; cleave to that which is good" (Rom. 12:9).

The worldly and carnal Christians will say, "Oh, you cannot win the lost if you denounce their sins and make them angry." But that is Satan's philosophy, not Christ's. Actually, Billy Sunday is an example in that he won thousands of drunkards as he preached with red-hot indignation against the liquor traffic. And every greatly used soul winner has found that unless there is preaching against sin, there is little repentance. And preachers are commanded, "Them that sin rebuke before all, that others also may fear" (I Tim. 5:20). A command for preachers is, "Cry aloud, spare not, lift up thy voice like a trumpet, and shew my people their transgression, and the house of Jacob their sin" (Isa. 58:1). At Ephesus they could not bear those who are evil.

False Apostles Exposed

God was pleased with those at Ephesus: *". . .thou hast tried them which say they are apostles, and are not, and hast found them liars"* (vs. 2). Should the Christian try and critically weigh even teachers and preachers in the churches? Yes, they should. These who claimed to be apostles were not really apostles sent of God, but false teachers. And the Lord Jesus commanded, "Beware of false prophets, which come to you in sheep's clothing, but inwardly they are ravening wolves. Ye shall know them by their fruits" (Matt. 7:15, 16). A false prophet can be known by his teaching. A man who does not believe in the virgin birth, the actual deity, the blood atonement, the bodily resurrection of Jesus Christ, is a false prophet. The man who does not believe the Bible nor count it the very Word of God is a false prophet. And so the one who denies these truths ought not be received as a good leader. In II John, verses 9 to 11, we are commanded:

"Whosoever transgresseth, and abideth not in the doctrine of Christ, hath not God. He that abideth in the doctrine of Christ, he hath both the Father and the Son. If there come any unto you and bring not this doctrine, receive him not into your house, neither bid him God speed: For he that biddeth him God speed is partaker of his evil deeds."

One who does not abide in the Bible teaching about Christ is not a Christian, he "hath not God." We are not to receive him into our houses nor bid him Godspeed. We are exhorted, ". . .that ye should earnestly contend for the faith" (Jude 3).

Will God's man sometimes need to speak out boldly against false teaching by those who are even Christian brothers? He will. Paul rebuked Peter openly as we learn in Galatians 2, because Peter was compromising and led Barnabas and others to compromise. Paul said, "All they which are in Asia be turned away from me; of whom are Phygellus and Hermogenes" (II Tim. 1:15). He said, "Demas hath forsaken me, having loved this present world" (II Tim. 4:10). And when people were wrong on essential doctrines, wrong on the plan of salvation, and thus, we presume, were unsaved, Paul's language was sharp and powerful.

He said in Galatians 1:8, 9, "But though we, or an angel from heaven, preach any other gospel unto you than that which we have preached unto you, let him be accursed. As we said before, so say I now again, If any man preach any other gospel unto you than that ye have received, let him be accursed." He said about these false teachers who had led the converts in Galatia wrong, led them to go back to ceremonial law, "I would they were even cut off which trouble you" (Gal. 5:12).

Those who claim to be apostles were not. John was the only living apostle at this time, and God did not appoint anybody else with apostolic authority after the New Testament was written, and all of us have the instructions of God to go by clearly. We need Spirit-filled preachers and teachers, not those who would initiate new doctrine.

And we are solemnly warned to beware of those who seek Christian leadership but are not true to the Word of God. What a sin it is for Christians to call a man a brother who denies the essential deity of Christ or the great doctrines of the Faith of the Gospel as stated in I Corinthians 15:3, 4, ". . .how that Christ died for our sins according to the scriptures; And that he was buried, and that he rose again the third day according to the scriptures."

These Patient, Persistent Christians at Ephesus

"And hast borne, and hast patience, and for my name's sake hast laboured, and hast not fainted" (vs. 3).

We are commanded to "count it all joy when ye fall into divers temptations," and we are commanded, "Let patience have her perfect work" (Jas. 1:2, 4).

Patience is used here as a synonym for persistence, unflagging zeal. And we are commanded in Hebrews 12:1, "Let us lay aside every weight, and the sin which doth so easily beset us, and let us run with patience the race that is set before us." That is, be persistent in spite of temptations and troubles.

And Isaiah 40:29-31 says:

"He giveth power to the faint; and to them that have no might he increaseth strength. Even the youths shall faint and be weary, and the young men shall utterly fall: But they that wait upon the Lord shall renew their strength: they shall mount up with wings as eagles; they shall run, and not be weary; and they shall walk, and not faint."

So these good Christians at Ephesus patiently bore their troubles, they opposed false doctrines, they labored hard to get out the Gospel and thus they were pleasing to the Lord. Oh, Christians ought not faint, ought not give up! It is true about prayer. Jesus "spake a parable unto them to this end, that men ought always to pray, and not to faint" (Luke 18:1). The Hebrew Christians who suffered great affliction and the loss of goods were counseled, "Cast not away therefore your confidence, which hath great recompence of reward. For ye have need of patience, that, after ye have done the will of God, ye might receive the promise" (Heb. 10:35, 36).

Dr. Bob Jones, Sr., used to say, "The greatest ability is dependability." Faithfulness, persistence in the will of God despite difficulties and disappointments, how blessed it is!

A Sad Complaint:

"Thou hast left thy first love" (vs. 4). It is striking and sad that good Christians who persistently serve God may lose some of the honeymoon sweetness of their early Christian life. Christians who may set out to serve God with genuine love and have blessed joy in His presence, may come to serve Him as a matter of duty, without the outflowing of love, without the constant sense of God's presence they once had.

Oh, an old Methodist hymn says,

> **Prone to wander, Lord, I feel it,**
> **Prone to leave the God I love.**

Yes, our human hearts have a tendency to backslide. And no matter how much our character is settled in the habits of Christian life, God wants the heart love, too, and the joy. We are not only to be resigned to tribulation, but we are to "count it all joy when ye fall into divers temptations." We ought to remember "in every thing give thanks" (I Thess. 5:18). We should remember that the apostles, James and John, went away from a terrible beating "rejoicing that they were counted worthy to suffer shame for his name" (Acts 5:41). Oh, duty is good, but duty with a happy heart is essential.

My song, "Let the Sun Shine Again in My Heart," says:

I remember the time when I first knew the Saviour,
   When the sunlight of blessing so flooded my heart.
Oh, the sweetness of "first love," with Jesus so near me,
   And I thought such devotion would never depart.

Then how sweet were the Scriptures, they spoke to me daily,
   How they guided my steps: but my zeal did not last.
And the sweet place of pray'r where I met with my Saviour
   I neglected, and so soon my joys were all past.

Oh, I loved well to walk in the way with God's children,
   When we met with glad heart in a fellowship sweet.
But the pull of the flesh and some worldly companions
   In the paths of sin's pleasure attracted my feet.

Lord, I come now again for forgiveness and blessing,
   As Thy penitent child I am seeking Thy peace.
For the blood paid my debt and Thy Spirit within me
   Bids me come to my Father, my wand'ring to cease.

Let the sun shine again, Let the flow'rs bloom again;
   Stir the embers of love in my heart!—
Holy Spirit reprove, then embrace me again;
   Let the sun shine again in my heart!

In the Lord's prayer we are taught to come daily to pray, "And forgive us our sins; for we also forgive every one that is indebted to us." You see, we need daily to be revived in heart, to have new cleansing, new anointing with power and new rejoicing.

The young convert instinctively has a desire to see other people saved. When I found Christ in the First Baptist Church of Gainesville, Texas, as a nine-year-old boy, I asked my father about my joining the church. He had not been present when I was saved. I didn't know how to tell him about it. He thought because I was so young, I probably was not saved. And I thought

my father knew everything, so I did not have full assurance for
three years. But God had put a burning in my heart when I got
saved.

So the next morning as I went to school, I knelt down on a
sandbar in the creek bottom and prayed for others. "Lord, I may
be too young to be saved but this one is not, and that one." I
named others who ought to be saved. Oh, I know now that was
good evidence that God had put that "first love" in my heart.

It was a joy in Spearman, Texas, to win a French war bride
who came back with her American husband after World War I.
She was a devout Catholic, but when I preached on, "Ye Must
Be Born Again," she saw she did not have that. Her husband
brought her to my room and there we went into the Scriptures
carefully. With many tears she prayed in French for the Lord to
save her. Then she claimed the Lord and trusted Him. We shook
hands on it and she embraced her husband gladly. Then I said,
"Now I must leave. I have promised to meet two young men to
talk to them about the Lord." And we went out the gate together.
I turned to the right and they to the left down the sidewalk. But
behind me soon I heard the clatter of a woman's heels running on
the sidewalk and her cry, "Brudder Rice! Brudder Rice!" (in her
quaint accent). This new convert came weeping to me, seized my
hand in both of hers, and sobbed. I wondered, Was she not sure
of salvation? She had seemed so glad and so sure. But she said,
"Oh, Brudder Rice! I do hope you save those boys!"

You see, first love must enter into the concern the Lord Jesus
has about saving sinners. And it is too bad when our churches get
cold and orthodox and formal and lose the passion and first love
that went out to get sinners and get them saved.

And will you note carefully here the Lord says, *"Remember
therefore from whence thou art fallen, and repent, and do the
first works; or else I will come unto thee quickly, and will remove
thy candlestick out of his place, except thou repent"* (vs. 5).

Dr. W. B. Riley says on this verse:

This is the parable of the barren fig tree repeated in the Epistle
to the Church of Ephesus. I often think of what Dr. A. J. Gordon

said, when on one occasion he was discussing the destitution of a spiritual life in the city of Boston.

"Ecclesiastical corpses lie all about us. The caskets in which they repose are lined with satin, and are decorated with solid silver handles and abundant flowers, and like other caskets they are just large enough for their occupants, with no room for strangers. These churches have died of respectability, and been embalmed in self-complacency. If, by the grace of God this church is alive [referring to the Clarendon Street Church, of which he was pastor] be warned to use your opportunity, or the feet of them that buried thy sisters will be at the door and carry thee out."

The church must be fruitful, and, if fruitless, it has its choice between reformation and removal.

These people who labored and were faithful, who stood for Christ and the truth, if they did not come back to the first love and joy in soul winning, then the Lord Jesus said, "I will. . . remove thy candlestick out of his place." What does He mean? He means that church will die. Churches are to be soul-saving stations. A church that does not win souls has missed its mission and is on its way to death.

We must say, then, that when Jesus said, ". . .upon this rock I will build my church; and the gates of hell shall not prevail against it," He was not speaking of local congregations. The gates of Hell do prevail against a church when it loses its soul-winning passion and concern. So this church at Ephesus passed out of existence, as did all other churches of the New Testament. The local church is not immortal. As Dr. B. H. Carroll said, "Churches are time organizations, not eternal organizations." That church which is the body of Christ is eternal, but local congregations of Christians are not. And every local congregation has a solemn warning that unless they come back to soul-winning zeal and joy, the Lord is likely to remove the church itself, the candlestick.

"But this thou hast, that thou hatest the deeds of the Nicolaitanes, which I also hate" (vs. 6). These Nicolaitanes were probably a local false cult not known in history. It was to the credit of the Christians at Ephesus that they were vigorously opposed to it and said so. They "hated" it as Christ did.

"He that hath an ear, let him hear" (vs. 7). God wants people

with a heart atuned to hear Him. How we need to beware lest a
preconceived opinion or the influence of a loved one or friend, or
self-interest, give us a bias that keeps us from instantly considering openly every word from God!

Dr. J. B. Gambrell, a Texas Baptist editor, said years ago,
"You cannot teach some people anything because they already
know so much that is not so."

"Overcomers"—not *because* they overcome but *after* that happy accomplishment should they look forward to the eternal
refreshing and renewal of everlasting life in the presence of God
eating from the tree of life which sinful man had left in the
Garden of Eden.

VERSES 8—11:

8 And unto the angel of the church in Smyrna write; These things saith the first and the last, which was dead, and is alive;

9 I know thy works, and tribulation, and poverty, (but thou art rich) and *I know* the blasphemy of them which say they are Jews, and are not, but *are* the synagogue of Satan.

10 Fear none of those things which thou shalt suffer: behold, the devil shall cast *some* of you into prison, that ye may be tried; and ye shall have tribulation ten days: be thou faithful unto death, and I will give thee a crown of life.

11 He that hath an ear, let him hear what the Spirit saith unto the churches; He that overcometh shall not be hurt of the second death.

To the Church at Smyrna

In the *Bible of the Expositor and the Evangelist,* Dr. W. B.
Riley defines Smyrna:

> The Church at Smyrna was in the place next nearest to Patmos,
> and in its strength it was second to that at Ephesus. This city of
> Smyrna, situated at the head of a beautiful bay about 40 miles
> northwest of Ephesus, still exists, and is a commerical center to-
> day, from which railroads radiate much after the fashion of our
> modern western cities.
>
> In its early days, Smyrna was one of the most beautiful cities of
> the Orient, celebrated for its games, its library, its temples, and
> its sacred festivals. It is probable that Paul preached the Gospel
> there and founded a church while acting pastor at Ephesus; and
> according to what seems an authoritative tradition, Polycarp was

for a long time the Bishop of Smyrna, and suffered his martyrdom in that place, after 86 years of loyal service to God.

Christ Knows Our Toil, Tribulation, Poverty

"I know thy works, and tribulation" (vs. 9). Does God know all the tribulations that come to good Christians? Yes, He knows! Paul's thorn in the flesh is in His dear plan. A humbled Paul, compelled to wait on God for help, will serve Him better and have greater reward than if Paul were "exalted above measure" by the great revelations given him. Since "the trying of your faith worketh patience" (Jas. 1:3), the patient Christian will have more reward and more joy as well as more fruit.

Job was left for a bit in Satan's hands for trial. But God still put a hedge about him. Then Satan could not take his life. Job was rewarded and newly blessed, but millions in Heaven will thank Job and thank God because he proved to all of us that "the Lord is very pitiful, and of tender mercy" (Jas. 5:11).

"DOES JESUS CARE?"

Does Jesus care when my heart is pained
   Too deeply for mirth and song;
As the burdens press, and the cares distress,
   And the way grows weary and long?

Does Jesus care when my way is dark
   With a nameless dread and fear?
As the daylight fades into deep night shades,
   Does He care enough to be near?

Does Jesus care when I've tried and failed
   To resist some temptation strong;
When for my deep grief I find no relief,
   Tho' my tears flow all the night long?

Does Jesus care when I've said "good-by"
   To the dearest on earth to me,
And my sad heart aches till it nearly breaks—
   Is it aught to Him? Does He see?

O yes, He cares; I know He cares,
   His heart is touched with my grief;
When the days are weary, the long nights dreary,
   I know my Saviour cares.

". . .and poverty. . ." (vs. 9). Poverty is known to God, and poverty, in the will of God, is blessed. "How hardly shall they

that have riches enter into the kingdom of God?" Riches are often a curse. They were to the prodigal son. Poverty may bring some pain but it often prevents far more. Jesus said, "Blessed be ye poor" (Luke 6:20). And Jesus came, we are told, "anointed . . .to preach the gospel to the poor" (Luke 4:18, quoting Isa. 61:1).

It was to poor shepherds that Christ's birth was announced at Bethlehem. When God cursed the ground so that it brought toil and burden and tended to poverty, God said to Adam, "Cursed is the ground for thy sake" (Gen. 3:17). Oh, it was for man's good that he must toil, for "an idle mind is the Devil's workshop."

"Now no chastening for the present seemeth to be joyous, but grievous: nevertheless afterward it yeildeth the peaceable fruit of righteousness unto them which are exercised thereby."—Heb. 12:11.

Prison for Some: Fear Not

". . .behold, the devil shall cast some of you into prison, that ye may be tried" (vs. 10). Don't be afraid of the future, the Lord tells the Christians at Smyrna. Satan will cast some of them into prison. So what? Paul in prison said, "I have learned, in whatsoever state I am, therewith to be content" (Phil. 4:11).

God was with Paul and Silas in prison. John the Baptist was in prison for preaching and went to Heaven from prison, as did many others. All the promises are still great for one in prison. God still has angels round about the prison, though unseen. God still answers prayer.

He was with Joseph in prison and brought him out to rule Egypt and save the lives of many. In answer to prayer, Peter was brought out of the prison by an angel in Acts 12. Daniel went to the lions' den but came out safely, and the three Hebrew children went through the fiery furnace without harm. Yes, and "one like the Son of God" came to walk with them there. I think they would never have seen Him but for the fiery furnace!

Oh, lions' dens and fiery furnaces and prisons are greatly overrated as terrors for obedient Christians! "Fear none of those things which thou shalt suffer," Jesus said.

It is marvelous how good a studio dungeons have made for God's men.

It was in prison that Joseph learned some of the best lessons of his life—courage, patience, interpretations.

It was in prison that Daniel tested the truths that he had been declaring, and found in them no failure for God was with him.

It was in prison that Paul and Silas caught the spirit of petition and from prison that some of the former's most splendid Epistles were sent.

It was in prison that John Bunyan saw the illuminated path of the just leading from Sodom to the Celestial City; and it was in prison that Judson learned the nature of true trust in God, and came into the full experience of the same. . . .

W. B. Riley in *The Bible of the Expositor.*

Israel was carried away to Babylon for their sins. Oh, but they were not forgotten there. If they only knew it, the loving, yearning heart of God followed them and promised well. In Jeremiah 29:11-13 God said:

"For I know the thoughts that I think toward you, saith the Lord, thoughts of peace, and not of evil, to give you an expected end. Then shall ye call upon me, and ye shall go and pray unto me, and I will hearken unto you. And ye shall seek me, and find me, when ye shall search for me with all your heart."

> Fear not, I am with thee, O be not dismayed,
> For I am thy God, I will still give thee aid;
> I'll strengthen thee, help thee, and cause thee to stand,
> Upheld by My gracious, omnipotent hand.
>
> When thro' the deep waters I call thee to go,
> The rivers of sorrow shall not overflow;
> For I will be with thee thy trials to bless,
> And sanctify to thee thy deepest distress.
>
> When thro' fiery trials thy pathway shall lie,
> My grace, all-sufficient, shall be thy supply;
> The flames shall not hurt thee, I only design
> Thy dross to consume, and thy gold to refine.

Satan's Time Limited: Then Have Joy!

They were to be *"tribulation ten days"* (vs. 10). God sets a limit for Christians in trouble. "Man proposes but God disposes." They are to be "faithful unto death" in order to get "a crown of life." That means sometimes Christians will die in persecution. But is that bad? I envy Paul's reception in Heaven when the headman's ax took him out of Rome's Mamertine dungeon! I envy Stephen the glory of his entrance into Heaven, as a rock broke his skull! He saw Jesus standing up from the throne beside the Father's throne to welcome home the martyr!

T. DeWitt Talmage said, "The tears of earth will be the wine of Heaven." So, be *"faithful unto death"* and whether released here or dying a martyr, the crown of life will follow. Says Dr. W. B. Riley:

Yes, it is a crown of life; no crown of gold, no crown of diamonds. These are dead and valueless things. When I get to Heaven, I do not expect to be wearing a crown of gold, studded with precious stones, any more than I expect, while yet on earth, to do the same. If they gave me one, I should not want to wear it. Instead of casting it at Christ's feet, I think I would fling it down to earth, in the hope that some saintly man would lay hold of it and sell it to the jeweler's and use the results to preach the Gospel to dying men.

But, the *"crown of life"*—that is a different thing. That is the thing that is promised. LIFE! That is a precious thing. Life, with all of its potencies, all of its possibilities, all of its opportunities! Life, with all of its service, with all of its sanctities! Ah, that is the crown I covet!

Trouble? Tribulation? Prison? Yes, sometimes; but a glorious end to it all. For at the end none of Christ's own can be *"hurt of the second death"* (vs. 11). We are to remember Heaven and the blessing coming, and not be too much troubled by present-day poverty, persecution and pain.

Death, a brief parting from pain into eternal rest and peace, is not bad. Departing from trouble to reward is not all bad. But the second death into eternal punishment is bad eternally, unspeakably bad. Thank God, no child of God enters the second death!

> Haste thee on from grace to glory,
>   Armed by faith, and winged by prayer;
> Heaven's eternal day's before thee,
>   God's own hand shall guide thee there.
> Soon shall close thy earthly mission,

Swift shall pass thy pilgrim days,
Hope shall change to glad fruition,
Faith to sight, and prayer to praise.

VERSES 12—17:

12 And to the angel of the church in Pĕr-́gă-mŏs write; These things saith he which hath the sharp sword with two edges;
13 I know thy works, and where thou dwellest, *even* where Satan's seat *is:* and thou holdest fast my name, and hast not denied my faith, even in those days wherein Antipas *was* my faithful martyr, who was slain among you, where Satan dwelleth.
14 But I have a few things against thee, because thou hast there them that hold the doctrine of Bā-́lāam, who taught Balac to cast a stumbling-block before the children of Israel, to eat things sacrificed unto idols, and to commit fornication.
15 So hast thou also them that hold the doctrine of the Nĭc-ō-lā-ĭ-́tānes, which thing I hate.
16 Repent; or else I will come unto thee quickly, and will fight against them with the sword of my mouth.
17 He that hath an ear, let him hear what the Spirit saith unto the churches; To him that overcometh will I give to eat of the hidden manna, and will give him a white stone, and in the stone a new name written, which no man knoweth saving he that receiveth *it.*

To the Church at Pergamos

PERGAMOS lies directly north of Smyrna, perhaps forty miles distant. . .At the time the Apocalypse was written, it was a sumptuous city, the home of rich chiefs, who had adorned it with magnificent residences, temples and groves. It had a library which rivalled that at Alexandria, a great medical school, and was famous for the rites which were there celebrated in honour of Aesculapius. It was not a commerical town such as Ephesus, but a union of a pagan Cathedral city, a university seat, and a royal residence. . .It was a city of heathen temples—a grand Pantheon of pagan worship—a metropolis of sacred sensuality—and hence "Satan's throne." Now half-buried arches, columns prostrate in the sand, and a few thousand Turkish and Greek huts, is about all that remains to mark the luxuriant and sensuous city, where the faithful Antipas suffered, and where so much glory reigned.—*The Apocalypse,* by J. A. Seiss.

Jesus is here called *"he which hath the sharp sword with two edges"* (vs. 12). That is warning for the wicked. It reminds us again that Christ is Judge. We are reminded of His return to the earth, pictured in Revelation 19, riding a white horse with the armies of Heaven following Him and "out of his mouth goeth a sharp sword." But it is also a comfort to Christians. We can remember that "the Lord executeth righteousness and judgment for all that are oppressed" (Ps. 103:6). Like the psalmist, the Christian can say, "Thy rod and thy staff they comfort me." Jesus not only is Saviour, but He is Judge.

". . .*where Satan's seat is*" (vs. 13). Halley's Handbook says about this verse: "Pergamum was a seat of emperor worship, where incense was offered before the statue of the emperor as to God. Refusal of Christians to do this often meant death. Also, an altar to Jupiter. And a temple of Esculapius, a healing god, worshiped in the form of a serpent, one of the names of Satan. Besides these, it was also a stronghold of Balaamite and Nicolaitan teachers. Thus, as a notorious center of heathenism and wickedness, it was called 'Satan's seat.' "

Dr. Scofield, in his reference Bible, thinks that means symbolically the period after Constantine's conversion and the church is taken over by the state. I think it refers to the time then present, certainly in Pergamos and in the last of the first century while John was alive. If Christ could have come in the time of the apostles, as He could have, then these churches have no meaning as periods of church history. Since we are plainly told about the Second Coming, "It is not for you to know the times or the seasons, which the Father hath put in his own power" (Acts 1:7), then Christians do wrong to presume they can figure out things God has determined to keep secret. There was a sense in which "Satan's seat" was there at Pergamos. A heathen idol was there at Pergamos in John's time. We may all learn from Christ's messages to these seven churches, but we dare not forget they were literal churches at the time John wrote. Do not put symbolic spiritual meaning here and ignore the literal meaning.

Christians there face their persecution. Antipas died a martyr. Christians there had not denied Christ in time of terrible persecution and danger. They held fast to His name. Does one imagine that persecution, pressure to deny Christ, or compromise to avoid loss or trouble or pain, is to be unusual? Then read again these messages to the seven churches in the early youth of the Gospel and see that persecution, struggles with false doctrine, and false teachers were met everywhere. So it is now. Satan's seat in some sense is in every city.

In one place a brewery or distillery helps corrupt the area and the nation. Sometimes it is a false prophet misleading thousands. Or it is a great university manned by infidels against the Bible. Or it may be a vile publishing house, or the center of a great denomination which has fallen into unbelief and deception. It is "Satan's seat"!

Woe to Those Who Follow Balaam!

"But I have a few things against thee, because thou hast them that hold the doctrine of Balaam" (vs. 14). Christ warns of a grievous sin they tolerated at Pergamos. Balaam taught Israel to fellowship with Midianites and they fell into worship of idols and committed adultery with the Midianite women. Numbers 31:14-16 tells us:

"And Moses was wroth with the officers of the host, with the captains over thousands, and captains over hundreds, which came from the battle. And Moses said unto them, Have ye saved all the women alive? Behold, these caused the children of Israel, through the counsel of Balaam, to commit trespass against the Lord in the matter of Peor, and there was a plague among the congregation of the Lord."

So a curse came on Israel, and Moses sent an army against the Midianites to kill all the males.

Fornication amid Christians is shocking. But a man living in incest with his stepmother at Corinth was first tolerated, then expelled, at Paul's plain command, until he repented (I Cor. 5).

In nearly every day's mail I read tragic stories of Christians taking up the unclean ways of the world and the sadness it brings in broken homes.

At Pergamos the Christians ate meat sacrificed to idols, some committed fornication, as did Israelites led into sin by Balaam. Oh, Christians need to beware not only of the example, the pressure and the customs of the outside world, but of the old carnal nature within that pulls one down. "The flesh lusteth against the

Spirit, and the Spirit against the flesh" (Gal. 5:17). Christians
have a new nature, but the old nature is still there until the time
of the resurrection. And a Christian must lament, as did Paul,
"For the good that I would I do not; But the evil which I would
not, that I do. . .O wretched man that I am! who shall deliver
me from the body of this death?. . .So then with the mind I
myself serve the law of God; but with the flesh the law of sin"
(Rom. 7:19, 24, 25). A Christian cannot commit the unpardonable sin, for all his sins are covered and he has "now received
the atonement" (Rom. 5:11). But Christians may still sin and
lose fellowship with God or may have drastic chastening at the
hand of God and may miss blessed rewards they ought to have.

Christians are taught to pray in our daily prayer, "Forgive us
our sins" (Luke 11:4). The repentance of a lost sinner, turning
from sin to trust in Christ, should be a continuing process in actual practice, although the heart has sincerely turned from sin to
Christ to get saved. In practice we need to say as the psalmist,
"He restoreth my soul" (Ps. 23:3). We need to remember the
command, "But be ye transformed by the renewing of your
mind. . ." (Rom 12:2). We can sometimes pray as did David
after he had committed such great sin, "Create in me a clean
heart, O God; and renew a right spirit within me" (Ps. 51:10).

Repent, or Face Judgment

*"Repent; or else I will come unto thee quickly, and will fight
against them with the sword of my mouth"* (vs. 16). These Christians at Pergamos must repent or face God's sword of judgment.
At Corinth some who were irreverent and worldly and even
drunken at the Lord's table, found that God said, "For this cause
many are weak and sickly among you, and many sleep" (I Cor.
11:30). Christians may be sick or may die prematurely because of
sin. For sin Moses missed going into the Promised Land. And
many a man has suffered in health or in business or through his
children because of unrepented sin.

James 5:16 tells us, "Confess your faults one to another, and
pray one for another, that ye may be healed." Our sickness often
is the result of sin. And we have the plain statement that God

"scourgeth every son whom he receiveth" (Heb. 12:6).

Christians, then, need to beware lest we fall into impatient unbelief as did Moses when he smote the rock instead of speaking to it as the Lord said, or lest we should fall into adultery and murder like David, or idolatry like Solomon, or to cursing and denying of the Lord like Peter! Oh, how we should hate and fear sin, and how we should be like Paul who said, "I keep under my body, and bring it into subjection: lest that by any means, when I have preached to others, I myself should be a castaway" (I Cor. 9:27), as far as service is concerned.

And the church of Pergamos is reminded again, as we are, that we should seek to be always tuned in, have an open ear, have an eager, listening heart to what God's Spirit says to us in the Scriptures as He said to them.

Here we have the sweet reminder to overcomers of *"a white stone"!* (vs. 17). On it a new name unknown to all but the one who receives it! Some have thought that meant a precious stone, a diamond. Not necessarily so. The value is what is written on the stone, a new and heavenly name. And what all does it mean? We do not know. "For now we see through a glass, darkly; but then face to face: now I know in part; but then shall I know even as also I am known" (I Cor. 13:12).

Ah, the joy of certainty now, the extra joy of a thousand mysteries made plain in Heaven!

VERSES 18—29:

18 And unto the angel of the church in Thȳ-ă-tī́-ră write; These things saith the Son of God, who hath his eyes like unto a flame of fire, and his feet *are* like fine brass;

19 I know thy works, and charity, and service, and faith, and thy patience, and thy works; and the last *to be* more than the first.

20 Notwithstanding I have a few things against thee, because thou sufferest that woman Jĕź-ĕ-bĕl, which calleth herself a prophetess, to teach and to seduce my servants to commit fornication, and to eat things sacrificed unto idols.

21 And I gave her space to repent of her fornication; and she repented not.

22 Behold, I will cast her into a bed, and them that commit adultery with her into great tribulation, except they repent of their deeds.

23 And I will kill her children with

death; and all the churches shall know that I am he which searcheth the reins and hearts: and I will give unto every one of you according to your works.

24 But unto you I say, and unto the rest in Thy̆-ă-tī-̆ră, as many as have not this doctrine, and which have not known the depths of Satan, as they speak; I will put upon you none other burden.

25 But that which ye have *already* hold fast till I come.

26 And he that overcometh, and keepeth my works unto the end, to him will I give power over the nations:

27 And he shall rule them with a rod of iron; as the vessels of a potter shall they be broken to shivers: even as I received of my Father.

28 And I will give him the morning star.

29 He that hath an ear, let him hear what the   Spirit saith unto the churches.

To the Church of Thyatira

Says Seiss: "Twenty or thirty miles to the southeast was Thyatira, the fourth in the list, and once a considerable town, founded by Seleucus Nicator. In the time of John, it was mainly inhabited by Macedonians, who had formed themselves into various guilds of potters, tanners, weavers, rope-makers and dyers. Lydia, the seller of purple stuffs, whom Paul met at Philippi, was from this place. . .It was a place of great amalgamation of race and religious observances. It now has about 30,000 and is full of ruins."

Don't forget the glory of the resurrected Jesus with *"eyes like unto a flame of fire, and his feet are like fine brass"* (vs. 19). Never let our conception of the Lord Jesus become common. Holy awe, "the fear of the Lord" is involved here.

"Charity," Brotherly Love

In verse 19 charity, or Christian love, is the first virtue praised and approved in these Christians at Thyatira. How great a quality of character! How strongly commanded by the Lord! Two commands sum up all the law and all duty:

"Thou shalt love the Lord thy God with all thy heart, and with all thy soul, and with all thy mind. This is the first and great commandment. And the second is like unto it, Thou shalt love thy neighbour as thyself."—Matt. 22:37-39.

How much? Even as yourself!

And I Corinthians 13 says it so compellingly: Without Christian charity, brotherly love, all faith, all sacrifice, all service, is no better than sounding brass or a tinkling cymbal! And this is the criterion that is to always mark a Christian before the world: "By this shall all men know that ye are my disciples, if ye have love one to another" (John 13:35).

Brotherly love is to suffer long and still be kind. It is to think no evil. It is to put the most favorable construction possible on the acts or words or reports about another Christian. And then, "Brethren, if a man be overtaken in a fault, ye which are spiritual, restore such an one in the spirit of meekness; considering thyself, lest thou also be tempted" (Gal. 6:1).

And failure to forgive one who does wrong so grieves God that we are commanded, "And when ye stand praying, forgive, if ye have ought against any: that your Father also which is in heaven may forgive you your trespasses" (Mark 11:25). And we are to remember it as we daily pray and be able to say, "And forgive us our debts, as we forgive our debtors."

There are Christians with whom we differ. But I must love born-again Christians who believe the Bible, who love the dear Lord Jesus, my Lord Jesus!

"Other sheep I have, which are not of this fold," He said. But, oh, glad day when all God's sheep will be of one fold!

And so with the same Lord, the same faith and with born-again ones baptized picturing Christ's death and resurrection (we have the same baptism). We must endeavor to "keep the unity of the Spirit in the bond of peace" (Eph. 4:3). Parents can discipline their children as they love them. Preachers can "reprove, rebuke, exhort with all longsuffering and doctrine," while they love Christians sincerely and help them. To be true to Christ in doctrine is necessary. To be true to Christ in Christian love is even more strongly commanded.

Oh, then, let us love one another even when we must sometimes express lovingly our differences and must sometimes correct the erring brother.

Service, Faith and Works

How they worked for God—these Christians at Thyatira! We

think they fed the poor. They worked to get out the Gospel. They were honest, hard-working Christians. We suppose they did not, like many congregations today, leave most of the church work to a few. Christian love, charity for all would mean help for all, attention to the poor, the neglected, the lonely, the sinning.

And *"thy works"* is repeated: *". . .and thy works; and the last to be more than the first"* (vs. 19). I have no doubt they gave liberally. That they visited the sick. That they were active Christians.

"And faith" they had. "Without faith it is impossible to please him: for he that cometh to God must believe that he is, and that he is a rewarder of them that diligently seek him" (Heb. 11:6). And "whatsoever is not of faith is sin" (Rom. 14:23). They believed the Bible. They believed God answered prayer. And they trusted God to bring things out well.

And the Lord knew more: *". . .and thy patience."* A great word which means persistence in doing right. So "the trying of your faith worketh patience" (Jas. 1:3). We are to "lay aside every weight, and the sin which doth so easily beset us, and let us run with patience the race that is set before us, Looking unto Jesus the author and finisher of our faith" (Heb. 12:1, 2). Faithfulness—what a virtue! "The greatest ability is dependability."

False Prophetess Jezebel

Was that actually her name? More likely she is here likened to and named after the wicked queen, Jezebel, wife of Ahab in Samaria who worshiped Baal and put God's prophets to death. Halley's Handbook says about Jezebel in verse 20:

> Thyatira was famous for its magnificent Temple of Artemis, another name for Diana. Jezebel, it is thought, may have been a prominent woman devotee of Diana, with a gift for leadership, who had a following of influential people and who, attracted to the growing cause of Christianity, attached herself to the church, militantly insisting, however, on the right to teach and practice licentious indulgence, claiming inspiration for her teaching.
>
> She was called "Jezebel" because, like Jezebel the devilish wife of Ahab who had introduced the abominations of Astarte worship

into Israel (I Kings 16), she was introducing the same vile practices into the Christian church.

Not all of the Thyatira pastors accepted her teaching. But, trying to be Liberal, and thinking that she might be a help in winning the whole city to the name of Christ, they accepted her as a fellow pastor.

With that the Lord was greatly displeased. And, in a stinging rebuke, He presented Himself "with eyes like fire and feet like brass" (2:18).

God has a clear teaching about the danger in women as prophets and religious teachers. "Let the woman learn in silence with all subjection. But I suffer not a woman to teach, nor to usurp authority over the man, but to be in silence" (I Tim. 2:11, 12). And again, "Let your women keep silence in the churches: for it is not permitted unto them to speak; but they are commanded to be under obedience, as also saith the law. And if they will learn any thing, let them ask their husbands at home: for it is a shame for women to speak in the church" (I Cor. 14:34, 35).

In history we have seen the abomination of the Fox Sisters and the Spiritist cult; Mrs. White, the seeress of Seventh-Day Adventists; Mary Baker Eddy, founder of so-called Christian Science, and many other women preachers teaching false doctines, overemphasizing healing, or in the modern tongues movement, claiming sinless perfection, etc. We remember there were no women preachers in the New Testament. Men, women, sons, daughters, servants and handmaids may all be filled with the Spirit and prophecy, that is, may witness in the power of the Holy Spirit as is plainly promised in Acts 2:15-21 quoting from Joel. But the leadership of the churches and over men is reserved only for men.

This "Jezebel" seduced Christians "to commit fornication, and to eat things sacrificed unto idols." The sin here is similar to that rebuked at Pergamos (vs. 14), a city not far away. There the leadership was by a woman.

Dr. Ironside's comment on verse 21, *"I gave her space to repent. . .and she repented not,"* is as follows:

> God gave her space to repent and she repented not. Go back to
> the days of Savonarola in Italy—Wickliffe and Cranmer of

England—John Knox in Scotland—Martin Luther in Germany—
Zwingle in Switzerland—Calvin in France—all those mighty
reformers whom God raised up throughout the world to call Rome
to repent of her iniquity, but "she repented not."

. . .In our day, we have a lot of foolish Protestants who believe
that the old Rome is now a harmless old pussy-cat sitting on the
banks of the Tiber: she purrs so contentedly. . .And so efforts are
being made to re-unite the various great bodies of Christendom
in one vast society headed by the Pope. . .What foolish people
these Protestants are!. . .They are dazzled with the thought of a
great united church, and are hurrying us on to a union with Rome
which Scripture shows clearly enough will yet take place. But,
thank God, not until the church of Christ has been caught up to
meet the Lord in the clouds, to be with Himself, according to His
promise (John 14:2, 3). God gave Rome space to repent. If she had
had any desire to get right with Him, she would have repented in
the 16th century.

Punishment for Offender

As a result of this wickedness, punishment will be *"great
tribulation"* (vs. 22), and the Lord will *"kill her children with
death"* (vs. 23).

We remember that because the high priest Eli's sons were vile
and he restrained them not, they were to be killed in battle.

And Eli, the old high priest, fell when he heard it and broke his
neck.

And here is a general rule, often repeated in the Bible,
*". . .and I will give unto every one of you according to your
works"* (vs. 23) as a divine law that "the way of transgressors is
hard" (Prov. 13:15). Moses was led to warn Israel, "But if ye will
not do so, behold ye have sinned against the Lord: and be sure
your sin will find you out" (Num. 32:23). And Romans 6:23 says,
"For the wages of sin is death."

God has laws that always work. Sin always brings punishment.
It does not always show immediately, but bit by bit there is a
reaping to that kind of sowing.

However, they were given the opportunity to repent. These
troubles will come *"except they repent of their deeds"* (vs. 22).
God has mercy for the penitent soul. Repentance does not always
stop the natural results of our sin. David was penitent after he

had taken Uriah's wife and had Uriah murdered, but trouble came through his children: a daughter raped, a son a murderer, the illegitimate baby's death, the two sons revolting against their father's kingdom. But the verdict of death for David, who had pronounced the death verdict about the rich man who took his neighbor's little ewe lamb, was revoked and David was spared.

What does it mean when Jesus said, *"Behold, I will cast her into a bed. . ."* (vs. 22)? Evidently a period of trouble. It is a figure of speech, like we sometimes say, "You have made your bed, now lie in it."

But the warnings of judgment here are not to affect all the Christians of Thyatira. To those who *"have not this doctrine, and which have not known the depths of Satan, as they speak,"* Jesus said, *"I will put upon you none other burden"* (vs. 24). But they should hold fast that which they have (vs. 25). This is the third mention of Satan in the Seven Letters. In Smyrna he cast Christians into prison (2:9, 10); in Pergamum, Satan's "throne": he was persecuting the church and corrupting it with false teachings (2:13, 14). Here in Thyatira, Jezebel's teachings were known as the "deep things of Satan" (2:24). And in 3:9 Satan is mentioned as the enemy of the church in Philadelphia.

And in verse 26 is a promise of power and rule to those who are faithful: *". . .power over the nations,"* which must refer to the kingdom age.

And to these that overcome, He says, *"I will give him the morning star"* (vs. 28). The Morning Star is Jesus, as we see from Revelation 22:16. Christ is offering Himself with all His wealth of love and power, to His people. At Christ's second coming He will appear when "the day dawn, and the day star arise in your hearts" (II Pet. 1:19). And when John the Baptist was born old Zacharias said:

"And thou, child, shalt be called the prophet of the Highest: for thou shalt go before the face of the Lord to prepare his ways; To give knowledge of salvation unto his people by the remission of their sins, Through the tender mercy of our God; whereby the dayspring from on high hath visited us, To give light to them that sit in darkness and in the shadow of death, to

guide our feet into the way of peace."—Luke 1:76-79.

Ah, when Jesus, the Bright and Morning Star, comes to reign on the earth, He will be "the Sun of righteousness" (Mal. 4:2). And in the Heavenly Jerusalem we are told, "And the city had no need of the sun, neither of the moon, to shine in it: for the glory of God did lighten it, and the Lamb is the light thereof" (Rev. 21:23).

Oh, the dear Lord Jesus, the Light of the World, will be the Light of Heaven as He is now the Light in the Christian's heart. Then, let us hear what the Spirit saith to the churches. God give us an open ear to hear!

Chapter 3

AND unto the angel of the church in Sardis write; These things saith he that hath the seven Spirits of God, and the seven stars; I know thy works, that thou hast a name that thou livest, and art dead.

2 Be watchful, and strengthen the things which remain, that are ready to die: for I have not found thy works perfect before God.

3 Remember therefore how thou hast received and heard, and hold fast, and repent. If therefore thou shalt not watch, I will come on thee as a thief, and thou shalt not know what hour I will come upon thee.

4 Thou hast a few names even in Sardis which have not defiled their garments; and they shall walk with me in white: for they are worthy.

5 He that overcometh, the same shall be clothed in white raiment; and I will not blot out his name out of the book of life, but I will confess his name before my Father, and before his angels.

6 He that hath an ear, let him hear what the Spirit saith unto the churches.

To the Church at Sardis

Seiss says:

> From Thyatira some thirty miles to the southward, is Sardis, at the foot of Mount Tmolus, on the banks of a rivulet famous for its golden sands. Here the Wealthy Croesus lived and reigned. Here the wise Thales, Cleobulus, and Solon had their homes. And on the plains around it once lay the hosts of Xerxes, on their way to find a sepulchre at Marathon. It was a rich and glorious city when Cyrus conquered it; and though subsequently destroyed by an earthquake, it obtained considerable distinction under the Romans, in the reign of Tiberias. It is now a scene of melancholy ruins, with a mill and a few shepherds' huts. . .The ancient city was noted for its temple of the goddess Cybele, whose worship resembled that of Diana of Ephesus.

And Dr. W. B. Riley added a few more facts about Sardis:

> Sardis was the capital of Lydia. . .Although almost 2500 years have passed since Croesus sat upon his throne in this city, and rich men have come and gone by the thousands, still the name of this ancient king is a very synonym of immeasurable wealth.
>
> It is stated on what seems to be good authority that when Cyrus, 548 B. C., conquered Croesus and took possession of his capital

city, he found there riches to the amount of six hundred million dollars—a matchless fortune in that day. What wonder that a church located in such a city should be tempted by the worldliness sweeping around it; and, while holding fast to apostolic teaching should, nevertheless, become infected with the spirit of the city, and grieve, and lose the Spirit of God.

Seven Spirits of God, Seven Stars

Jesus is *"he that hath the seven Spirits of God, and the seven stars"* (vs. 1). Why seven Spirits of God? Well, could you describe the Holy Spirit? Not looks, nor weight, nor size. Is He beautiful? No one can see Him. How tall? How much does He weigh? He is a Spirit, not a physical body. Terms that describe human beings are not adequate, but the number seven is a number that goes with perfection, with deity.

God put seven days in a week. There were seven lamps on the golden lampstand or candlestick in the Tabernacle in the Old Testament which pictured Christ as the "light of the world." Seven times ten, or seventy weeks of years, were prophesied from the command to rebuild Jerusalem after the captivity of Israel to the coming of the Messiah (Dan. 9:27).

God put the number seven prominent in nature referring to life processes. There are four weeks in a woman's menstrual period ordinarily. It takes three weeks to hatch chicken eggs, four weeks for turkey eggs, and two weeks for some birds.

The term "the seven Spirits of God" is used elsewhere. It does not mean that the Holy Spirit is seven different persons but that He is deity and so is infinite. He can be in and with millions of people at the same time all around the world and deal with each one separately. So one divine Person is equal to an infinite number of persons. Thus the term "seven Spirits." It pictures the perfection, deity and infinity of the Holy Spirit.

The divers manifold works in nature of the Holy Spirit are referred to in Isaiah 11:2 where of Christ, returning to reign on David's throne in the power of the Holy Spirit, it is said, "And the spirit of the Lord shall rest upon him, the spirit of wisdom and understanding, the spirit of counsel and might, the spirit of knowledge and of the fear of the Lord." Note that the "spirit of the Lord" is the spirit of wisdom, the spirit of understanding, the spirit of counsel, the spirit of might or power, the spirit of knowledge, the spirit of the fear of the Lord.

Christ also has "*the seven stars*" in His hands (vs. 1). As the seven churches are given messages that apply to all local churches and Christians in them, so the seven stars not only represent the seven messengers of these seven churches but in a sense, all the Christian leaders in all offices. All these are in Christ's hands.

"A Name That Thou Livest, and Art Dead" (Vs. 1)

There are churches that are thought to be alive spiritually but are spiritually dead.

First, a church is made up of members and church members who claim to be and are listed as Christians or children of God but are not. They are dead. Jesus said, "Enter ye in at the strait gate: for wide is the gate, and broad is the way, that leadeth to destruction, and many there be which go in thereat: Because strait is the gate, and narrow is the way, which leadeth unto life, and few there be that find it" (Matt. 7:13,14.)

Sadly, then, we must note that there are relatively "few" who find the narrow way to Heaven by way of Christ, the Door and the "strait gate." But "Many there be," Jesus said, who go in the broad way of human righteousness, false religions and false hopes, to eternal destruction. Let us say there are more unsaved persons claiming the name of Christ than there are saved. There are more people going to Hell than there are going to Heaven.

Again in Matthew 7:21 and 22 the Lord Jesus said:

"Not every one that saith unto me, Lord, Lord, shall enter into the kingdom of heaven; but he that doeth the will of my Father which is in heaven. Many will say to me in that day, Lord, Lord, have we not prophesied in thy name? and in thy name have cast out devils? and in thy name done many wonderful works?"

That is, one who does the will of God, as to being saved by penitent faith in Christ, is saved. And one who has his own way of salvation by good deeds or by churches or rites or a priest, is not saved.

Many who are active in churches and will say to Christ that they have prophesied in Christ's name and cast out devils, yet these have never been converted. Jesus will say, "I never knew you." He is not saying that they were once saved and lost salvation, but they never were saved. They are in the broad way. They have not come to know personally Christ as Saviour.

We see also that those who are in churches but unconverted "work iniquity," Jesus said. Morality without Christ is a fake, surface morality from a wicked and unregenerate heart.

Nicodemus, though a religious leader and morally upright when unsaved, was dead and needed to be born again, even as Judas who was unconverted and spiritually dead, though he was an apostle and preached, we suppose, and cast out devils and healed the sick as did the other apostles (Matt. 10:1).

In the parable in Matthew 13 we find that the tares are tares among the wheat, unsaved people claiming and appearing to be saved to the outsider. In the parable in Matthew 25, we find five of the ten virgins did not have the oil of salvation, that is, they were not born of the Spirit, and although they hoped to meet the bridegroom, were left outside. And at the king's wedding feast for his son in Matthew 22 Jesus tells of a man who tried to attend without the prescribed wedding garment and was cast outside. So there are many warnings of unconverted people who are religious but lost.

We remember that Martin Luther was a praying, devout monk long before he understood that "the just shall live [should have life] by faith."

John Wesley came to America to save Indians and went on preaching, when he found that he himself had never yet personally trusted Christ for salvation.

Sadly we must conclude that many are outwardly religious and profess to be Christians, though they are lost. There are many religious groups that claim the name Christian but do not hold to the essentials of the Christian Faith. Where a group, local or denominational, teaches salvation by priestly rites, by church, by actual righteousness and does not hold to the Gospel of salvation by grace through faith, we must assume that those who are so taught and so profess are usually not saved. They have a name that they live but they are dead.

And local churches or groups with no saving Gospel are dead. They cannot bring living, producing Christians if they do not have the Christian Gospel.

Dead mothers do not produce living children.

When there is no Gospel clearly preached, and when religious forms and ceremonies of "worship" prevail, sinners are not told they are lost and have to be saved, then such churches are dead as far as bringing forth children of God.

Powerless orthodoxy may be called dead also. Those who do not know a saving Christ and a saving Gospel are dead. But there are preachers who believe the Bible, who claim Christ as Saviour, who preach to congregations that are, in the main, believers, but who do not seek and do not have the holy anointing of the Spirit of God. They do not weep over sinners nor present the Gospel to them. No sinners are taught they are lost and need to be saved, and there are no repenting sinners coming to Christ in such churches. Like the barren fig tree the Lord Jesus cursed, they live but they are fruitless and are, in effect, dead as far as fruitbearing is concerned. And like that fig tree was cursed and withered and forbidden to bear fruit forever in the future, so they die. The former fruitless orthodoxy is open to cults and modernism and dies out, becoming the victim of open unbelief.

In Christ's parable of the vine, Jesus said, "Every branch in me that beareth not fruit he taketh away" (John 15:2). And again He said, "If a man abide not in me, he is cast forth as a branch, and is withered" (vs. 6). And then He says of that kind of grape branches, "Men gather them, and cast them into the fire, and they are burned" (John 15:6).

Deadness follows fruitlessness.

"Strengthen the Things Which Remain" (Vs. 2)

Charles Spurgeon has this comment on verse 2:

Have you ever read *The Ancient Mariner*? I dare say you

thought it one of the strangest imaginations ever put together, especially that part where the old mariner represents the corpses of dead men rising up to man the ship; dead men pulling the rope; dead men at the oars; dead men steering; dead men spreading the sails! I thought what a strange idea, and yet I have lived to see that. I have gone into churches where there was a dead man in the pulpit, a dead man reading the notices, a dead man singing, a dead man taking a collection, and the pews were filled with the same.

Among those spiritually dead at Sardis where some living Christians. Verse 4 says, *"Thou hast a few names even in Sardis which have not defiled their garments."* For these there is hope if they *"hold fast, and repent"* (vs. 3). "Hold fast"—to what? That they had *"received and heard"* (vs. 3). They were to hold fast to the faith of the Gospel (Phil. 1:27) and the Gospel itself, that is, the historic Christian Faith. And all the blessings they must hold that come with the Gospel.

"Repent," Jesus said. Of what? Of fellowship with infidels, of supporting programs of false teachers. For Christians today it would mean coming out of any yoke with unbelievers (II Cor. 6:14-18). It should mean not receiving into our houses (or churches or colleges) any who do not hold to the Bible doctrine about Christ, not even to bid them "God speed." Second John 9 to 11 says:

"Whosoever transgresseth, and abideth not in the doctrine of Christ, hath not God. He that abideth in the doctrine of Christ, he hath both the Father and the Son. If there come any unto you, and bring not this doctrine, receive him not into your house, neither bid him God speed: For he that biddeth him God speed is partaker of his evil deeds."

So to repent would mean leaving the empty formalism and going back to the saving Gospel and trying to reach "every creature" with the Gospel, as Christians are commanded.

Ruin, punishment, destruction are certain to come to fruitless, dead churches and to the few living who stay with the dead and do not repent.

But though trouble, punishment and public exposure will come to those who do not repent, born-again Christians, with the saving faith that overcomes the world, will be clothed in white raiment and their names will not be blotted out of the book of life and they will be confessed by the Saviour as His own before the Father and the angels!

Oh, to be faithful, you remnant Christians who need to repent and restore!

Reader, does your spiritual ear find itself tuned to God's message here?

VERSES 7—13:

7 And to the angel of the church in Philadelphia write; These things saith he that is holy, he that is true, he that hath the key of David, he that openeth, and no man shutteth; and shutteth, and no man openeth;

8 I know thy works: behold, I have set before thee an open door, and no man can shut it: for thou hast a little strength, and hast kept my word, and hast not denied my name.

9 Behold, I will make them of the synagogue of Satan, which say they are Jews, and are not, but do lie; behold, I will make them to come and worship before thy feet, and to know that I have loved thee.

10 Because thou hast kept the word of my patience, I also will keep thee from the hour of temptation, which shall come upon all the world, to try them that dwell upon the earth.

11 Behold, I come quickly: hold that fast which thou hast, that no man take thy crown.

12 Him that overcometh will I make a pillar in the temple of my God, and he shall go no more out: and I will write upon him the name of my God, and the name of the city of my God, *which is* new Jerusalem, which cometh down out of heaven from my God: and *I will write upon him* my new name.

13 He that hath an ear, let him hear what the Spirit saith unto the churches.

To the Church at Philadelphia

Again we look to Seiss for a description of the Church at Philadelphia: "Southeastward, less than forty miles, stood Philadelphia, the great winemarket of Phrygia, rocked with oft-recurring earthquakes, and with a population once large and powerful, but never very distinguished. It took its name from the king who found it. . .Those who constituted the Church to which John was commanded to write, are supposed to have been poor people, living on the outskirts, and heavily taxed for public purposes."

And Halley's Bible Handbook says that "the great earthquake of A.D. 17 ruined it completely. The 'new name' is certainly a reference to the proposal to rename the city Neocaesarea in gratitude for Tiberius' generous earthquake relief."

The name "Philadelphia" means "city of brotherly love." Other cities in Bible times had this name. But here the Philadelphia is in the small province of Asia now a part of Asiatic Turkey.

The Letter Is From "He That Is Holy, He That Is True" (Vs. 7).

This greeting is that of deity. These are not the words of greeting from John but from the Lord Jesus Christ Himself. They fit Him and no mere mortal man. Even of men speaking for God. Isaiah wrote as a prophet of God, in whose mouth God put His words (Isa. 51:16). Paul wrote as an apostle of Christ. John wrote his first, second and third epistles as from "the elder unto the elect lady," and "the elder unto the wellbeloved Gaius." James and Jude each wrote as "the servant of Jesus Christ." But the book of Revelation is "the Revelation of Jesus Christ, which God gave unto him." These are direct letters from Jesus Christ to the seven churches recorded by John. So the greeting is directly from Christ.

But all through this book, Christ is elevated, not as a meek and lowly Saviour dying for sinners, but as the Christ of the Second Coming to reign. He is still the God-Man, but now His deity is accented as was His humanity in the Gospels.

Verse 7 reminds us that *"He. . .is holy."* That is, He is separate, set apart in a way nobody else is. He is "the only begotten Son of God," that is, the only Person physically begotten of God.

On the Mount of Transfiguration, a voice from Heaven said they were not to worship nor exalt Moses and Elijah but, "This is my beloved Son, in whom I am well pleased; hear ye him" (Matt. 17:5). So Moses and Elijah disappeared and "they saw no man, save Jesus only." Ah, He has "a name which is above every name: That at the name of Jesus every knee should bow, of things in heaven, and things in earth, and things under the earth" (Phil. 2:9,10).

He is "true" as no man is true. He is "the way, the truth, and the life" (John 14:6).

When He returns to earth with the armies of Heaven, we are told, ". . .he was called Faithful and True" (19:11).

Christ "Hath the Key of David" (Vs. 7)

This is the Lord Jesus of whom was promised in Luke 1:32, "He shall be great, and shall be called the Son of the Highest: and the Lord God shall give unto him the throne of his father David." He is the Sprout from the cut-down dynasty of King David. He is the "Branch" of Isaiah 11:1. The disciples had asked Him once, "Wilt thou at this time restore again the kingdom to Israel?" (Acts 1:6). He told them then it was not for them to know a set time for prophetic fulfillment, and it is not for us to do so. But when we think of Christ's coming, we are to remember that following the rapture and the judgment seat of Christ in Heaven and Daniel's seventieth week, including the Great Tribulation on earth, the Lord will return to reign on David's throne. "He hath the key of David."

"He That Openeth, and No Man Shutteth; and Shutteth, and No Man Openeth" (Vs. 7).

We should have a holy exaltation here. Great Nebuchadnezzar of the first world empire in the world had to learn this:

"While the word was in the king's mouth, there fell a voice from heaven, saying, O king Nebuchadnezzar, to thee it is spoken; The kingdom is departed from thee. And they shall drive thee from men, and thy dwelling shall be with the beasts of the field: they shall make thee to eat grass as oxen, and seven times shall pass over thee, until thou know that the most High ruleth in the kingdom of men, and giveth it to whomsoever he will."—Dan. 4:31,32.

Ah, men of God, neither wicked men nor governments nor circumstances, can shut doors that Christ opens for us, nor open doors that Christ closes. Rome could not stop the ministry of

Martin Luther. The Church of England could not shut up the ministry of John Wesley. And many a believing Christian has found it so.

We remember when a committee of two seminary teachers and a pastor, representing denominational leadership, threatened this writer that if I continued my open exposure of modern unbelief in a denominational university, every door among the churches would be closed to my ministry and my ministry as an evangelist would be ended. It did not happen so.

Another time a proud and domineering man threatened that "no man will get anywhere in the Northeast and outside of Texas" without his approval and that of his great church. He was wrong. I answered him kindly that "promotion cometh neither from the east, nor from the west, nor from the south. But God is the judge. . ." (Ps. 75:6, 7). He could not shut the doors that Christ opened. And despite his vigorous opposition, God led us out into great citywide revival campaigns in many cities.

So verse 8 here promises to the Christians at Philadelphia an open door that no man can shut. Paul, imprisoned at Caesarea, preached to King Agrippa and Festus. Imprisoned at Rome, He won Onesimus and made converts of the Praetorian Guard and wrote the prison epistles. Whenever a man is in the will of God, God will set before him an open door.

They had *"a little strength,"* but that is enough when Omnipotence is with them! Isaiah 40:29-31 says:

"He giveth power to the faint; and to them that have no might he increaseth strength. Even the youths shall faint and be weary, and the young men shall utterly fall: But they that wait upon the Lord shall renew their strength; they shall mount up with wings as eagles; they shall run, and not be weary; and they shall walk, and not faint."

And Paul was inspired to write, "I can do all things through Christ which strengtheneth me."

Weak but Keeping God's Word, Not Denying Christ

What a tribute to these tempted and troubled Christians! You remember that these letters to the seven churches are all written while John is exiled on the Island of Patmos for the testimony of Christ and when the Roman Empire had started a vigorous persecution of any who would not worship the emperor or offer sacrifices to heathen gods. So this handful, this remnant of faithful Christians in Philadelphia, needed encouragement. And what a tribute to these tempted, troubled Christians it was that they have *"kept my word, and hast not denied my name"* (vs. 8).

They must deal with *"the synagogue of Satan"* (vs. 9), we suppose with fanatical Jews, that is, physical Jews, not spiritual, who hated Christ and the Gospel as did those at Jerusalem, and Jews to whom Paul approached in every city in his missionary journeys. But to these Christians, Christ said, *"Thou hast kept my word, and hast not denied my name."*

Here is the great dividing issue. Those who seek "error" in the Scripture, who think it may *contain* the Word of God, in some sense, but that it is not the verbally inspired, inerrant Word of God, still say nice things about the Lord Jesus and pretend to follow Him.

The World Council of Churches, I understand, claims to be based on "Jesus Christ as Saviour and Lord." But its principal leaders openly deny the infallible inspiration of the Scriptures and much of the historic Christian Faith.

But those at Philadelphia kept the Word of Christ and did not deny Christ's name.

You see, Christ and the Bible stand or fall together. Jesus said in Mark 8:38, "Whosoever therefore shall be ashamed of me and of my words in this adulterous and sinful generation; of him also shall the Son of man be ashamed, when he cometh in the glory of his Father with the holy angels."

No man is true to Christ who doesn't believe the Bible, the Word of Christ.

Jesus said, "Think not that I am come to destroy the law, or the prophets: I am not come to destroy, but to fulfil. For verily I say unto you, Till heaven and earth pass, one jot or one tittle shall in no wise pass from the law, till all be fulfilled" (Matt. 5:17,18).

Again He said in Matthew 4:4, "It is written, Man shall not

live by bread alone, but by every word that proceedeth out of the mouth of God."

And after His resurrection He said to the doubters, "O fools, and slow of heart to believe all that the prophets have spoken . . ." (Luke 24:25).

It must be Christ and His Word, the Bible, or no Christ who is God and no Bible which is the Word of God! They stand or fall together.

"Which Say They Are Jews, and Are Not" (Vs. 9).

Could a Jewish synagogue be a "synagogue of Satan"? Yes, if it opposed Christ and rejected Him. Although they might be physically of the race of Israel they are not real Jews in the Bible sense. Romans 2:28, 29 tells us:

"For he is not a Jew, which is one outwardly; neither is that circumcision, which is outward in the flesh: But he is a Jew, which is one inwardly; and circumcision is that of the heart, in the spirit, and not in the letter; whose praise is not of men, but of God."

The promises of Christ and His blessing were promised to "Abraham and his seed," but the future seed of Abraham were promised to be like the sand of the seashore and so a great group of literal Israelites. But the seed were likened also to the stars of Heaven, which we think mean a heavenly seed of the faith of Abraham. So Galatians 3:29 says, "And if ye be Christ's, then are ye Abraham's seed, and heirs according to the promise."

Unsaved Jews claimed to be Abraham's seed, but Jesus denied it as John 6:39 tells us: "And this is the Father's will which hath sent me, that of all which he hath given me I should lose nothing, but should raise it up again at the last day." So those who are descended physically from Abraham are not spiritually his children unless they have faith in Christ as did Abraham.

Ah, but these unregenerate Jews would one day come to bow before Philadelphia Christians. Would some of them be saved like at Jerusalem when "a great company of the priests were obedient to the faith" (Acts 6:7)? And like Crispus, chief ruler of the synagogue in Corinth, who was saved (Acts 18:8)? Yes, probably some were so saved and honored the faithful Christians they joined. But others, perhaps, wait still for the time when "every knee shall bow to me, and every tongue shall confess to God" in a future accounting. And then when people acknowledge Christ they will acknowledge His people.

The Hour of Temptation Coming

Clouds of trouble gathered around God's people everywhere in the Roman Empire when John wrote these letters from Jesus to the seven churches. John himself was in prison, in exile. He was to them "your brother, and companion in tribulation" (1:9). At Pergamos, Antipas had died a martyr to the faith (2:13). At Smyrna, Satan would cast some of them into prison for ten days. The cult of the Nicolaitanes rose to plague sound Christians and deceive the unwary. Worldliness came in like a flood. There were those who like Balaam led people to fornication and eating meats offered to idols. At Thyatira, a Jezebel led Christians into sin. Christians at Ephesus had left their first love. There were only "a few names even in Sardis" that were faithful, who would not defile their garments (3:4).

Here at Philadelphia they had only *"a little strength,"* not much. So they should expect tribulation, temptation, trouble. However, they would be kept from the great temptation (or in the great temptation) and trial and persecution that was forming in all the Roman Empire. God takes care of His own who trust in Him.

"Behold, I Come Quickly" (Vs. 11)

The idea is not "immediately" but suddenly, unexpectedly. There is probably a double meaning here. First, a sudden coming in judgment and punishment for sin is warned. To the church at Ephesus, Jesus said, ". . .or else I will come unto thee quickly, and will remove thy candlestick," that is, destroy the church (Rev. 2:5). To the church at Pergamos, Jesus had warned, ". . . else I will come unto thee quickly, and will fight against them with the sword of my mouth" (2:16).

To the church at Sardis, He had warned, "If therefore thou shalt not watch, I will come on thee as a thief, and thou shalt not know what hour I will come upon thee" (Rev. 3:3).

So here the Lord speaks first of all in coming in a providential way bringing judgment. But He may be also emphasizing what He so often said in the Gospels, like "Watch therefore, for ye know neither the day nor the hour wherein the Son of man cometh" (Matt. 25:13). So in Matthew 24:36 and 42; Mark 13:32 and the following verses and elsewhere.

In closing the canon of inspiration this book says to all of us what it said then to the seven churches, "Surely I come quickly" (22:20). And in this case He certainly speaks of His personal, physical, bodily return. It will be sudden. It is impending. It does not mean immediately but certainly.

Ah, yes, overcomers! We have more reminder to encourage us: the prospect of becoming a pillar in the Temple of God in Heaven, with no more wandering and with the name of God and of the new Jerusalem and the new name of Christ upon us. We do not know all it means, but it is a great incite to godly living.

Have you ears to hear what Christ is saying to you here?

VERSES 14—22:

14 And unto the angel of the church of the Lā-ŏd-ĭ-çē-̒ăns write; These things saith the Amen, the faithful and true witness, the beginning of the creation of God;

15 I know thy works, that thou art neither cold nor hot: I would thou wert cold or hot.

16 So then because thou art lukewarm, and neither cold nor hot, I will spue thee out of my mouth.

17 Because thou sayest, I am rich, and increased with goods, and have need of nothing; and knowest not that thou art wretched, and miserable, and poor, and blind, and naked:

18 I counsel thee to buy of me gold tried in the fire, that thou mayest be rich; and white raiment, that thou mayest be clothed, and that the shame of thy nakedness do not appear; and anoint thine eyes with eyesalve, that thou mayest see.

19 As many as I love, I rebuke and chasten: be zealous therefore, and repent.

20 Behold, I stand at the door, and knock: if any man hear my voice, and open the door, I will come in to him, and will sup with him, and he with me.

21 To him that overcometh will I grant to sit with me in my throne, even as I also overcame, and am set down with my Father in his throne.

22 He that hath an ear, let him hear what the Spirit saith unto the churches.

To the Church of the Laodiceans

Jesus Is "the Amen, the. . .True Witness" (Vs. 14)

Jesus is *"the Amen."* He echoes God's Word and work. He says "Amen" to all God says and does.

He is *"the true witness"* (vs. 14). First, this means Christ is the perfect representative of God. In Genesis 31:50 Laban said of a covenant with Jacob, "God is witness." God sees all and judges it perfectly. So Christ claims to be the always faithful, true Witness. God had given witness to Christ at His baptism and at the Mount of Transfiguration (Matt. 3:17; Luke 3:22; Matt. 17:5; II Pet. 1:17).

So Christ claims to be the same perfect true witness just as He claimed that "I and my Father are one" (John 10:30). Jesus is the true and faithful witness and in I John 5:9,10 He is identified likewise with the Holy Spirit who witnesses within us.

Jesus is not simply *a* true witness, He is *the* true Witness, a perfection putting Him above all men. He is God, not a fallible, limited man. But as Christ is *"the. . .true witness,"* He is thus put equal to and aligned with the Father and the Holy Spirit. He is unique. In the perfect, complete sense no man is a perfectly true witness.

A man may tell the truth as far as he knows it, but human knowledge is not complete or perfect knowledge. A man may testify to what he thinks he hears or sees but may be mistaken. Or his concepts and vocabulary are limited. He does not know how to express all he saw nor even to understand it all. Only Jesus is *"the. . .true witness."*

Of Jesus, Judas said in tragic lamentation, "I have betrayed the innocent blood" (Matt. 27:4). Note not only one of innocent blood but the only innocent blood this side the Garden of Eden! As Christ's sinlessness and omnipotence and omniscience are unique, so His witness is unique.

Christ here involves the Word of God also. As Christ and the Word are inextricably combined in Mark 8:38 so that one who is ashamed of Jesus is ashamed of the Word and entails shame before God the Father and the holy angels, so if Christ be the eternal Son of God, deity, the Bible must be the eternal Word of

God. If Christ is "the. . .true witness," then the Bible which Jesus calls "my words" (Mark 8:38) and which is called "the word of Christ," is the inerrant, infallibly correct, verbally inspired Bible, as unique among literature as Christ is among men. There can be no separation between the written Word of God and the incarnate Word of God. Christ and the Bible stand or fall together.

". . .*the beginning of the creation of God"* (vs. 14). That does not mean that Christ is a created being. For John 1:1-3: says: "In the beginning was the Word, and the Word was with God, and the Word was God. The same was in the beginning with God. All things were made by him; and without him was not any thing made that was made."

Jesus is God, an eternal, infinite being like the Father and equal with the Father. Was Jesus created? Only the human body of Jesus was created. This Scripture may infer that before the world began God had determined and decreed that Jesus would be born of a virgin, have a human body and die for our sins. He was "the Lamb slain from the foundation of the world" (Rev. 13:8). Jesus was "the only *begotten* Son" of God, that is, the only Son physically begotten in a virgin's womb, miraculously begotten of God.

But there is more meaning here, we think. Jesus is "the beginning of the creation of God" in the sense that He is Himself the Creator. He made all things that were made (John 1:3; Col 1:15-17). Let us say the Lord Jesus was the One who began all the creation of God, not that He was created but that He was the Creator.

"Neither cold nor hot" (vs. 15). Here is a lamentation and complaint that the Christians of Laodicea are neither cold nor hot. Here God speaks of the sin of lukewarmness. It is a sin of small fervor, of little zeal, the sin of divided loyalty. At the very best a Christian's love for God is less than God deserves and less than the love commanded, ". . .with all thy heart, and with all thy soul, and with all thy mind" (Matt. 22:37). Every Christian must admit to the battle between the flesh and the Spirit, must say even if with tears, "Lord, I believe; help thou mine unbelief,"

as did the father of the demon-possessed boy in Mark 9:24. But the devout Christian is pointed toward God, striving to please God. At least God has a right to demand fervent love from His people, zeal for His cause. There are no perfect Christians but Christians can have a consistently earnest, fervent heart.

"Neither cold nor hot" obviously accents a truth that even though one be a born-again Christian he will not automatically do right, not automatically be a fervent Christian, but must earnestly seek to grow in grace and knowledge of God. How many admonitions in the Bible prove that!

"I beseech you therefore, brethren, by the mercies of God, that ye present your bodies a living sacrifice, holy, acceptable unto God, which is your reasonable service. And be not conformed to this world: but be ye transformed by the renewing of your mind, that ye may prove what is that good and acceptable, and perfect, will of God."—Rom. 12:1,2.

We need the daily renewing of our minds.

Hebrews 12:1 says, "Wherefore seeing we also are compassed about with so great a cloud of witnesses, let us lay aside every weight, and the sin which doth so easily beset us, and let us run with patience the race that is set before us. . . ."

So a Christian must lay aside his weights and the besetting sin of unbelief. In II Peter 1:5-9 we read:

"And beside this, giving all diligence, add to your faith virtue; and to virtue knowledge; And to knowledge temperance; and to temperance patience; and to patience godliness; And to godliness brotherly kindness; and to brotherly kindness charity. For if these things be in you, and abound, they make you that ye shall neither be barren nor unfruitful in the knowledge of our Lord Jesus Christ. But he that lacketh these things is blind, and cannot see afar off, and hath forgotten that he was purged from his old sins."

Here those who have been "purged from his old sins," that is, saved, need to work to have Christian virtues and blessings. And in the model prayer we are taught to come daily confessing our sins and seek to avoid temptation.

"I Would Thou Wert Cold or Hot" (Vs. 15)

Does that mean that lukewarm, undedicated Christians without holy zeal, are so hurtful to Christ's cause that He would rather they were entirely cold, unconverted, not professing Christians at all? It seems so. For the mass of worldly Christians about us are a handicap to hinder all who would win souls. The lukewarm criticise the soul winner. The fervent soul is "too emotional," "a fanatic" to the lukewarm. The lukewarm in zeal may be politically active to control churches and to handicap the fervent pastor. Even as there are many religious leaders unsaved (Matt. 7:21-23), so there are leaders saved but not consecrated, who are lukewarm spiritually, who slow down all who would press forward earnestly in soul winning, in defense of the Faith and in loving fellowship.

It is not the unconverted world that hinders revival and soul winning but lukewarm Christians. The Lord Jesus plainly said, "The harvest truly is great, but the labourers are few" (Luke 10:2). The problem is not the harvest but the laborers. In II Chronicles 7:14 we read it is "my people, which are called by my name" who need to meet God's demands for revival.

The marvelous spread of the Gospel and the manifest power of God in the early church show how fruitful Christians can be without the encumbrance and the hindrance of the lukewarm. We think that a few Spirit-filled Christians, willing to die or to suffer prison or loss of property, wholly dedicated to God, would win more souls than a host of Christians, most of whom are lukewarm, halfhearted about serving God. *"I would thou wert cold or hot,"* instead of lukewarm, the Lord Jesus said!

Lukewarm? How?

Lukewarmness about the Bible, even among born-again Christians, is startling! It is shocking to find that probably more than half the Christians never have one time read the Bible through. Inevitably they are not well established in truth, so they are the prey of false cults and of many temptations. They would not be strong for the defense of the Faith nor indignant against the liberals who deny the verbal inspiration. They fall into many sins not having the protection of the Word hidden in their heart (Ps. 119:11).

They are often lacking in fervent love for Christians. So like the Corinthians they follow man, they cultivate divisions and strife and so are "babes in Christ," "carnal" Christians (I Cor. 3:1-4).

These Christians whose halfhearted and inadequate zeal disgust God are likely to be halfhearted and little concerned about holy living. They may be opinionated and critical about some traditions of life style among others but without any deep-felt concern to please God in their secret hearts. The Hollywood movies, tobacco, beer and cocktails, immodest dress and undisciplined children—all these are common place among these worldly Christians.

Indifferent hearts do not have a burden for soul winning. No tears of entreaty. No impassioned prayers. No zeal to get the Gospel out to every creature in reach. What a farce is the Christian's attitude that ignores the one great thing Jesus Christ died for—the saving of souls, that which He commanded so sternly in the Great Commission!

"I will spue thee out of my mouth" (vs. 16). Does that mean that God will disown His own born-again child? That the way to Heaven is by good works and only the deserving get there? Certainly not. We must remember that Jesus said, "Verily, verily, I say unto you, He that heareth my word, and believeth on him that sent me, hath everlasting life, and shall not come into condemnation; but is passed from death unto life" (John 5:24). Jesus said of His sheep, ". . .they shall never perish" (John 10:28). And Romans 8:33-39 says:

"Who shall lay anything to the charge of God's elect? It is God that justifieth. Who is he that condemneth? It is Christ that died, yea rather, that is risen again, who is even at the right hand of God, who also maketh intercession for us. Who shall separate us from the love of Christ? shall tribulation, or distress, or persecution, or famine, or nakedness, or peril, or sword? As it is written, For thy sake we are killed all the day long; we are accounted as sheep for the slaughter. Nay, in all these things we

*are more than conquerors through him that loved us. For I am
persuaded, that neither death, nor life, nor angels, nor principalities, nor powers, nor things present, nor things to come,
Nor height, nor depth, nor any other creature, shall be able to
separate us from the love of God, which is in Christ Jesus our
Lord."*

Paul was inspired to write, "I know whom I have believed, and
am persuaded that he is able to keep that which I have committed unto him against that day" (II Tim. 1:12b).

No, man's failure does not cancel God's promises. God does
not here deny salvation by grace without works which He so
clearly promised. Then what does it mean that inspired the picture of one vomiting out a disgusting and sickening matter?

A Christian can be "spued out" of fellowship with Christ. "If
we say that we have fellowship with him, and walk in darkness,
we lie, and do not the truth" (I John 1:6). One can thus lose all
the "joy of salvation" as David did, and then prayed for that joy
to be restored (Ps. 51:8, 12).

One may, by his indifference, become a vessel God cannot use.
Paul feared that "when I have preached to others, I myself
should be a castaway" (I Cor. 9:27). That is, he may be laid aside
as a worker. Many a Christian once greatly used has been cast
aside. I think of a gifted preacher now selling church furniture, of
another selling church bonds, cast aside as far as usefulness is
concerned. I knew a college and seminary graduate with great
gifts and wide influence over many states, an evangelist who
stepped out to make money and did but later wished and
earnestly tried to get back into God's work but could not. God
had no open doors for him. God had no blessing for him. As a soul
winner in great public leadership he was cast out. I do not say he
couldn't win souls privately if he tried, but a great ministry was
laid aside because he had been lukewarm and concerned more
about money-making and taking care of his family than about
the ministry.

Sometimes there are Christians who disgust God because they
have no holy passion to serve Him and die prematurely because
of their sin. Many did at Corinth who were carnally-minded

about the Lord's Supper (I Cor. 11:30), and many more were "weak and sickly" because of their heart attitude.

What These Lukewarm Christians Should Seek

Note carefully that God does not suggest that these are not saved or that they should seek salvation.

They thought they were rich but were not. They counted only worldly wealth. They were really "wretched, and miserable, and poor, and blind, and naked." How poor a Christian if he has only the fleeting, outward, unsatisfying things of this world! They should *"buy,"* that is, earn and gain *"gold tried in the fire,"* spiritual riches (vs. 18). Surely that would mean Holy Spirit power. The powerful presence of Christ through the Holy Spirit is wealth indeed. That would bring the peace of Philippians 4:6, 7; the contentment Paul found in prison (Phil. 4:11); the enduement of power the disciples were to tarry for and seek. The command, "And be not drunk with wine, wherein is excess; but be filled with the Spirit" (Eph. 5:18) is for every Christian. D. L. Moody said, "It is foolish to try to do the work of God without the power of God."

These poor Christians should seek *"white raiment, that thou mayest be clothed, and that the shame of thy nakedness do not appear"* (vs. 18). Surely Christians are to seek God's help to live a holy life. Isaiah 61:10 says, "I will greatly rejoice in the Lord, my soul shall be joyful in my God; for he hath clothed me with the garments of salvation, he hath covered me with the robe of righteousness, as a bridegroom decketh himself with ornaments, and as a bride adorneth herself with her jewels."

Well, every Christian has the garment of salvation which is Christ's imputed righteousness. That is the wedding garment without which no one can sit at the wedding feast of the king's Son (Matt. 22:11-14). But imputed righteousness ought to lead us to seek the imparted righteousness also. One who now is a "new man" (Col. 3:10) should "put off all these; anger, wrath, malice, blasphemy, filthy communication out of your mouth" (Col. 3:8). He should "put on therefore, as the elect of God, holy and beloved, bowels of mercies, kindness, humbleness of mind,

meekness, longsuffering; Forbearing one another, and forgiving
one another. . ." (Col. 3:12, 13). One who is counted
righteous for Christ's sake should become outwardly righteous to
show a holy concern for righteousness.

Oh, for the robe of righteousness to cover the shameful disgrace of a worldly life before the world!

Lukewarm Christians should *"anoint thine eyes with eyesalve,
that thou mayest see"* (vs. 18). The farmer who rejoiced in
houses, barns and plenty died as a fool because he was not rich
toward God. Then if even a lost man is a fool for putting things of
the flesh first, is not a worldly-minded Christian more so?

But the main concern of a Christian should be in all things for
"the glory of God" (I Cor. 10:31). We know that Christ died to
save sinners and the saving of sinners is the dearest thing to
God's heart.

Oh, for eyes to see the value of a soul to be saved from eternal
death as Jesus sees it, for whom He paid such an awful price!
Only those who put soul winning first fulfill the Great Commission. Only they have anointed eyes to see poor lost souls and their
danger and their value to God.

Oh, may God anoint our eyes to a vision of lost souls about us.

> Lord, give me a vision,
>   Oh, help me to see,
> The needs all around me;
>   Souls dying for thee,
> Oh, make me a blessing,
>   As onward I go.
> By telling the story;
>   That others may know.
>
> Lord, give me a vision,
>   Of fields that are white,
> Souls that we must gather;
>   E're cometh the night,
> Dark shadows are gath'ring,
>   And some will be lost.
> Some neighbor or brother;
>   How awful the cost.
>
> Lord, give me a vision,
>   Lest empty I stand,
> There at the great judgment;
>   No sheaves in my hand,

No labour of love,
  To offer my King.
With nothing but leaves then;
  The Master to bring.

Lord, give me a vision,
  Oh, help me to see,
Some neighbor today, Lord,
  And bring him to Thee,
That on that glad morning,
  Some soul there may say,
" 'Twas your pray'rs that saved me;
  You showed me the way."

God Loves and Chastens the Lukewarm

These are dearly loved children of God, so He will chasten them. "For whom the Lord loveth he chasteneth, and scourgeth every son whom he receiveth" (Heb. 12:6). Chastening may be by sickness or accident or trouble, by spiritual darkness, by the loss of joy, by the loss of loved ones. So those who are neither cold nor hot but lukewarm should repent. There is mercy for the penitent, and God's people need to repent again and again (See 2:5, 16, 22; 3:3, 19; II Cor. 7:9).

Now Christ stands at the heart's door of every Christian (vs. 20) and wants to restore fellowship that has been broken by their worldliness and lukewarmness. But the truth applies to all men everywhere. Christ is at the door. A lost man who wants salvation has only to open the door. That means that he wants forgiveness, he believes Christ will come in, and trusts Christ to do it.

This is like John 1:11, "He came unto his own, and his own received him not." Just receive Christ by faith. He is offered. He comes to you. It is like in Revelation 22:17, "And the Spirit and the bride say, Come. And let him that heareth say, Come. And let him that is athirst come. And whosoever will, let him take the water of life freely." Everyone who will can take the cup of salvation; so Jesus said, "All that the Father giveth me shall come to me; and him that cometh to me I will in no wise cast out" (John 6:37). One who comes to Christ is not rejected, and "whosoever shall call upon the name of the Lord shall be saved" (Rom. 10:13). These failing Christians are invited to overcome and to reign with Christ and join Him in sweet fellowship.

Do you have ears to hear? Does Christ speak to your heart about your lukewarmness?

We have seen a number of times in St. Paul's Cathedral in London the moving picture of "The Light of the World," by W. Holman Hunt. Hunt has depicted Christ standing before a closed door, with His right hand upon the knocker. It is evident the door has been long closed. Weeds have grown up in front of it, and vines across the top. Critics complained that the artist had forgotten to put a knob, a latch, on the door, but Hunt replied, "This door opens only from the inside."

Some Pertinent Comments by J. A. Seiss

In EPHESUS, even among the warm, patient, fervent, enduring and faithful ones, there were fallen ones, and some whose love had cooled, and some whose first works had been abandoned, and some giving place to the base deeds of the Nicolaitanes, and some false ones claiming to be apostles and were not.

In SMYRNA were faithless blasphemers, and those of Satan's synagogue, as well as faithful, suffering ones, and those whom Christ is to crown in Heaven.

In PERGAMOS were those who denied the faith, and followed the treacherous teachings of Balaam, and the doctrines of the detested Nicolaitanes, as well as those who held fast the name of Jesus, and witness for Him unto death.

In THYATIRA we find a debauching and idolatrous Jezebel and her death-worthy children, and multitudes of spiritual adulterers, as well as those whose works, and faith, and charity, and patience are noted with favour, and who had not been drawn into Satan's depths.

In SARDIS there was incompleteness, deadness, defalcation, need for repentance, and threatened judgment, as well as names of those who had not defiled their garments.

In PHILADELPHIA we discover "the synagogue of Satan," falsifiers, those who had settled themselves upon the earth, and such as had not kept Christ's word, as well as such as should be kept from the sifting trial, and advanced to celestial crowns.

And in LAODICEA there was found disgusting lukewarmness, empty profession, and base self-conceit, with Christ Himself excluded.

In all ages and dispensations, the plants of grace have ever found the weeds upspringing by their sides, their roots intertwining, and their stalks and leaves and fruits putting forth together. The Church is not an exception, and never will be, as long as the present dispensation lasts. Even in its first and purest periods, as the scriptural accounts attest, it was intermixed with what pertained not to it. There was a Judas among its apostles; an Ananias and a Simon Magus among its first converts; a Demas and a Diotrephes among its first public servants. And as long as it continues in this world, Christ will have His Antichrist, and the temple of God its men of sin. He who sets out to find a perfect Church in which there are no unworthy elements and no disfigurations, proposes to himself a hopeless search. Go where he will, worship where he may, in any country, in any age, he will soon find tares among the wheat, sin mixing in with all earthly holiness; self-deceivers, hypocrites, and unchristians in every assembly of saints; Satan insinuating himself into every gathering of the sons of God to present themselves before the Lord. No preaching—however pure; no discipline—however strict or prudent; no watchfulness—however searching and faithful, can ever make it different. . . .

The Saviour Himself has taught us that in the Gospel field wheat and tares are to be found; that it is forbidden to pluck up the bad, lest the good also be damaged; and that both are to "grow together until the harvest," which is the end of the economy—the winding up of the present order of things—"the end of the world."

Chapter 4

VERSES 1—3:

AFTER this I looked, and, behold, a door *was* opened in heaven: and the first voice which I heard *was* as it were of a trumpet talking with me; which said, Come up hither, and I will shew thee things which must be hereafter.

2 And immediately I was in the spirit; and, behold, a throne was set in heaven, and *one* sat on the throne.

3 And he that sat was to look upon like a jasper and a sardine stone: and *there was* a rainbow round about the throne, in sight like unto an emerald.

A Door Opened in Heaven

It is obvious that chapter 4 begins a new subject. Chapter 1 is the introduction to the book. Then chapters 2 and 3 are addressed to the seven churches in the province of Asia. The messages are for the then present time, to messengers and churches then living during John's lifetime.

But the book of Revelation plainly professes to be about the future ". . .to shew unto his servants things which must shortly come to pass" (1:1). John was to write not only "things which are" (messages to the seven churches then existing) but "things which shall be hereafter" (1:19). Moreover, we are distinctly told "things which shall be" revealed here concerning Christ's return.

The theme of all the book of Revelation is stated in chapter 1, verse 7, "Behold, he cometh with clouds; and every eye shall see him, and they also which pierced him: and all kindreds of the earth shall wail because of him. Even so, Amen." And Christ announces Himself not as only the Saviour "which was" with John on earth but the Lord "which is to come, the Almighty."

Note again the theme is not the course of this age, but Christ's coming. And note more specifically it is the second climactic phase of Christ's coming that is the theme. It is not His coming into the air to receive His saints, when living Christians will be changed and sleeping saints raised, as discussed in I Thessalonians 4:13-17 and I Corinthians 15:51,52.

We suppose the rapture of saints taken to Heaven is hinted at in the words to John, *"Come up hither"* (vs. 1), but none of the events and details connected with the rapture are mentioned. No mention of "the shout," the "voice of the archangel." There is a "trumpet" sound, but no mention of the resurrection, no change of the living, no "one. . .taken, and the other left." The book of Revelation is not especially about the rapture of saints taken to Heaven and before the judgment seat of Christ and for the wedding supper. It is rather about the somewhat later event or part of the same great event, Christ's return with saints and angels to destroy the government of this world, convert a remnant of Jews and set up His promised kingdom on earth.

Why no discussion of the first phase of Christ's coming? First, no doubt, because the time of that first phase of His coming was a secret known only to God (Matt. 24:36; Mark 13:32). "But of that day and hour knoweth no man, no, not the angels of heaven, but my Father only." Christians are commanded to "watch therefore, for ye know neither the day nor the hour wherein the Son of man cometh" (Matt. 25:13). And that instruction to watch for a surprising, unforeseen, instant coming for His own is emphasized again and again in the Olivet Discourse. Plainly "it is not for you to know the times or the seasons, which the Father hath put in his own power" (Acts 1:7). Certainly His reticence here would match His reticence before. No hint is given as to how we may know when the rapture of saints approaches.

In my book, *The Coming Kingdom of Christ,* one entire chapter is given answering the so-called "signs" by which people think they can know what God plainly said they could not know.

And the other reason for the emphasis on the physical, bodily return of Christ to reign, not His preliminary phase of taking up the saints at the rapture, is that this matter of God's covenant to restore the throne of David, to gather and save a remnant of Israel and to take over the governments of this world, is the great teaching of the Old Testament prophecy. The Old Testament does not center on the rapture but on Christ's return to reign. So, the simple question of the apostles, "Lord, wilt thou at this time restore again the kingdom to Israel?" (Acts 1:6). And the Angel

Gabriel had told Mary, in announcing the birth of the Lord Jesus, "He shall be great, and shall be called the Son of the Highest: and the Lord God shall give unto him the throne of his father David: And he shall reign over the house of Jacob for ever; and of his kingdom there shall be no end" (Luke 1:32,33).

Preaching to the Jews at Pentecost, Peter said of David, "Therefore being a prophet, and knowing that God had sworn with an oath to him, that of the fruit of his loins, according to the flesh, he would raise up Christ to sit on his throne" (Acts 2:30). Remember, the rapture is a preliminary detail of a much larger plan that involves centuries. The oft foretold "day of the Lord" is not when Christ calls out His saints but when Jesus comes to reign on earth and the events to follow. The rapture of saints is not the end, the climax of God's plan. Christ's glorious appearing with saints and angels as foretold in Revelation 1:7, and more in detail in Revelation 19:11-16, is the climax, and that and the things that surround it, all except the secret time of the rapture, are the theme of the book of Revelation.

Now Revelation, in chapter 2, leaves "things that are" to tell of "the things that shall be."

So chapters 4 and 5 are introductory to the prophecies of the future which follow.

The Throne in Heaven

In chapter 1 John saw Christ on the Lord's day on the isle of Patmos. Now, looking into the far future, Christ is shown in Heaven. Was it Christ on the throne? Verse 11 designates the One on the throne as the Creator. John 1:1-3 says about creation: "In the beginning was the Word, and the Word was with God, and the Word was God. The same was in the beginning with God. All things were made by him; and without him was not any thing made that was made."

Again Colossians 1:16 says, "For by him were all things created, that are in heaven, and that are in earth, visible and invisible, whether they be thrones, or dominions, or principalities, or powers: all things were created by him, and for him."

However, Genesis 1:1 says, "In the beginning God created the heaven and the earth."

At first glance, we would think that the One on the throne in verse 2 and praised in verse 11 is the Saviour. However, in chapter 5, verses 6 and 7 indicate the Lamb in the midst of the elders and that He comes to the One on the throne to take the seven-sealed book. That indicates it is God the Father on the throne, praised for creation, even though the Lord Jesus was the active One of the Trinity and the Agent of the Father in creation. Or there could be here two different pictures, each with a separate truth.

What beauties are about the throne are only briefly mentioned. All the beauties belong to God. All the colors of the rainbow surround Him.

Unger discusses the rainbow:

> The rainbow, (Ezk. 1:28), is a token of God's mercy based on the accepted sacrifice of His Son, as the Noachic bow was the sign of a covenant based on the sacrifice offered by Noah (Gen. 8:20-22) which looked forward to Christ. John's bow was emerald colored (green) guaranteeing God's fidelity to His covenant with Noah not to destroy the earth again, as in the Flood, despite the terrible judgment to come (Chap. 5-19) and despite the fact that the throne is a throne not of grace but of judgment.

"Like a jasper. . ." (vs. 3). Does that refer to a sparkling diamond? Ironside says this about the jasper: "The jasper of the Revelation is not the opaque stone we know by that name. It is later described as clear as crystal (21:11). It is probably the diamond, the most brilliant of all the precious jewels."

"Like. . .a sardine stone," and ". . .like unto an emerald" (vs. 3). How can gems and gold and brass like in the furnace and white garments show the beauty and majesty of the throne in Heaven and of God and Christ? But the terms can make us pause, make us eager to see "the glory that shall be revealed." Our poor, clouded, dull minds take not easily to glory! But the bush burning not burned, the pillar of cloud and fire in the wilderness, the Heavenly Jerusalem, the beauties described to us but scarcely grasped—these all promise glories our eyes will see when the mists are rolled away, when we see face to face, and when we know what we now see so darkly.

VERSES 4,5:

4 And round about the throne *were* four and twenty seats: and upon the seats I saw four and twenty elders sitting, clothed in white raiment; and they had on their heads crowns of gold.

5 And out of the throne proceeded lightnings and thunderings and voices: and *there were* seven lamps of fire burning before the throne, which are the seven Spirits of God.

The Twenty-Four Elders

These elders have crowns. Their seats or thrones are about the throne of God or of Christ. Who are they? They are literal people. Chapter 5, verse 9, tells that they are redeemed by the death of Christ so they are human beings, Christians. They are "out of every kindred, and tongue, and people, and nation." The following verse tells us they are to reign on the earth.

Jesus promised the apostles, "That ye which have followed me, in the regeneration when the Son of man shall sit in the throne of his glory, ye also shall sit upon twelve thrones, judging the twelve tribes of Israel" (Matt. 19:28).

He had a reason for having twelve apostles since there were twelve tribes, and the number is meaningful. Perhaps the twelve more (making twenty-four elders to reign) will be blessed Christians from Gentile nations, men chosen to rule with Christ on the earth. We are told in the parable of the pounds some faithful ones will be given "authority over ten cities," and some "over five cities" (Luke 19:17-19). At any rate, these born-again elders will reign on the earth with Christ.

A. T. Robertson quotes Swete as saying regarding verse 5: "The thunderstorm is in Hebrew poetry a familiar symbol of the Divine power: cf., e.g., I Sam. 2:10; Ps. 18:9f.; Job 37:4f."

Seiss comments on the lightnings and thunderings:

These demonstrate that the throne is one of judgment, and that wrath is about to proceed from it. When God was about to visit

Egypt's sins upon her, He "sent thunder [in Heb. "voices"], and hail, and fire ran along upon the ground." And Pharaoh sent and said, "Intreat the Lord that there be no more voices of God" (Exod. 9:23,28). When He wished to show Israel the terribleness of His anger with sin, "there were thunders and lightnings, and a thick cloud upon the mount, and the voice of the trumpet exceeding loud" (Exod. 19:16). When He sent forth His wrath upon the Philistines, "the Lord thundered with a great thunder on that day upon the Philistines, and discomfited them, and they were smitten before Israel" (I Sam. 7:10). So also was His displeasure expressed at Israel's demand for a king. Samuel said, "The Lord shall send thunder and rain [in wheat harvest], that ye may perceive and see that your wickedness is great, which ye have done in the sight of the Lord, in asking you a king. And the Lord sent thunder and rain that day, and all the people greatly feared" (I Sam. 12:17,18).

These instances show us, that this is not a throne of grace, but a throne of judgment. These lightnings, thunders, and voices, proceeding from it, tell of justice and wrath to be visited upon transgressors. The river of water of life is gone, and in its place is the terror and fire of judgment and death.

Note the *"seven lamps. . .the seven Spirits of God"* (vs. 5). This is symbolic. (See the discussion on Revelation 3:1.) The number seven pictures deity, infinity, with the Spirit of God everywhere at all times.

VERSES 6—8:

6 And before the throne *there was* a sea of glass like unto crystal: and in the midst of the throne, and round about the throne, *were* four beasts full of eyes before and behind.

7 And the first beast *was* like a lion, and the second beast like a calf, and the third beast had a face as a man, and the fourth beast *was* like a flying eagle.

8 And the four beasts had each of them six wings about *him;* and *they were* full of eyes within: and they rest not day and night, saying, Holy, holy, holy, Lord God Almighty, which was, and is, and is to come.

The Four Living Creatures

These "beasts" should better be called "living creatures." That is the term defining them in *Young's Analytical Concordance.* They are not men, they are not angels, but are heavenly creatures made to honor God. Compare these "living creatures" with those of Ezekiel 1:5-10:

"Also out of the midst thereof came the likeness of four living creatures. And this was their appearance; they had the likeness of a man. And every one had four faces, and every one had four wings. And their feet were straight feet; and the sole of their feet was like the sole of a calf's foot: and they sparkled like the colour of burnished brass. And they had the hands of a man under their wings on their four sides; and they four had their faces and their wings. Their wings were joined one to another; they turned not when they went; they went every one straight forward."

Dr. Scofield says of these: "The 'living creatures' are identical with the Cherubim." They are angelic beings who represent God in some manner. There are similarities and differences. In Ezekiel the creatures had four wings, and in Revelation each had six wings. We may suppose that as angels can appear and disappear, and as they can look like men (Gen. 18:2, 16; Gen. 19:2, 15, 16) or not, so these heavenly creatures might appear in whatever form would fit the message intended.

Here in Revelation 4 the four creatures picture the character of Christ—like a lion for strength and kingship, like a calf for sacrifice, like a man picturing Christ's incarnation, like an eagle as seeing all things. These heavenly creatures cry day and night to announce and praise Christ, God, and we believe they mean that Jesus Christ is God and, as God, Creator.

VERSES 9—11:

9 And when those beasts give glory and honour and thanks to him that sat on the throne, who liveth for ever and ever,

10 The four and twenty elders fall down before him that sat on the throne, and worship him that liveth for ever and ever, and cast their crowns before the throne, saying,

11 Thou art worthy, O Lord, to receive glory and honour and power: for thou hast created all things, and for thy pleasure they are and were created.

Heavenly Creatures and Human Elders Join in Praise

Here we are reminded of the promise, "That at the name of Jesus every knee should bow, of things in heaven, and things in earth, and things under the earth; And that every tongue should confess that Jesus Christ is Lord, to the glory of God the Father" (Phil. 2:10, 11). Angelic creatures and elders who are to reign on the earth with Christ unite in thanks and praises, particularly for God as Creator and for Christ. Ah, these most blessed among apostles and saints bow low to Christ and worship Him. Crowns—thrown down before Christ! To rule with Christ is great. To be ruled by Him and worship Him still is greater for these. Ah, let the Lord Jesus have all the praise and glory for whatever honor He may lovingly bestow upon us.

We remember that on the Mount of Transfiguration, when Peter would have somewhat rated Jesus, Moses and Elijah alike as deserving special tabernacles or tents for staying on the mount, Moses and Elijah disappeared, they saw Jesus only and a voice from Heaven said, "This is my beloved Son, in whom I am well pleased; hear ye him" (Matt. 17:5).

Oh, all the apostles and elders in the world are not to be compared with the Lord Jesus and would properly cast their crowns before Him in worship. Christ created all things and all are for His pleasure. So the same thing is stated in Colossians 1:16.

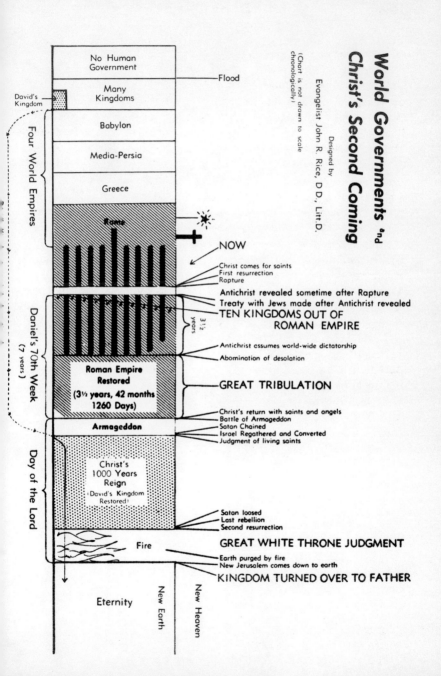

World Governments and Christ's Second Coming

Designed by
Evangelist John R. Rice, D.D., Litt.D.

(Chart is not drawn to scale chronologically)

No Human Government

— Flood

David's Kingdom

Many Kingdoms

Babylon

Media-Persia

Greece

Four World Empires

Rome

NOW

Christ comes for saints
First resurrection
Rapture

Antichrist revealed sometime after Rapture
Treaty with Jews made after Antichrist revealed
TEN KINGDOMS OUT OF ROMAN EMPIRE

3½ years

Antichrist assumes world-wide dictatorship
Abomination of desolation

Daniel's 70th Week (7 years)

Roman Empire Restored (3½ years, 42 months 1260 Days)

GREAT TRIBULATION

Christ's return with saints and angels
Battle of Armageddon
Satan Chained
Israel Regathered and Converted
Judgment of living saints

Armageddon

Day of the Lord

Christ's 1000 Years Reign (David's Kingdom Restored)

Satan loosed
Last rebellion
Second resurrection

Fire

GREAT WHITE THRONE JUDGMENT

Earth purged by fire
New Jerusalem comes down to earth

KINGDOM TURNED OVER TO FATHER

Eternity

New Earth

New Heaven

Chapter 5

VERSES 1—4:

AND I saw in the right hand of him that sat on the throne a book written within and on the backside, sealed with seven seals.

2 And I saw a strong angel proclaiming with a loud voice, Who is worthy to open the book, and to loose the seals thereof?

3 And no man in heaven, nor in earth, neither under the earth, was able to open the book, neither to look thereon.

4 And I wept much, because no man was found worthy to open and to read the book, neither to look thereon.

The Book of Future Woes

The book sealed with seven seals is a book of the future. As each seal is opened in the next chapter, we will see revealed great trouble and plagues on the earth. But they are sealed up, shut up from the knowledge of men. *"No man in heaven, nor in earth, neither under the earth"* [in Hell] (vs. 3) can unseal the book of the future. No historian can foretell it. No spiritist nor student of the stars nor astrologer can tell it. No religious leader has it revealed to him.

Here is another witness that, as Jesus told the apostles in Acts 1:7, "It is not for you to know the times or the seasons, which the Father hath put in his own power."

Ironside comments on this book with seven seals:

> The ancient books of Israel were generally sheepskin rolls; and when we are told that this book was sealed with seven seals, we are to understand that the book was rolled up to a certain point, and there a seal was put upon the edge, so that it could not be opened until that seal was broken. It was rolled up a little farther and another seal put on, and so on, until there were six seals on the edge of the book and one seal closing the entire scroll. When the first seal was opened a certain portion of the book was exposed to view, and so with each one following. When the seventh was broken then the entire book would be unrolled.

A. T. Robertson says, "A will in Roman law bore the seven seals of the seven witnesses. But this sealed book of doom calls for no witnesses beyond God's own will."

It is a folly of men that they try to foretell the time of Christ's coming. It was folly in the year 1,000 when people reasoned that this age ought to last only a thousand years, and they expected Christ's return immediately. It was folly when Martin Luther thought the pope was the Antichrist. It was a folly when Farmer Miller in New York State figured that he knew Christ would return in 1843 or 1844.

Only Christ can reveal the future, and the book of Revelation does not hint as to when we may expect the end of the age and the return of Christ for us.

There are seven seals. Seven means that God reminds us that here is a divine wisdom infinitely correct, not to be ferreted out by human wisdom. There are many sevens in this book indicating the completeness and God-revealed, God-controlled perfection of the book of Revelation. There were seven churches, seven stars, seven Spirits of God (1:4; 3:1; 4:5. In 4:5 they are pictured by seven lamps.) There are seven angels and seven trumpets (8:2). There are seven thunders (10:3). There are "seven angels having the seven last plagues" in seven vials (15:1).

VERSES 5—7:

5 And one of the elders saith unto me, Weep not: behold, the Lion of the tribe of Juda, the Root of David, hath prevailed to open the book, and to loose the seven seals thereof.

6 And I beheld, and, lo, in the midst of the throne and of the four beasts, and in the midst of the elders, stood a Lamb as it had been slain, having seven horns and seven eyes, which are the seven Spirits of God sent forth into all the earth.

7 And he came and took the book out of the right hand of him that sat upon the throne.

Christ Alone Worthy to Control and Tell Future

How God must delight in the beautiful descriptive names and titles of Jesus. He is "Messiah" or "Christ," the Hebrew and Greek terms for Anointed. He is Son of God, Son of Man, Son of David. He is the Branch of David's dynasty. He is the First and

Last. He is the Beginning and Ending, the Alpha and Omega of the Greek alphabet. He is the Morning Star. He is to rise as "the Sun of righteousness." He is the Good Shepherd. He is the Way, the Truth, the Life. He is the Light of the World. He is our High Priest, Redeemer, King of the Jews, the Hope of Israel. A great Christian layman, Dr. Clinton Howard, had a famous address on "Pearls of Paradise," dwelling on the wonderful names of the Lord Jesus. It would be a blessing for each one to list all the names and titles you can of Jesus.

Here Jesus is called *"the Lion of the tribe of Juda"* (vs. 5). That suggests not only the past but that at Christ's coming He will deal with Israel again, according to His eternal purpose as Judge and Ruler. Of all Judah, He is the Lion, the Ruler, and inherent in the nature of His second coming He is to be not only as a lamb, but as a lion to destroy His enemies.

He is "the Root of David." Elsewhere he is "Son of David," but here He is listed as before David, Lord of David, as Creator of David, in fact. His deity is involved. Jesus brought this question to unbelieving Pharisees:

"While the Pharisees were gathered together, Jesus asked them, Saying, What think ye of Christ? whose son is he? They say unto him, The son of David. He saith unto them, How then doth David in spirit call him Lord, saying, The Lord said unto my Lord, Sit thou on my right hand, till I make thine enemies thy footstool? If David then call him Lord, how is he his son? And no man was able to answer him a word, neither durst any man from that day forth ask him any more questions."—Matt. 22:41-46.

So Jesus is David's Son physically, but long before then and always after He is David's Lord.

Then Jesus appears as *"a Lamb as it had been slain"* (vs. 6). The authority over men to save and judge is given to Jesus because He died to save. He, then, of all the universe is counted worthy to open the book of the seven seals.

Seiss explains the significance of the Greek word used for Jesus as the Lamb here:

> He is here described, not by the ordinary word *(amnos)* used to signify a lamb, but by another *(arnios)* more intensely significant of gentleness and domesticity—a pet lamb—in sharp contrast with the wild beasts, in opposition to whom He is arrayed. This the more fully brings out His particular mildness and familiar identification with His people, and the utter inexcusableness and guilt of those savage and untamable ones who persist in rejecting, persecuting, and warring against Him. They wrong and injure the gentlest and most inoffensive of beings—they murder the pet Lamb of the family of God.

The Lamb had *"seven horns"* (vs. 6). Horns speak of kingly power to rule. The ten horns of the beast in Daniel 7:24 are ten kings that shall arise. The little horn arising in the midst of them is to be the world dictator, the Antichrist. So Christ is to have power, rulership and kingship. And since there are seven horns, He is to have eternal, unlimited, infinite power. All things are in His hands.

The Lamb has *"seven eyes, which are the seven Spirits of God sent forth into all the earth"* (vs. 6). Consider the continual connection, the liaison between Christ and the Holy Spirit of God. He is also called "the Spirit of Christ" (Rom. 8:9; I Pet. 1:11).

Jesus and the Holy Spirit

Jesus was "conceived. . .of the Holy Ghost" (Matt. 1:20). He did not begin His ministry, never preached a sermon nor worked a miracle, until he was baptized (Luke 3:21, 22). Then the Holy Spirit came upon Him visibly and He was "anointed. . .to preach the gospel" and began (Luke 4:14-22; Isa. 61:1). Then, Acts 10:37, 38 tells us:

> *"That word, I say, ye know, which was published throughout all Judaea, and began from Galilee, after the baptism which John preached; How God anointed Jesus of Nazareth with the Holy Ghost and with power: who went about doing good, and healing all that were oppressed of the devil; for God was with him."*

As Light of the World, He was pictured by the golden lampstand in the Old Testament Tabernacle, burning the oil of the

Holy Spirit. All His power was as a perfect, Spirit-filled Man, our Example.

David, as a shadow of Jesus' coming to Kingship, was anointed with oil; so Jesus will reign as a Spirit-filled Man, as we see in Isaiah 11:1-3. Aaron the high priest was anointed, picturing Jesus our High Priest ever interceding for us now in Heaven, with a physical body risen from the dead but acting still in the fullness of the Spirit.

Jesus was perfectly, completely filled with the Spirit without measure (John 3:34). So the abundance of oil, when Aaron was anointed was "like the precious ointment upon the head, that ran down upon the beard, even Aaron's beard: that went down to the skirts of his garments" (Ps. 133:2). So all the seven Spirits of God—divine, infinite, completeness—are with the Lord Jesus.

And in Heaven He still is, through the Spirit, manifest to every Christian.

"He that hath my commandments, and keepeth them, he it is that loveth me: and he that loveth me shall be loved of my Father, and I will love him, and will manifest myself to him. Judas saith unto him, not Iscariot, Lord, how is it that thou wilt manifest thyself unto us, and not unto the world? Jesus answered and said unto him, If a man love me, he will keep my words: and my Father will love him, and we will come unto him, and make our abode with him."—John 14:21-23.

And He is to deal with men "unto all the earth." And Christ, through the Holy Spirit, has promised, "Lo, I am with you alway, even unto the end of the world" (Matt. 28:20).

So Christ is able and worthy to open the book and show what is coming in the future. Remember, the book is "The Revelation of Jesus Christ, which God gave unto him, to shew unto his servants things which must shortly come to pass" (1:1).

8 And when he had taken the book, the four beasts and four *and* twenty elders fell down before the Lamb, having every one of them harps, and golden vials full of odours, which are the prayers of saints.

9 And they sung a new song, saying, Thou art worthy to take the book, and to open the seals thereof: for thou wast slain, and hast redeemed us to God by thy blood out of every kindred, and tongue, and people, and nation;

10 And hast made us unto our God kings and priests: and we shall reign on the earth.

Living Creatures Worship Christ Because of Redemption

In the preceding chapter, in verses 9 to 11, the living creatures and the twenty-four elders worshiped and praised God for creation. Here the elders sing a new song of the worthiness of the Lamb because of His death on the cross as an atonement for sin. What is ahead is largely judgment and only He who died to save sinners is given authority and judgment over those who refuse Him.

All beautiful things are of God. Dr. Bob Jones, Sr., used to say, "If the Devil has any beautiful things he stole them." So the basic principles of music are of God. Man did not invent the music scales or the harmony in chords or the beat in rhythm. Man discovered them. Those are what God had created. Men learn to record music on lines and spaces, but he records good music he has discovered.

God made music to be the handmaid of truth, the instrument of the Holy Spirit, the spiritual expression of joy. When Elisha sought God's Spirit to learn the will of God, he said, "Bring me a minstrel" (II Kings 3:15). "And it came to pass, when the minstrel played, that the hand of the Lord came upon him." Christians are commanded, "And be not drunk with wine, wherein is excess; but be filled with the Spirit; Speaking to yourselves in psalms and hymns and spiritual songs, singing and making melody in your heart to the Lord" (Eph. 5:18, 19). Again in Colossians 3:16 God commands, "Let the word of Christ dwell in you richly in all wisdom; teaching and admonishing one another in psalms and hymns and spiritual songs, singing with grace in your hearts to the Lord."

The Spirit of God has an affinity for music. Music expresses praise, rejoicing. Often it is praise of great victories. "Songs of deliverance" are promised in Psalm 32:7, and a "song in the night" in Psalm 77:6. Moses taught Israel a song of victory after delivering from Pharaoh who died in the Red Sea (Exod. 15:1-20). That song was, we suppose, called "the song of Moses the servant of God, and the song of the Lamb" (15:3), over victory and over the destruction of the wicked. And that reminds us that Pharaoh was a shadow or type of the coming Antichrist, and the slavery of Israel and the plagues in Egypt seem to picture the plagues in the tribulation time as revealed in Revelation.

"A new song" (vs. 9), a mark of fresh revelation or new blessing is mentioned in Psalm 33:3 and Isaiah 42:10. And when Christ returns to reign and a remnant of Israel is gathered to Palestine, we are told that "the desert shall rejoice, and blossom as the rose. It shall blossom abundantly, and rejoice even with joy and singing" (Isa. 35:1, 2). Then "the ransomed of the Lord shall return, and come to Zion with songs and everlasting joy upon their heads: they shall obtain joy and gladness, and sorrow and sighing shall flee away" (Isa. 35:10). My song says:

> **Sorrow and sighing shall flee away**
> **When Jesus comes to reign.**
> **Eyes of the blind will be opened then;**
> **Tongue of the dumb shall sing.**
>
> **Raptured with Christ, then a honeymoon**
> **With Him in gloryland.**
> **With Him to earth, when the angels bring**
> **Israel to Holy land.**
>
> **Lame men shall leap as an hart, for then**
> **All sickness gone, all sore.**
> **Deserts will bloom and the thorns, and briars**
> **Shall curse the earth no more!**
>
> **Kingdoms shall fall, and old Satan's rule**
> **Shall end with all its tears.**
> **Righteousness fill all the earth, and peace**
> **Reign for a thousand years.**
>
> **We pray, dear Lord, may Thy Kingdom come,**
> **On earth Thy will be done.**
> **But we have now all Thy peace and joy**
> **And in our hearts Thy throne.**
>
> **Sorrow and sighing shall flee away!**

> **Flee away that glory day!**
> **Garden of Eden restored that day!**
> **When Jesus comes to reign.**

Then we are told "the mountains and the hills shall break forth before you into singing, and all the trees of the field shall clap their hands" (Isa. 55:12).

The Lord Jesus is to be the theme of the song the elders sing to Jesus in verse 9.

Note again these twenty-four elders are men who shall reign with Christ as kings and priests in the kingdom age.

VERSES 11—14:

11 And I beheld, and I heard the voice of many angels round about the throne and the beasts and the elders: and the number of them was ten thousand times ten thousand, and thousands of thousands;

12 Saying with a loud voice, Worthy is the Lamb that was slain to receive power, and riches, and wisdom, and strength, and honour, and glory, and blessing.

13 And every creature which is in heaven, and on the earth, and under the earth, and such as are in the sea, and all that are in them, heard I saying, Blessing, and honour, and glory, and power, *be* unto him that sitteth upon the throne, and unto the Lamb for ever and ever.

14 And the four beasts said, Amen. And the four *and* twenty elders fell down and worshipped him that liveth for ever and ever.

Angels Join With Every Living Creature to Praise Jesus Christ

How many angels in Heaven? Ten thousand times ten thousand would be a hundred million, and add to these "thousands of thousands." That is at least two thousand times two tousands or a minimum of four million more. So there are at least 104 million angels. These were all called to worship Christ at His birth. "And again, when he bringeth in the first begotten into the world, he saith, And let all the angels of God worship him" (Heb. 1:6).

We suppose that the "multitude of the heavenly host" of Luke 2:13, chanting "Glory to God in the highest, and on earth peace, good will toward men," included all those angels that covered the sky.

So angels praised Christ, the "Worthy Lamb"; so does every

creature on earth and under the earth and such as are in the sea. Here is a fulfillment of Philippians 2:9-11, when every knee is to bow and every tongue is to confess that Christ is Lord. Will those *"under the earth"* (vs. 13), which surely means Hell, praise Christ, too? Oh, yes. So has promised Zechariah 12:10; John 19:37; Revelation 1:7. "They shall look on him whom they pierced," and, "every eye shall see him," even to the wicked. To the high priest involved in Christ's execution, Jesus said, "Thou hast said: nevertheless I say unto you, Hereafter shall ye see the Son of man sitting on the right hand of power, and coming in the clouds of heaven" (Matt. 26:64).

"Every creature!" The Greek word for "creature" here is *ktisma*, anything made or created. Could that be animals, too, and not only men? Yes. When all the "trees of the field. . .clap their hands" and when "mountains and. . .hills shall break forth. . .into singing," and when the rocks cry out to honor Christ (Luke 19:40), we need not be surprised when Christ gives voices to animals to praise Him!

Oh, then, let us be sure to be full of praises for the Saviour who is ours. He never saved angels nor heavenly creatures, so no one has such a proper duty and right to praise Him as those redeemed by the Saviour's blood!

Is the Saviour yours? H. A. Ironside said, "What a host! You would think that God had enough without us. Old John Bunyan says, 'Oh, this Lamb of God! He had a whole Heaven to Himself, myriads of angels to do His pleasure, but this could not satisfy Him. He must have sinners to share it with Him!' If you are ever going to sing up there you will have to start in down here. Can you say, 'Thou wast slain, and hast redeemed me by Thy blood'?"

AN INTERLUDE
Between
Chapters 5 and 6

Daniel Lays Groundwork for Revelation

Here we must insert an interlude.

We do not here plan to give a detailed explanation of the book of Daniel but only of such portions as help directly to understand the book of Revelation. Daniel is inspired prophecy. Some details of the course of the age, the tribulation time, the rise and reign of the Antichrist as revealed in Daniel, are essential. After chapter 5 in Revelation, we need the background of prophecy in Daniel.

Four World Empires Before Christ's Kingdom on Earth

In Daniel, chapter 2, Nebuchadnezzar, the founder of the Babylonian Empire, had a dream. He saw a great image of a man and was told:

"Thou, O king, sawest, and behold a great image. This great image, whose brightness was excellent, stood before thee; and the form thereof was terrible. This image's head was of fine gold, his breast and his arms of silver, his belly and his thighs of brass. His legs of iron, his feet part of iron and part of clay. Thou sawest till that a stone was cut out without hands, which smote the image upon his feet that were of iron and clay, and brake them to pieces. Then was the iron, the clay, the brass, the silver, and the gold, broken to pieces together, and became like the chaff of the summer threshingfloors; and the wind carried them away, that no place was found for them: and the stone that smote the image became a great mountain, and filled the whole earth."—Dan. 2:31-35.

The interpretation was given: Nebuchadnezzar as the ruler of Babylon was the head of gold. The breast and arms of silver pictured Media-Persia to follow Babylon. Then the belly and thighs of brass pictured the Grecian kingdom established by Alexander the Great. The legs of iron pictured the Roman Empire to be divided into Eastern and Western Rome. The feet and toes of part iron and part clay represented the ten nations coming out of the Roman Empire when the Empire fell apart. And the stone cut out of the mountain pictured Christ at His return to destroy human government and to rule the whole world.

Again Daniel Saw Beasts Representing the Four World Empires and Further, the Rise of Antichrist

Daniel 7:3-7 tells us:

"And four great beasts came up from the sea, diverse one from another. The first was like a lion, and had eagle's wings: I beheld till the wings thereof were plucked, and it was lifted up from the earth, and made stand upon the feet as a man, and a man's heart was given to it. And behold another beast, a second, like to a bear, and it raised up itself on one side, and it had three ribs in the mouth of it between the teeth of it: and they said thus unto it, Arise, devour much flesh. After this I beheld, and lo another, like a leopard, which had upon the back of it four wings of a fowl; the beast had also four heads; and dominion was given to it. After this I saw in the night visions, and behold a fourth beast, dreadful and terrible, and strong exceedingly; and it had great iron teeth: it devoured and brake in pieces, and stamped the residue with the feet of it: and it was diverse from all the beasts that were before it; and it had ten horns."

Then the explanation is given. Again these four beasts picture the same four world empires as the image in Nebuchadnezzar's dream in Daniel 2. The lion was Babylon. The bear with three ribs in its mouth pictured Media-Persia made up of three parts, Babylon, Media and Persia. The leopard pictured Greece. The four heads pictured the empire after Alexander's death, divided to his four generals. The fourth beast "dreadful and terrible" pictured Rome, the last world empire. The ten horns here are like the ten toes of the image in Daniel 2. They represent the ten kingdoms out of the dissolved Roman Empire.

But here is further revelation. Another little horn is shown arising among the ten, and behold, he is a man, a world dictator, the Antichrist.

And Daniel 7:21 says: "I beheld, and the same horn made war with the saints, and prevailed against them."

Daniel 7:25,26 says: "And he shall speak great words against the most High, and shall wear out the saints of the most High, and think to change times and laws: and they shall be given into his hand until a time and times and the dividing of time. But the judgment shall sit, and they shall take away his dominion, to consume and to destroy it unto the end."

So here is a hater of God, the Antichrist, who will persecute the saints and shall be allowed to reign over Christians "A time and times and the dividing of time." A time here is a year, two more make three, and the dividing of time or a half year make three and a half years. This three and a half years is the last half of the seventieth week of Daniel's prophecy in chapter 9.

This is the time of the Great Tribulation. All this is after the rapture, and in the period discussed in some of the book of Revelation.

Antichrist More Explicitly Foretold in Daniel 9

Daniel 9:24-27 is the essential background of prophecy of the future:

"Seventy weeks are determined upon thy people and upon thy holy city, to finish the transgression, and to make an end of sins, and to make reconciliation for iniquity, and to bring in everlasting righteousness, and to seal up the vision and prophecy, and to anoint the most Holy. Know therefore and understand, that from the going forth of the commandment to restore and to build Jerusalem unto the Messiah the Prince shall be seven weeks, and threescore and two weeks: the street shall be built again, and the wall, even in troublous times. And after threescore and two weeks shall Messiah be cut off, but not for himself: and the people of the prince that shall come shall destroy the city and the sanctuary; and the end thereof shall be with a flood, and unto the end of the war desolations are determined. And he shall confirm the covenant with many for one

week: and in the midst of the week he shall cause the sacrifice and the oblation to cease, and for the overspreading of abominations he shall make it desolate, even until the consummation, and that determined shall be poured upon the desolate."

Some facts stand out here:

1. Seventy weeks of years, a history of Israel as a nation in the land, are here mentioned.

2. Sixty-nine weeks of years were promised from the command of Cyrus (we think) to rebuild Jerusalem, down to the birth of Christ. So the Wise Men and others from Babylon expected His birth.

3. After the seven weeks of years to build Jerusalem and the other sixty-two weeks, 69 weeks of years, 'the Messiah shall be cut off,' that is, Christ would come and be crucified.

4. The armies of Rome would destroy Jerusalem. Notice they are the people "of the prince that shall come," that is, of the Antichrist. He will be a dictator of Rome, as a revived Roman empire.

Now there is a great leap, a parenthetical period; between the destruction of Jerusalem and the Jews' being scattered to all the world and the temporary end of the national history of Israel down to the time of the Antichrist. For centuries Jews have had no national existence. Even now they have no Temple, no priesthood, no sacrifices, are not counted a scriptural religious Israel.

5. Then the seventieth week of Daniel's seventy weeks of years begins, when the Man of Sin, the Antichrist, will make a covenant with many to re-establish the Temple and sacrifices of Israel. Here is a great gap between the 69 weeks of years, (the first 483 years from the time of Cyrus to the coming of Christ), and the last week of the seventy, after the rapture and after the Man of Sin himself rises up in the ruins of the Roman Empire to restore it and then makes a treaty with Israel purporting to be for seven years. Jews will have a Temple and priesthood and sacrifices again and the national life of Israel as a nation worshiping God will continue.

6. But in the midst of the seventieth week of prophesied Jewish history the Antichrist will stop the Jewish sacrifices, will commit the "abomination of desolation" referred to in Daniel 9:27 and which Jesus foretold in Matthew 24:15, 16, "When ye therefore shall see the abomination of desolation, spoken of by Daniel the prophet, stand in the holy place, (Whoso readeth, let him understand:) Then let them which be in Judaea flee into the mountains." This Man of Sin will claim to be God on earth and demand worship. And his awful reign will be the darkest time of trouble this world ever saw.

All that will come out clearer in the book of Revelation.

Here we have the outline briefly of prophecy. A ruler of the revived Roman empire will gain power over other kings until he becomes absolute. He will make a treaty with Jews to have a Temple and sacrifices and worship there for seven years. Then after three and a half years he will break his treaty and the last three and a half years of his reign will be the Great Tribulation.

Neither Daniel nor Revelation Point Out Rapture When Christ Is to Take His Own to Heaven

We must bear in mind God's clearly defined plan. He has kept secret from everybody the time of Christ's return to gather His own when the Christian dead will be raised and the Christian living will be changed.

The Bible does tell clearly one fact that makes us know it is the next thing on God's program. Again and again we are warned, "What I say unto you I say unto all, Watch," and, "Watch therefore, for ye know neither the day nor the hour wherein the Son of man cometh" (Mark 13:37; Matt. 25:13).

That warning is so clearly given again and again in the Olivet discourse in Matthew 24, also in the parable of the ten virgins in Matthew 25, in Luke 13, etc. The return of Christ for His own, this first step in the Second Coming, is imminent, impending, expected momentarily, any time, day or night. That means that the other things that are prophesied to come in the future—the Antichrist, the Great Tribulation, the regathering of Israel, and such things—could not come until after the rapture. The rapture itself is not in the schedule of events. It is to be before them.

The Lord plainly foretold the first coming of Christ and told how long it would be from the command to rebuild Jerusalem down to the coming of the Messiah. After the rapture, when we are all gone to Heaven, God has a very clearly outlined schedule of seven years. We do not know whether it will begin immediately after the rapture or some time after, but seven years are promised when the nation Israel will have a covenant to worship their God and have the sacrifices and a Temple in Jerusalem. Meantime the Man of Sin will be gaining power and arrogance and in the middle of the seven years he will claim to be God on earth, will enter into the Temple, showing himself that he is God (II Thess. 2:4). Then "Immediately after the tribulation of those days," as Jesus foretold in Matthew 24:29 and following, Christ will return in glory with all the saints and angels, will fight the battle of Armageddon, will regather a remnant of Israel into the wilderness of wandering. There the rebels will be purged out. There the rest of the Jews will be saved, and then the Lord Jesus will set up His kingdom and reign on the throne of David as the angel promised Mary in Luke 1:32.

When will come the rapture, this first phase or the first step of Christ's second coming? No one can know. We simply know that is the next step in prophecy, the one thing we are to watch for. And no prophesied event can come before that except the regular course of this age.

Chapter 6

VERSES 1, 2:

AND I saw when the Lamb opened one of the seals, and I heard, as it were the noise of thunder, one of the four beasts saying, Come and see.

2 And I saw, and behold a white horse: and he that sat on him had a bow; and a crown was given unto him: and he went forth conquering, and to conquer.

First Seal: Rise of a Dictator

Here is one riding *a white horse* (vs. 1). We are reminded of Jesus, pictured in Revelation 19:11-16. But this is another ruler, evidently the rise of the Antichrist. A man on a fine horse represents power. Great generals are often sculptured on horses. Great warriors ride, they do not walk. Robert E. Lee rode Traveler. Alexander the Great rode Bucephalus. In ordinary matters men rode in carriages or on camels and lesser men on donkeys. Conquerors in war rode horses.

In the Old Testament the horse is often the emblem of war (Job 39:25; Ps. 76:6; Prov. 21:31; Ezek. 26:10). Seiss reminds us that in dealing with these seal-openings, we must bear in mind that we are dealing with the scenes of the judgment. They relate to "the day of the Lord." "Anticipatory fulfillments have occurred, but the proper breaking of these seals, and whatever is connected with their opening, belongs to the future, and to that momentous period, now at hand, which is to close up the entire order of things now existing. The whole scene presents the action of the judgment-throne in Heaven toward those then living upon the earth."

"A bow" (vs. 2) for war. This is not a peaceable ascent to an inherited throne. Rather, it is a battle to conquer men and nations. We remember the "little horn," picturing the rise of the Antichrist in the midst of the ten kings who are to rule over ten kingdoms from the dissolved Roman empire, pictured in Daniel 7:8. He is to pluck up or take the kingdom from three of the ten

kings. Of him it is explained: "And he shall speak great words against the most High, and shall wear out the saints of the most High, and think to change times and laws: and they shall be given into his hand until a time and times and the dividing of time" (Dan. 7:25).

Here first is the rise of this "man of sin" (II Thess. 2:3) to power. He is given a crown, so he who was not a king becomes one, usurping thrones and overthrowing others. Here is probably pictured his beginning. Later he will commit the "Abomination of desolation," will break the covenant with Israel, stop the worship and sacrifices to God in the midst of the covenant, a week of years.

The rise of the "man of sin" cannot be until after the rapture. Here read II Thessalonians 2:1-8 and find an order of events that will help us.

"Now we beseech you, brethren, by the coming of our Lord Jesus Christ, and by our gathering together unto him, That ye be not soon shaken in mind, or be troubled, neither by spirit, nor by word, nor by letter as from us, as that the day of Christ is at hand. Let no man deceive you by any means: for that day shall not come, except there come a falling away first, and that man of sin be revealed, the son of perdition; Who opposeth and exalteth himself above all that is called God, or that is worshipped; so that he as God sitteth in the temple of God, shewing himself that he is God. Remember ye not, that, when I was yet with you, I told you these things? And now ye know what withholdeth that he might be revealed in his time. For the mystery of iniquity doth already work: only he who now letteth will let, until he be taken out of the way. And then shall that Wicked be revealed, whom the Lord shall consume with the spirit of his mouth, and shall destroy with the brightness of his coming."

Note now the term "the day of Christ," the same as "the day of the Lord," when Christ sets up His kingdom. It is not at hand until certain things occur (vs. 2).

1. First, there needs to be a "falling away," literally a depar-

ture, that is, as we understand it the rapture of the saints, the "gathering together unto him" of verse 1. The Greek word here is *apostacio,* so it is natural for people to think that it means a religious apostasy, a falling from grace. But it can hardly mean that. The word is sometimes used for departure, and "the day of the Lord" is the time of Christ's return to conquer and reign. It waits not on a religious apostasy but on the departure of the saints. The Man of Sin cannot appear until that time. (See the book by E. Schuyler English entitled *Re-thinking the Rapture.*) Dr. Ironside and other scholars agreed that the falling away here means the departure of the saints.

2. Nothing here is preliminary to the rapture, but a regular schedule of events to follow the rapture. Since we are often warned to expect daily the rapture, the first phase of Christ's coming at any moment, "in the twinkling of an eye," there cannot be and are not any prophesied events to come before that rapture. So before the rise of the Antichrist, before Daniel's seventieth week of years can begin, before the tribulation period, must come the rapture of the saints.

3. But then Someone "who now letteth" or restrains the course of history so that the Man of Sin cannot appear—who is He? That Restrainer is the Holy Spirit. His worldwide influence through born-again Christians makes it so the restored Roman empire cannot rise nor the Antichrist appear until Christians are taken out and thus the influence through them of the Holy Spirit is removed from its restraining power on this wicked world.

How many men have tired to build a world empire after the decay of Rome, as such an empire! Charlemagne, the pope, Napoleon, Kaiser Wilhelm, Mussolini, Hitler! But none can succeed until Christians and the Holy Spirit's influence on society through them, is taken away.

That does not mean that the Holy Spirit Himself will be gone, no more to convict and save or dwell in the Christians who will be converted in the tribulation, to help and empower them. A multitude will be converted and saved by Holy Spirit power during the Great Tribulation (see 7:9-14).

Also, Joel 2:28-30 and Acts 2:14-21 plainly say that the period

called "the last days," the pouring out of the Holy Spirit on all
flesh so they will witness to Christ, runs right on through this age
to "the great and notable day of the Lord." So the Holy Spirit
will not be gone from the world. But the accumulated influence
of the Holy Spirit on society through Christians is now a constant
check. "The mystery of iniquity doth already work" (II Thess.
2:7) but cannot succeed until after the rapture. The one *"conquering, and to conquer"* (vs. 2) will be a "prince" of the people
who destroyed Jerusalem in A.D. 70, that is, of Rome (Dan. 9:26;
Dan. 7:7, 8). He will restore that Roman empire. Note that
Revelation 13:3 tells us that one head of Rome was wounded to
death "and his deadly wound was healed," so that Rome will live
again as a world empire under the Antichrist.

VERSES 3,4

3 And when he had opened the
second seal, I heard the second beast
say, Come and see.
4 And there went out another horse
that was red: and *power* was given
to him that sat thereon to take peace
from the earth, and that they should
kill one another: and there was given
unto him a great sword.

Second Seal: Peace Taken From Earth

Seiss reminds us: "We are not to suppose, however, that the
action of one horse ceases entirely, before the other comes into
play. They are consecutive in their incoming, in the main stress
of them, and in some of their more marked circumstances, but
they are all, in a measure, contemporaneous.

The red horse of war follows the white horse of dictatorship.
War, oppression and trouble to multitudes follow where usurpers
seize power. Give Mussolini absolute power in Italy, he dreams of
world conquest and begins his slaughter in Ethiopia. Give Hitler
unchallenged power in Germany, he sets out to conquer the
world. Let the little Corporal Napoleon Bonaparte seize power in
France, he aims then at all Europe and bathes the nations in
blood. The troubles of war will ensue with nations soaked in
blood till the lone armies and navy of England at last put him

down. Here is the law of God in nature that sin brings death, that dictatorship leads to war.

Jesus said about the course of this age:

"And ye shall hear of wars and rumours of wars: see that ye be not troubled: for all these things must come to pass, but the end is not yet. For nation shall rise against nation, and kingdom against kingdom: and there shall be famines, and pestilences, and earthquakes, in divers places. All these are the beginning of sorrows."—Matt. 24:6-8.

So the wars and slaughter of this age are only the beginning of sorrows that shall follow when God's people are taken out and the Holy Spirit's influence on the world through them is removed. The red horse pictures the end of peace on earth when the Antichrist seizes power.

Lot could have won nine more to be righteous and with ten righteous could have restrained the wrath of God on Sodom and Gomorrah. But he failed and was taken out, and Sodom and Gomorrah, Admah and Zeboim were destroyed. So the wrath of God on wicked men would result in death during Daniel's seventieth week. The *"great sword"* goes with the tragic red horse.

VERSES 5, 6:

5 And when he had opened the third seal, I heard the third beast say, Come and see. And I beheld, and lo a black horse; and he that sat on him had a pair of balances in his hand.

6 And I heard a voice in the midst of the four beasts say, A measure of wheat for a penny, and three measures of barley for a penny; and *see* thou hurt not the oil and the wine.

Third Seal: Famine

Weigh out the food carefully! It is scarce. Wars have taken men from the plow and reaping. Opposing armies have burned the fields and ravished the storehouses. Now stark famine comes, the third woe pictured when the third seal is opened on the book. Three quarts (or measures) of barley for a denarius, a day's wages, one quart of wheat—not enough wheat for two persons a day. Prices rise in the scarcity. That is the price of dictatorship, wars and bloodshed. Careful of the scarce oil and wine; there is not enough to go around! Note the famine in Samaria when besieged by Roman armies as described in II Kings 6:24-29.

In America government interference with crops and prices, wild spending, prodigal welfare programs, mean inflated prices and threaten eventual disaster unless checked. The black horse of famine, inflated prices, scarcity, will follow dictatorship and war in the seventieth week of Daniel.

On these verses, Seiss adds this:

> People do not generally suppose that God has much to do with price lists. They go up and down, and millions higgle over them every day, but no one thinks of anything Divine connected with them. But whether men realize it or not, price lists are made in Heaven. John hears the rates of corn and bread announced by the same heavenly powers by which these mystic horses are called into action. Whatever the weather, the crops, the quantities of money in the country, the extent of speculation in the market, or other subordinate causes may have to do with it, the prime and all-controlling cause is the decree of the throne. It is God from whom we have our daily bread, and it is by His will that it is plentiful and cheap, or scarce and costly.

VERSES 7, 8:

7 And when he had opened the fourth seal, I heard the voice of the fourth beast say, Come and see.
8 And I looked, and behold a pale horse: and his name that sat on him was Death, and Hell followed with him. And power was given unto them over the fourth part of the earth, to kill with sword, and with hunger, and with death, and with the beasts of the earth.

Fourth Seal: Death

The conquering dictator on the white horse with the sword of war and oppression of the red horse and famine and scarcity and starvation of the black horse are followed by the *"pale horse"* by the name of *"Death, and Hell followed after"* (vs. 8). Note here a *"fourth part of the earth."* Does it mean a fourth part of the earth's surface, or a fourth part of the population of the world? At any rate millions will die.

But this is only the beginning of the death that will curse the earth. Revelation 8:11 tells of men dying because of poisoned water, and verse 15 of chapter 9 tells of angels loosed "for to slay the third part of men." Again an earthquake will kill seven thousand (11:13). Then the demon-possessed army of the Antichrist of two hundred million men (9:16) is to be destroyed at Armageddon (14:14-20).

These seals are not to end. The seventh seal reveals seven trumpets and woe is to follow. The seventh trumpet reveals other woes, and the fact that the number seven is repeated indicates that the judgments are of God, though He will allow wicked men to do their part. God allowed Judas to betray Christ for thirty pieces of silver though Christ was "delivered by the determinate counsel and foreknowledge of God" (Acts 2:23). God allowed heathen nations to punish Israel for Him, then He judged those nations.

Note that the death by wild beasts as well as by sword and hunger is mentioned in verse 8. In Luke 13:1-5 Jesus taught that death, whether at Pilate's hands or the falling of a wall, was all the act of God and a warning to all men.

VERSES 9—11:

9 And when he had opened the fifth seal, I saw under the altar the souls of them that were slain for the word of God, and for the testimony which they held:

10 And they cried with a loud voice, saying, How long, O Lord, holy and true, dost thou not judge and avenge our blood on them that dwell on the earth?

11 And white robes were given unto every one of them; and it was said unto them, that they should rest yet for a little season, until their fellow-servants also and their brethren, that should be killed as they *were*, should be fulfilled.

Fifth Seal: Martyrs of Tribulation Time

Who are these *"slain for the word of God, and for the testimony which they held"* (vs. 9)? Remember these are after

the Christians are taken up to Heaven, the living changed and
those who were "asleep" raised. So there are martyrs to be killed
after the rapture. This is one of the woes revealed in the sealed
book along with the conquerer on the white horse, the war pictured by him on the red horse, the famine and death pictured by
the black and pale horses. And in Heaven they ask how long
those who kill them will remain unpunished. Those haters of
Christians will still be alive on the earth. J. A. Seiss says : "It appears from this that their murderers are then still living. Conse-
quently these crying ones are a specific class of martyrs, who had
then very recently been slain. . . .It was an utterance from the
world of disembodied saints, somewhat akin, in feeling and
meaning, to that which John the Baptist sent from his prison to
the Saviour (Matt. 11:2-10)."

Bede has remarked upon this passage, that "those souls which
offered themselves a living sacrifice to God pray eternally for His
coming to judgment; not from any vindictive feeling against
their enemies, but in a spirit of zeal and love for God's glory and
justice, and for the coming of that day when sin, which is rebellion against Him, will be destroyed, and their own bodies
raised."

With the awful loosing of sinful men, with the restraint of millions of born-again Christians gone, Satan will know that "he
hath but a short time" (12:12). So he will storm against God and
God's saints. Satan will enter into a man who will become "the
son of perdition," "the man of sin" (II Thess. 2:3), the Antichrist. He will be Satan incarnate. He will set out to kill Christians, will even bring the armies of "the kings of the east"
(16:12), will bring Gog and Magog, then all the armies of the
restored Roman empire, against the heavenly armies of the Lord
Jesus in the valley of Megiddo where all that wicked army will be
destroyed (19:21).

So those who get saved after the rapture will face terrible
persecutions, with many put to death for their faith and "the
saints. . .shall be given into his hand" (the Antichrist), for three
and one half years (Dan. 7:25).

Those martyrs in Heaven are to be given *"white robes"* (vs.11).

We suppose they are only spirits, "souls," in Heaven until given white robes. Are they to be given temporary bodies? How else would a Spirit wear a robe? Paul was inspired to say:

"For we know that if our earthly house of this tabernacle were dissolved, we have a building of God, an house not made with hands, eternal in the heavens. For in this we groan, earnestly desiring to be clothed upon with our house which is from heaven: If so be that being clothed we shall not be found naked. For we that are in this tabernacle do groan, being burdened: not for that we would be unclothed, but clothed upon, that mortality might be swallowed up of life."—II Cor. 5:1-4.

Paul expected "not for that we would be unclothed but clothed upon." Garments are physical and indicate a physical body. Moses from Heaven appeared visibly on the Mount of Transfiguration as if he had a physical body though his body had been buried on Mount Nebo. We may be sure that at their resurrection, it is foretold that those who "were beheaded for the witness of Jesus. . .they lived and reigned with Christ a thousand years" (20:4). John saw all this and recorded it as if it were past, but only the vision of it, the revelation of it, is past. This is all part of the "things which must shortly come to pass" (1:1), that is, future events.

And these martyrs in Heaven are told that fellowservants and brethren should also suffer martyrdom. This, we suppose, is in the first three and one-half years of the Antichrist before the awful persecution that will follow in the last three and one-half years, "the great tribulation." So then the Antichrist will claim to be God, will demand worship of himself, the emperor of Rome; will demand that men will no more buy nor sell without his mark. Thus multitudes of Christians saved after the rapture will be slain.

Note also these souls in Heaven know what goes on on earth. Moses and Elijah from Heaven discussed with Jesus "his decease which he should accomplish at Jerusalem" (Luke 9:31). Those in Heaven know all about that. In Heaven they know and rejoice every time a soul on earth is saved (Luke 15:10). The great cloud of witnesses in Heaven 'compass about' and watch our race on earth (Heb. 12:1). In Heaven they watch and know about us. Why not, when the angels come and go daily caring for us (Heb. 1:14)? And saints going to Heaven would surely communicate to others in Heaven. They watch us and know about us.

VERSES 12—14:

12 And I beheld when he had opened the sixth seal, and, lo, there was a great earthquake; and the sun became black as sackcloth of hair, and the moon became as blood; 13 And the stars of heaven fell unto the earth, even as a fig tree casteth her untimely figs, when she is shaken of a mighty wind. 14 And the heaven departed as a scroll when it is rolled together; and every mountain and island were moved out of their places.

Sixth Seal: Chaos and God's Wrath in Nature

The former seals opened revealed the plagues brought by wicked men and in the economy as the result of sin. But the fifth seal, the murder of Christians, shows open hate and opposition to God. Now we must expect such sins to bring the wrath of God, so God will send a mighty earthquake. When Jesus died, "the earth did quake, and the rocks rent" (Matt. 27:51). Another earthquake is to follow (8:5), another (11:13) and another (16:18). All nature is disturbed and manifests the wrath of God.

Seiss reminds us:

In very many places, great convulsions of nature are spoken of in connection with special manifestations of Deity.

When God gave the law, "mount Sinai was altogether on a smoke, because the Lord descended upon it in fire, and the smoke thereof ascended as the smoke of a great furnace, and the whole mount quaked greatly" (Exod. 19:18).

When Elijah made complaint unto the Lord that Israel had shed the blood of His prophets, and trembled for his own safety, ". . .the Lord passed by, and a great and strong wind rent the mountains, and brake in pieces the rocks. . .and after the wind an earthquake" (I Kings 19:11).

When Jesus was murdered, "the veil of the temple was rent in twain from the top to the bottom; and the earth did quake, and the rocks rent" (Matt. 27:50, 51).

When Paul and Silas were beaten, imprisoned, and put into the stocks, and appealed unto the Lord in songs and prayers, "suddenly there was a great earthquake, so that the foundations of the prison were shaken, and all the doors were opened, and every one's bands were loosed" (Acts 16:26).

Especially are such convulsions prophesied of in connection with the judgment, and the approach and consummation of the end of the world. Jesus has plainly told us that famines, and pestilences, and earthquakes are more and more to characterize the coming of the end (Matt. 24:7-9).

". . .*and the sun became black as sackcloth of hair*" says verse 12. There was a plague of midnight darkness in Egypt (Exod. 10:21, 22). When Jesus died on the cross, ". . .from the sixth hour there was darkness over all the land unto the ninth hour" (Matt. 7:45). Other marvels will disrupt nature. Stars fall, the canopy of heaven disappears. Convulsions of the earth move mountains and islands from their places. These events are foretold more than once. (See Matt. 24:29; Joel 2:30, 31 quoted in Acts 2:19-21). These last two passages show that the Great Commission and the promise of Holy Spirit enduement are good through the whole age beyond the rapture, through the tribulation to "that great and notable day of the Lord."

VERSES 15—17:

15 And the kings of the earth, and the great men, and the rich men, and the chief captains, and the mighty men, and every bondman, and every free man, hid themselves in the dens and in the rocks of the mountains;

16 And said to the mountains and rocks, Fall on us, and hide us from the face of him that sitteth on the throne, and from the wrath of the Lamb:

17 For the great day of his wrath is come; and who shall be able to stand?

Men Shall Greatly Fear Wrath of Lamb

These woes and plagues are part of the wrath of God. The fear of Christ will be on kings and rulers. Revelation 1:7 says, "Behold, he cometh with clouds; and every eye shall see him, and they also which pierced him: and all kindreds of the earth shall wail because of him. Even so, Amen." Christ's wrath against the governments of the earth which are to climax in the world dictatorship of the Antichrist is pictured in stone cut out of a mountain without hands which is to smite the image of Nebuchadnezzar's dream, that image picturing world empires and smitten in his feet. That stone will destroy the whole image and then rule the whole world, the picture of Christ's reign. Matthew 24:30 tells how all the tribes of the earth will mourn at Christ's return to reign. The destruction of kings is foretold in Psalm 2:4-12. Note the universal despair of lost men, great and small, as they face Christ's coming.

Kings and generals, statesmen, common people everywhere alike, men who are unconverted and adherents of the Antichrist, will hide themselves in dens and caves, will wish the mountains to fall upon them so they may not face the wrath of Jesus Christ! Could they not be saved? Probably these have all so definitely and finally rejected Christ that they cannot repent, cannot change their stubborn, hardened heart against God and so cannot bring themselves to turn to Him.

We read in Revelation 13:8, "And all that dwell upon the earth shall worship him, whose names are not written in the book of life of the Lamb slain from the foundation of the world." So all who worship the beast (the Antichrist) are not written in the book of life.

Revelation 14:9-11 says:

"And the third angel followed them, saying with a loud voice, If any man worship the beast and his image, and receive his mark in his forehead, or in his hand, The same shall drink of the wine of the wrath of God, which is poured out without mixture into the cup of his indignation; and he shall be tormented with fire and brimstone in the presence of the holy angels, and in the presence of the Lamb: And the smoke of their torment ascendeth up for ever and ever: and they have no rest day nor night, who worship the beast and his image, and whosoever receiveth the mark of his name."

So all who take the mark of the beast and worship him, we

believe, will have committed the unpardonable sin. After great enlightenment and conviction "it is impossible. . .if they shall fall away [from such conviction and enlightenment] to renew them again unto repentance: seeing they crucify to themselves the Son of God afresh, and put him to an open shame" (Heb. 6:4-6).

It was so with Judas Iscariot who had gone so far against such light that though he was so miserable he committed suicide, yet he could not bring himself to want Jesus or to ask for mercy. For those who crucified Him, Jesus prayed on the cross, "Father, forgive them: for they know not what they do" (Luke 23:34). So one who is perfectly enlightened and then makes final choice against Christ and salvation has passed the place of repentance.

The unpardonable sin does not mean that God's offer of mercy is withdrawn or that if the sinner would come to Christ, he would be rejected. The promise is still good that "all that the Father giveth me shall come to me; and him that cometh to me I will in no wise cast out" (John 6:37). And again we are promised, "For whosoever shall call on the name of the Lord shall be saved" (Rom. 10:13). But a sinner may go so far that he cannot turn because he does not desire to turn. The unpardonable sin does not change Christ but the sinner and forever he turns himself away from God.

As far as we know everybody in Hell after death has passed that point of no return and cannot repent.

Chapter 7

Dr. J. Sidlow Baxter in *Explore the Book* calls attention to the fact that chapters 12 through 19 are parallel to and repeat the teachings of chapters 6 through 11. Note his outline showing that the events and plagues in the second section are not necessarily following consecutively but are a repeat, with different figures, of the teachings in the first section. Here he places the parallel teaching in two columns as follows:

Chapters vi.-xi.	*Chapters xii.-xix.*
Ch. vi. The seven seals.	The seven persons (xii., xiii.).
vii. Parenthetical:	Parenthetical (xiv.):
(1) Israel remnant sealed	(1) Israel remnant sealed.
(2) Blessedness of saints in heaven.	(2) Blessedness of the saints.
viii., ix. SEVEN TRUMPETS.	SEVEN VIALS (xv., xvi.).
1. On the earth.	1. On the earth.
2. On the sea.	2. On the sea.
3. On the rivers.	3. On the rivers.
4. Sun, moon, stars.	4. Sun.
5. Darkness, scourge.	5. Darkness, scourge.
6. Euphrates: army.	6. Euphrates: kings.
7. "Nations angry"; "Wrath"; "Great voices"; "Time no more."	7. "Nations fell"; "Wrath"; "Voices"; "Thunderings"; "It is done."
x., xi. Parenthetical: Jerusalem in the "Great Tribulation."	Parenthetical (xvii.-xviii.): Babylon in "Wrath of God."
xi. 15 End of seventh trumpet.	After seventh vial (xix.)
1. "Kingdom of the Lord."	1. "Lord God reigneth."
2. The 24 elders worship.	2. The 24 elders worship.
3. "Wrath" is come.	3. "Armageddon."

This concurrent parallel can easily be looked up and verified, for which purpose it is better to use the American Revised Version. There can surely be no mistaking it. It is really there; and the interpretation of the book hangs upon it.

VERSES 1—3:

AND after these things I saw four angels standing on the four corners of the earth, holding the four winds of the earth, that the wind should not blow on the earth, nor on the sea, nor on any tree.

2 And I saw another angel ascending from the east, having the seal of the living God: and he cried with a loud voice to the four angels, to whom it was given to hurt the earth and the sea,

3 Saying, Hurt not the earth, neither the sea, nor the trees, till we have sealed the servants of our God in their foreheads.

A. T. Robertson here reminds us that "instead of the seventh seal being opened, two other episodes or preliminary visions occupy chapter 7—the sealing of the servants of God (1-8) and the vision of the redeemed before the throne (9-17)."

Many to Be Saved During Great Tribulation

Now comes a parenthetical interlude. While the woes and plagues of God's wrath and man's hate go on, the book of Revelation turns aside to discuss those who will be saved in that tribulation period. Remember the Great Commission and its promise, in Matthew 28:19, 20 continue "even unto the end of the world," or more exactly, "to the consummation of the age." And this age, "the times of the Gentiles" (Luke 21:24), does not end until the last Gentile ruler, the Antichrist himself, is to be put down. Acts 2:14-21, quoting Joel 2:28-32 tells us that the pouring out of the Holy Spirit so that God's people may prophesy, that is, witness in the power of the Holy Spirit, will go on until "that great and notable day of the Lord." The "day of the Lord" involves the return of Christ in glory to destroy the governments of the world and take over His kingdom. And these Scriptures expressly say that all the time up to Christ's return to reign, "the day of the Lord," and "whosoever shall call on the name of the Lord shall be saved." So many will be saved in the tribulation time.

Some Bible teachers think that one who has heard the Gospel before the rapture and was not saved cannot be saved during the tribulation. I think they are mistaken. There is no change in the

Gospel nor in the promise, and "whosoever will, let him take the water of life freely" (22:17).

In the parable of the ten virgins, those five who did not have the oil of salvation but only a burning torch which soon went out, could not get in to see the bridegroom. They picture some who will miss the rapture and the wedding feast in Heaven. But they are told to "go ye rather to them that sell, and buy for yourselves" (Matt. 25:9). That indicates that they could get the oil of salvation but too late for the heavenly wedding.

Only one who has committed the unpardonable sin, finally, with full light, rejecting Christ forever, could not be saved later. God calls again and again. If one turns to trust Christ, he is then saved forever. God never changes the plan of salvation. Acts 10:43 says, "To him give all the prophets witness, that through his name whosoever believeth in him shall receive remission of sins." And John 6:37 says, "All that the Father giveth me shall come to me; and him that cometh to me I will in no wise cast out."

God's Care for His Own Midst Judgment and Trial

Four angels hold back the four winds that they can do no harm to God's own by land or sea or tree! Another angel comes to seal the servants of God in their foreheads and all the elements are withheld from hurting the earth, the sea and vegetation until then. So in the Great Tribulation God's saints are "sheltered in the arms of God." They are "covered with his wings." No harm can come to them except as God allows it for their eternal good and His own glory.

We do not mean that no trouble, no persecution will come to the Christian. We mean that in all troubles God will be with them to control or temper or withstand all the troubles. Trouble came to Job but only as God allowed it. Satan complained, "Hast thou not made an hedge about him, and about his house, and about all that he hath. . .?" (Job 1:10). And we know from the end of Job "that the Lord is very pitiful, and of tender mercy" (Jas. 5:11).

The children of Israel suffered sore bondage in Egypt and when plagues came they had light in their dwellings when all Egypt was dark; their cattle were kept when others died in the hail. God may allow His own to suffer hardship or even death, but like Paul and Silas they may pray open the jail and see the jailer saved (Acts 16:31) or like Paul in prison they may learn, ". . .in whatsoever state I am, therewith to be content" (Phil. 4:11) and then gladly suffer execution. Remember God has all Christians marked. Only what He lovingly and wisely approves can come to the Christian.

Hold the winds, ye angels! Hurt nothing till God's saints be sealed!

So Ezekiel, grieving in captivity, was shown how God had marked and preserved those 'that sighed and cried' over all the abominations going on in Israel when their sin caused God to send Nebuchadnezzar against Jerusalem. Behind the scenes an unseen angel marked all those fervent souls grieved by sin about them so they would be kept and God's angels with slaughter weapons destroyed others (Ezek. 9:1-7). Angels, you hold up the destruction of Sodom until Lot can be led out—you can do nothing in judgment on others before he is preserved (Gen. 19:22).

And every Christian is "sealed unto the day of redemption" (Eph. 4:30). We are marked as belonging to Christ, preserved by Him, "kept by the power of God through faith unto salvation . . ." (I Pet. 1:5). None can take us out of the hand of Christ and of the Father (John 10:27-30). We may be "cast down, but not destroyed" (II Cor. 4:9), "chastened, and not killed" (II Cor. 6:9).

VERSES 4—8:

4 And I heard the number of them which were sealed: *and there were* sealed an hundred *and* forty *and* four thousand of all the tribes of the children of Israel.

5 Of the tribe of Juda *were* sealed twelve thousand. Of the tribe of Reuben *were* sealed twelve thousand. Of the tribe of Gad *were* sealed twelve thousand.

6 Of the tribe of Aser *were* sealed twelve thousand. Of the tribe of Nĕp̓-thă-lĭm *were* sealed twelve thousand. Of the tribe of Mă-năs̓-

sēs *were* sealed twelve thousand.

7 Of the tribe of Simeon *were* sealed twelve thousand. Of the tribe of Levi *were* sealed twelve thousand. Of the tribe of Ĭs-sä-chär *were* sealed twelve thousand.

8 Of the tribe of Ză-bū-lon *were* sealed twelve thousand. Of the tribe of Joseph *were* sealed twelve thousand. Of the tribe of Benjamin *were* sealed twelve thousand.

144,000 of Israel Sealed

Here are the twelve tribes of Israel. A strange fact appears. The tribe of Dan is omitted. Why? No one knows. The Scripture does not say. Instead two tribes are named from the sons of Joseph—Manasseh and Ephraim—and that makes twelve tribes including the priestly tribe of Levi. Was the tribe of Dan largely absorbed in other tribes at the captivity and after? Or was Dan thus given no place here because of disgrace? We do not know. The number twelve is Israel's number and so counting Ephraim and Manesseh, the two sons of Joseph, as separated tribes, it makes twelve, leaving out Dan. Ironside says: "The rabbis used to say that the false Messiah (the Antichrist) would arise from Dan, and they based the supposition on Jacob's words in Genesis 49:17, 'Dan shall be a serpent by the way, an adder in the path, that biteth the horse heels, so that his rider shall fall backward.' We note from the historical record, in the book of Judges, that Dan was the first tribe to go into idolatry, and it would not be a matter of surprise if Dan would be the leader in the last great idolatry—worship of Antichrist."

One hundred and forty-four thousand is the square of twelve, multiplied a thousandfold, and some think it to be understood, not numerically but symbolically, representing the sum total of the elect of Israel, the firstfruits of the Gospel, or the sum total of Christians.

Is there some similarity here to the case of the twelve apostles? But Judas being disgraced and dead, they must elect another apostle to take his place (Acts 1:15-26).

We believe there will be this literal number of 144,000 Israelites especially chosen as servants of God, 12,000 from each tribe of the children of Israel. We remember the Great Tribulation is specifically related to Israel—it is called "the time of Jacob's trouble" (Jer. 30:7).

This is in Daniel's seventieth prophesied week of years of Jewish national Israel. A treaty by the Antichrist with Israel will allow them to restore the Temple, priesthood and sacrifices (Dan. 9:24). In the midst of the seven-year covenant this Man of Sin will break this covenant and commit the "abomination of desolation" and set out to persecute, oppress and kill Jews and Christians for the last three and one-half years (Dan. 9:27).

When the tribulation is over the Lord Jesus will regather all of Israel (Matt. 24:29-31, Deut. 30:1-6, Jer. 23:3-6, Ezek. 36:24-28). Then the Israelites will all be taken to the wilderness of wanderings and the rebels purged out (Ezek. 20:33-38). They will see the Saviour, will be convicted and saved (Zech. 12:10; 13:1-6; Heb. 10:16-18). This is the great grafting in of the tame olive branches (Israel) which were broken off but will be restored (Rom. 11:13-26).

So there is reason to tell of Jews of twelve tribes sealed during the tribulation. Note that relatively few Jews are mentioned here as being saved—144,000 compared to "a great multitude, which no man could number" of Gentiles of all countries of the earth, mentioned as saved in the following verses. Many more of Israel will be saved when Christ returns personally.

VERSES 9-14:

9 After this I beheld, and, lo, a great multitude, which no man could number, of all nations, and kindreds, and people, and tongues, stood before the throne, and before the Lamb, clothed with white robes, and palms in their hands;

10 And cried with a loud voice, saying, Salvation to our God which sitteth upon the throne, and unto the Lamb.

11 And all the angels stood round about the throne, and about the elders and the four beasts, and fell before the throne on their faces, and worshipped God,

12 Saying, Amen: Blessing, and glory, and wisdom, and thanksgiving, and honour, and power, and might, be unto our God for ever and ever. Amen.

13 And one of the elders answered, saying unto me, What are these which are arrayed in white robes? and whence came they?

14 And I said unto him, Sir, thou knowest. And he said to me, These are they which came out of great tribulation, and have washed their robes, and made them white in the blood of the Lamb.

Multitudes of Gentiles Saved During Tribulation

We are expressly told that there are ". . .*they which came out of great tribulation, and have washed their robes, and made them white in the blood of the Lamb*" (vs. 14). How will these be won to Christ?

1. No doubt many will have heard the Gospel but will not turn to Christ until suddenly their loved ones are taken away. They know how to be saved, so turn to Christ too late for the rapture.

Once a man heard me preaching in a great tent revival, went home under great conviction, went to the barn and in a corn crib he knelt and trusted Christ some hours after he heard the Gospel. Another time a man heard me preach and was deeply convicted. He went away, drove around in the night for hours and then came home and was saved. No doubt many who have heard the Gospel will turn to Christ when arrested by the amazing visitation, when Christ comes and takes His own, when one is taken and the other left (Matt. 24:29-41).

2. These converts certainly will win others.

3. Two special, miraculous witnesses will prophesy in 1,260 days, that is, 3½ years during the Great Tribulation.

4. Revelation 14:6, 7 says: "And I saw another angel fly in the midst of heaven, having the everlasting gospel to preach unto them that dwell on the earth, and to every nation, and kindred, and tongue, and people, Saying with a loud voice, Fear God, and give glory to him; for the hour of his judgment is come: and worship him that made heaven, and earth, and the sea, and the fountains of waters."

So those who will be saved will hear the Gospel, will be convicted by the Holy Spirit just as people are saved now.

Remember Acts 10:43 shows that there is only one plan of salvation in all ages. It is the same "everlasting gospel" that will be preached during the tribulation fulfilling the same Great Commission we now obey (Matt. 28:19,20).

VERSES 15—17:

15 Therefore are they before the throne of God, and serve him day and night in his temple: and he that sitteth on the throne shall dwell among them.

16 They shall hunger no more, neither thirst any more; neither shall the sun light on them, nor any heat.

17 For the Lamb which is in the midst of the throne shall feed them, and shall lead them unto living fountains of waters: and God shall wipe away all tears from their eyes.

Blessed Relief and Reward Promised These Saved in Such Troublous Times

We are reminded of the letters to seven churches in chapters 2 and 3. Always Christ reminds the overcomers of great blessings ahead. So here, those who will have suffered under the Antichrist and many doubtless martyred, are reminded they will serve the Lord before His throne in Heaven, will be done with the pains and trials of life, will be led to fountains of living waters and the tears of imprisonment, persecution and martyrdom will be all wiped away by the Saviour! Read what Dr. H. A. Ironside says:

The struggle for daily bread will be over—they shall hunger no more; the ofttimes vain effort to quench their thirst will be at an end—they shall thirst no more. Even the unpleasant and disagreeable things with which men have been afflicted because of the way sin has jarred God's creation will be at an end. The sun shall not light upon them, nor any heat.

In that day all the saved of the nations will be able to take up, in the fullest sense, the beautiful words of the psalmist, which we but feebly enter into now: "The Lord is my shepherd; I shall not want. He maketh me to lie down in green pastures: He leadeth me beside the still waters. He restoreth my soul: He leadeth me in the paths of righteousness for his name's sake."

What a long, dreary night, with what frightful disturbing nightmares, if I may so speak, has this world known, since sin, with all its attendant evils, came in to wreck man's hopes of joy and gladness! But how precious to know that evil shall not always have the upper hand; that a time is coming, aye, and is very near, when the curse will be lifted, the desert shall rejoice and blossom like the rose; even the lower creation will be changed and revert to former habits ere sin entered; "the lion shall eat straw like the ox"; the little child need not fear the most savage of beasts; for they shall not hurt nor destroy in that day. The government will be righteously regulated; abuses of every kind will be stopped, and for a thousand glorious years our Lord Himself shall reign in righteousness.

Chapter 8

VERSE 1:

AND when he had opened the seventh seal, there was silence in heaven about the space of half an hour.

Be Quiet! Attention: Tragic Announcement

In Habakkuk 2:20 the Old Testament prophet was inspired to say, "The Lord is in his holy temple: let all the earth keep silence before him."

In the courtroom perfect silence is required, every ear waiting to hear the report of the jury, innocent or guilty; every ear waits to hear the sentence of the judge.

One enters softly and sits quietly at a funeral.

In London when the warning siren started, all the city stopped deathly still to hear where the bomb would drop in World War II.

So a serious warning of deadly import is about to be revealed. Silence in Heaven for half an hour!

Take to heart most seriously what is coming!

"Calm before the coming storm—the most awful storm that shall ever break over this poor world. . .When this last seal is broken, it will be clearly manifested then just what side God takes in all the affairs of earth," says Dr. Ironside. "He will judge according to the holiness of His character and the righteousness of His throne. The seventh seal introduces the final drama of the Great Tribulation. No wonder there is silence in Heaven for half an hour before that seal is broken!"

VERSES 2—6:

2 And I saw the seven angels which stood before God; and to them were given seven trumpets.

3 And another angel came and stood at the altar, having a golden censer; and there was given unto him much incense, that he should offer *it* with the prayers of all saints upon

the golden altar which was before the throne.

4 And the smoke of the incense, *which came* with the prayers of the saints, ascended up before God out of the angel's hand.

5 And the angel took the censer, and filled it with fire of the altar, and cast *it* into the earth: and there were voices, and thunderings, and lightnings, and an earthquake.

6 And the seven angels which had the seven trumpets prepared themselves to sound.

Dr. H. A. Ironside comments further here:

> Careful readers of the Bible will connect the seven trumpets with the fall of Jericho: that great city just across the Jordan that barred the progress of the people of Israel into the promised land—the city that fell with the blast of God alone. The priests of Israel were given the trumpets of judgment, and for seven days they marched about the city blowing the trumpets; seven times on the seventh day they did so and at the seventh blast the walls fell down flat. Jericho is a type of this present world in its estrangement from God, with enmity to the people of God. Jericho fell at the sound of seven trumpets, and the world, as you and I know it, is going to fall at the sound of the seven trumpets of doom, blown by these angels of judgment.

Before Plagues, God Remembers Prayers of Saints

What a beautiful way to show how sweet, how important are the prayers of the saints in the mind of God! They are pictured here as offered to God along with sweet incense on the golden altar before the throne.

In Revelation 5:8 we are reminded that the living creatures and the twenty-four elders "fell down before the Lamb, having every one of them harps, and golden vials full of odours, which are the prayers of saints." Prayers, serious, heartfelt prayers from the hearts of God's people, are forever. Not the casual, routine, not pious repetitions, not formal speeches to God, but the cries of an earnest heart, rise like incense to God.

And these are prayers that are recorded, that are retained and are remembered. Since they are the prelude to the judgments of God, no doubt these are the prayers of those who look to God for help in their troubles and look to God for vengeance that the oppressed ones would not take for themselves. These are prayers, no doubt, like those "souls of them that were slain for the word of God, and for the testimony which they held" who in Heaven plead why are not these awful oppressors punished (6:9-11).

Prayers and tears go very closely together. In Psalm 56:8 is the plea, "Thou tellest my wanderings: put thou my tears into thy bottle: are they not in thy book?"

Oriental saints sometimes had tiny bottles in which were preserved the tears in times of great grief, to be a constant reminder of their griefs. And the psalmist wants God to save up the tears as here He saves up the prayers of the saints and lets them come before Him as sweet incense.

We remember how Hezekiah, who had been ordered, "Set thine house in order; for thou shalt die, and not live," prayed to God earnestly so that God sent him word, "I have heard thy prayer, I have seen thy tears: behold, I will heal thee: on the third day thou shalt go up unto the house of the Lord. And I will add unto thy days fifteen years" (II Kings 20:5, 6).

Sometimes prayers seem to pile up and accumulate and then altogether through the years they accomplish their goal. There is virtue in persistent prayer, in a heart cry often brought to God.

Zecharias and Elisabeth prayed for many, many years before God answered their prayer with the babe John the Baptist. So Sarah and Abraham prayed so long before God, in loving mercy, gave them Isaac.

Oh, the prayer you prayed yesterday and the day before and long before that, the prayer that still lingers, the heart cry of your soul—do not think God has forgotten! Do not think the prayer was wafted away on the wind and gone! Those "golden vials full of odours, which are the prayers of saints" (5:8), are kept securely to the appointed time for God to answer.

These prayers are offered on the golden altar before God, with sweet incense. It is surely intended that we remember the altar of incense God had Moses prepare in Exodus 30:1-10. And the incense itself was especially prepared as Exodus 30:34-38 says:

"And the Lord said unto Moses, Take unto thee sweet spices, stacte and onycha, and galbanum; these sweet spices with pure frankincense: of each shall there be a like weight: And thou shalt make it a perfume, a confection after the art of the apothecary, tempered together, pure and holy: And thou shalt

beat some of it very small, and put of it before the testimony in the tabernacle of the congregation, where I will meet with thee: it shall be unto you most holy. And as for the perfume which thou shalt make, ye shall not make to yourselves according to the composition thereof: it shall be unto thee holy for the Lord. Whosoever shall make like unto that, to smell thereto, shall even be cut off from his people."

It was a sacred kind of incense, set apart for this worship of God. No one could make such a perfume for himself or his lady.

And that sweet incense was to be burned every morning by Aaron when he dressed the lamps in the tabernacle and when he lighted the lamps at evening (Exod. 30:7, 8).

We remember that the great altar of judgment was of brass and was out in the court before the Temple. But this altar of incense was of gold and was inside the Tabernacle, before the veil, before the ark of the testimony and the mercy seat. As the brazen altar pictures Christ dying for sinners, atoning for our sins, so the golden altar of incense inside the holy place pictures the approach of one already forgiven and saved with his praises and prayer to God!

Are prayers like sweet perfume to God? Oh, yes. "The prayer of the upright is his delight" (Prov. 15:8). I think you would pray more, brokenhearted, troubled Christian in need, if you realized your prayer was a sweet smelling savor to God!

And here is another thought implied: the prayers of saints are offered with incense. These prayers go to a God who is already reconciled, but does not the incense indicate that the prayers of the Saviour Himself are added to our prayers? Is not Jesus our High Priest? Does He not pray for us as He did for the Apostle Peter, "I have prayed for thee, that thy faith fail not" (Luke 22:32)? And since God loves prayers so much, is it not wonderful that the Lord Jesus could say, "Father. . .I knew that thou hearest me always" (John 11:42).

Oh, trumpets at the mouth of angels do not blow yet; do not blow until we are reminded that God will bring the answer to our prayers, He will bring judgment on those who persecuted the saints. Just as the blood of Ahab was licked up by the dogs in the vineyard which he stole from murdered Naboth (I Kings 21:17-19; 22:37,38), eventually God brings judgment to defend His saints and vindicate them.

VERSE 7:

7 The first angel sounded, and there followed hail and fire mingled with blood, and they were cast upon the earth: and the third part of trees was burnt up, and all green grass was burnt up.

First Trumpet

A strange trilogy is here in this curse: *"hail and fire mingled with blood."* God sent a very grievous hail to destroy trees and livestock in Egypt (Exod. 9:18, 24,25). And there in Egypt also there was "hail, and fire mingled with the hail." The hail in Egypt killed men and beasts and trees. There was fire with the hail and thunder; we suppose the fire was some form of lightning. God uses nature to punish men or to bless them. The blood here reminds us of the plagues in Egypt when the water was turned to blood.

Again, when Joshua and Israel fought against Adonizedec to deliver Gibeon, Joshua 10:11 says, "And it came to pass, as they fled from before Israel, and were in the going down to Beth-horon, that the Lord cast down great stones from heaven upon them unto Azekah, and they died: they were more which died with hailstones than they whom the children of Israel slew with the sword."

"Great hail" is mentioned again in Revelation 11:19. And again Revelation 16:21 says, "And there fell upon men a great hail out of heaven, every stone about the weight of a talent: and men blasphemed God because of the plague of the hail; for the plague thereof was exceeding great." In Egypt hail broke every tree.

In this case in verse 7, we are told that John sees *"the third part of trees was burnt up, and all green grass was burnt up."* As God said to Adam, "Cursed is the ground for thy sake" (Gen.

3:17). God used a storm and "A great whale" to stop Jonah. As "The stars in their courses fought against Sisera" (Judges 5:20), so God's judgment will appear in nature during the time of God's wrath, the Great Tribulation.

Israel was slow to build God's house. Haggai says:

"Ye have sown much, and bring in little; ye eat, but ye have not enough; ye drink, but ye are not filled with drink; ye clothe you, but there is none warm; and he that earneth wages earneth wages to put it into a bag with holes. . .And I called for a drought upon the land, and upon the mountains, and upon the corn, and upon the new wine, and upon the oil, and upon that which the ground bringeth forth, and upon men, and upon cattle, and upon all the labour of the hands."—Hag. 1:6, 11.

And when they robbed God their crops failed (Mal. 3:7-10). God controls nature for blessing and for punishment.

Man is dependent on nature. Animals and plants are interdependent. Plants furnish oxygen for animals to breathe. The animals breathe out carbon dioxide which plants absorb.

And all animals ever eat must come either directly from the plant world, or secondarily, from other animals that eat plants. A rabbit eats grass and vegetation, and the wolf eats the rabbit. Cattle eat the grass, and men eat the beef and milk and butter. All about us are the wonderfully balanced forces of nature which God controls for our happiness and welfare. A curse on nature is a curse on mankind and on the earth.

VERSES 8, 9:

8 And the second angel sounded, and as it were a great mountain burning with fire was cast into the sea: and the third part of the sea became blood;

9 And the third part of the creatures which were in the sea, and had life, died; and the third part of the ships were destroyed.

Second Trumpet

Before, when the first trumpet sounded, *"the third part of*

trees was burnt up, and all green grass was burnt up.'' Now the
second trumpet brings a like curse upon the sea: *". . .and the
third part of the sea became blood; And the third part of the
creatures which were in the sea, and had life, died; and the third
part of the ships were destroyed.''* That *"great mountain burning
with fire. . .cast into the sea,''* is a picture of volcanic activity.
Sodom and Gomorrah were destroyed with the fire and brimstone from Heaven. The two Italian cities of Herculaneum and
Pompeii were destroyed when Mount Vesuvius erupted in 79
A.D.—they are still digging out some of the remains of houses
and people covered and destroyed in that great explosion. Port
Royal, a great city of wickedness in Jamaica, was destroyed by a
great earthquake in 1692.

We are reminded of what happened when the flood came on
the earth to destroy the whole race of mankind and everything
that hath breath except those spared in the great ark that God
had instructed Noah to build for his family and selected animals.
And it is not generally remembered that the convulsions that
covered the earth so that, first, the great canopy of water above
the earth fell and flooded the whole earth: and then sea bottoms
were lowered and mountain ranges lifted and tidal waves,
perhaps thousands of feet high, went around the earth destroying
everything so that fossil remains are on the top of every mountain, the giant forests of the earth were packed into coal beds and
covered some a mile deep. So the flood and the attendant convulsions of nature lasted about a year.

It is not surprising, then, that during the Great Tribulation the
wrath of God will be made known again and tragic plagues on
man by a nature which pictures and manifests the wrath of God.

God has promised that the earth will never again be
overflowed by water, and the time when the earth will be utterly
burned over and destroyed by fire (as it was destroyed by water
before) waits to the end of the millennium the "day of judgment
and perdition of ungodly men" (II Pet. 3:7). But in the tribulation time, a thousand years before fire will destroy the world, and
change all that fire will change in this planet so it can be planted
into a new Garden of Eden—these plagues still will show the

wrath of God in the tribulation time.

VERSES 10, 11:

10 And the third angel sounded, and there fell a great star from heaven, burning as it were a lamp, and it fell upon the third part of the rivers, and upon the fountains of waters;
11 And the name of the star is called Wormwood: and the third part of the waters became wormwood; and many men died of the waters, because they were made bitter.

Third Trumpet

". . .*there fell a great star from heaven*"—evidently a meteor. We need not be surprised for every "falling star" we see is some fragment of meteoric material coming into the earth's atmosphere. Often the friction burns up that lump of matter before it comes to the earth, but not always.

In Russia a giant crater proves that an enormous meteor from outer space struck there years ago. Many scientists have thought that what is called "the great rift," which includes the Jordan Valley, the Sea of Galilee and the Dead Sea (all below sea level) and which valley goes on down a straight line into the continent of Africa, was caused by some planet or heavenly body striking the side of the earth.

Some have thought it possible that collision with some other planet caused the flood. They think that the earth's axis now being twenty-three degrees off the center of its planetary path around the sun may have been caused by either a touch or the violent gravity pull of a nearby planet. And thus good men think that the uniform climate of the earth before the flood, when dry and tropical forests and tropical animals lived at the North and South Poles, was changed into the seasons we now have, after the flood.

The scientist Velikovsky who, though not a Christian, still believes that the Bible is historically true, thinks there is evidence of such giant collisions causing chaos (see his books, *Worlds in Collision* and *Ages in Chaos*). And it was after the flood when the Lord promised Noah, "While the earth remaineth, seedtime and harvest, and cold and heat, and summer and winter, and day and night shall not cease" (Gen. 8:22). There is no reference to the seasons on the earth before the flood.

We can well understand how a meteor from outer space and the cloud of meteor dust that might go with it might poison the waters so that many people would die from the chemicals thus brought into the water.

VERSES 12, 13:

12 And the fourth angel sounded, and the third part of the sun was smitten, and the third part of the moon, and the third part of the stars; so as the third part of them was darkened, and the day shone not for a third part of it, and the night likewise.

13 And I beheld, and heard an angel flying through the midst of heaven, saying with a loud voice, Woe, woe, woe, to the inhabiters of the earth by reason of the other voices of the trumpet of the three angels, which are yet to sound!

Fourth Trumpet

Note a progression in these plagues. The first one, in verse 7, affected the trees and grass of the earth and went not far beyond plagues that come with nature. Only there was blood to show the anger of God.

The next trumpet (vss. 8, 9) brought volcanic activity, which while still natural, under control of an angry God would kill many.

Next, there is a meteor from outer space, some heavenly body, to bring poison to the earth and great destruction and death (vss. 10, 11).

And now the plague in the fourth trumpet extends to the sun, moon and stars. The heavens themselves are affected by the judgment resulting from the blowing of the fourth trumpet. Life on the earth depends largely on the sun, and even though the skies may be overcast, the sun goes on doing its work to warm the earth, to give life to plants and make life possible for animals and men. But the indication here is that the sun itself will have only two-thirds as much light as before, at least for a time. And so with the moon and the stars.

Why "the third part" in verse 7, in verses 8 and 9 and 10? You must remember that God has reserved part of His judgments. There are saved men still on the earth. Not until later, when all the men of the universe are assembled out in space at the great white throne, in the "day of judgment and perdition of ungodly men," will this earth be completely burned over and every mark and habitation and work of men destroyed, so God can start over and plant the earth a new Garden of Eden and bring to it the Heavenly Jerusalem as the capital city!

But more woes are to come. "Woe, woe, woe"—three woes for three more trumpets yet to sound!

Chapter 9

AND the fifth angel sounded, and I saw a star fall from heaven unto the earth: and to him was given the key of the bottomless pit.

2 And he opened the bottomless pit; and there arose a smoke out of the pit, as the smoke of a great furnace; and the sun and the air were darkened by reason of the smoke of the pit.

Fifth Trumpet: First Woe

The *"star"* that fell from Heaven is a person. *"Him"* evidently an angel acting for Christ, "the angel custodian of the pit of the abyss, the prison house of the demons" (Luke 8:30,31) says Unger. Remember Jesus said, "All power is given unto me in heaven and in earth" (Matt. 28:18). Christ has "the keys of hell and death" (Rev. 1:18). He has all power over demons and over Satan. So here Christ gives the key of Hell to an angel, and Hell, the bottomless pit, is opened up. And from it comes the plague of the fifth trumpet.

There are many indications that Hell is in the center of the earth. A star falls "to the earth" and the bottomless pit is opened on the earth, the smoke of it rises to fill the air of the earth and to hide the sun. Jesus said, "Capernaum. . .shalt be brought down to hell" (Matt. 11:23). The meaning is certainly in a spiritual sense, but also in a literal meaning. The Christ-rejecters in Capernaum went to Hell. On earth "down" means toward the center of the earth.

Again and again it is said that sinners will be "cast. . .into outer darkness" (Matt. 22:13) or "cast. . .into a furnace of fire" (Matt. 13:42,50) or "cast out into outer darkness" (Matt. 8:12) or "cast into hell" (Matt. 5:29,30). So sinners are to be "cast into the lake of fire" (20:10), and the term "to cast" in the Bible seems always to mean to throw down, not up. So "cast into hell" or "cast into the lake of fire" must mean toward the center of the earth.

Hell is "the bottomless pit." At the center of the earth where there is no gravity and no down, and so, no bottom, but at the center of the earth with attraction the same in every direction, a person or thing could float with no pressure to go in any direction. Surely that kind of a situation would be "the bottomless pit."

When Korah, Dathan, Abiram and their friends rebelled against the rule of Moses, God had Moses to call the people to separate from these wicked men and said:

"If these men die the common death of all men, or if they be visited after the visitation of all men; then the Lord hath not sent me. But if the Lord make a new thing, and the earth open her mouth, and swallow them up, with all that appertain unto them, and they go down quick into the pit; then ye shall understand that these men have provoked the Lord."—Num. 16:29,30.

The next two verses say:

"And it came to pass, as he had made an end of speaking all these words, that the ground clave asunder that was under them: And the earth opened her mouth, and swallowed them up, and their houses, and all the men that appertained unto Korah, and all their goods. They, and all that appertained to them, went down alive into the pit, and the earth closed upon them: and they perished from among the congregation."

Here the men went "down quick into the pit" (vs. 30) or "went down alive into the pit" (vs. 33), but the word "pit" is the word *sheol,* the Hebrew word used everywhere in the Old Testament for Hell, or sometimes a general term for death. Men went down alive into Hell. We think that the body perished, of course, in the cataclysm, but, no doubt, they went immediately to Hell in the center of the earth. Surely that is intended as a picture showing that lost sinners go immediately to Hell when they die.

The wicked high priest who pressed for the crucifixion of the Lord Jesus and, no doubt, went to Hell, "shall see the Son of man. . .coming in the clouds of heaven," Jesus said (Matt. 26:64). And Philippians 2:10 promises, "That at the name of

·Jesus every knee should bow, of things in heaven, and things in earth, and *things under the earth.*" Surely that means people in Heaven and on earth, and those in Hell who are "under the earth."

VERSES 3—12:

3 And there came out of the smoke locusts upon the earth: and unto them was given power, as the scorpions of the earth have power.

4 And it was commanded them that they should not hurt the grass of the earth, neither any green thing, neither any tree; but only those men which have not the seal of God in their foreheads.

5 And to them it was given that they should not kill them, but that they should be tormented five months: and their torment *was* as the torment of a scorpion, when he striketh a man.

6 And in those days shall men seek death, and shall not find it; and shall desire to die, and death shall flee from them.

7 And the shapes of the locusts *were* like unto horses prepared unto battle; and on their heads *were* as

.it were crowns like gold, and their faces *were* as the faces of men.

8 And they had hair as the hair of women, and their teeth were as *the teeth* of lions.

9 And they had breastplates, as it were breastplates of iron; and the .sound of their wings *was* as the sound of chariots of many horses running to battle.

10 And they had tails like unto scorpions, and there were stings in their tails: and their power *was* to hurt men five months.

11 And they had a king over them, *which is* the angel of the bottomless pit, whose name in the Hebrew tongue *is* Abaddon, but in the Greek tongue hath *his* name Ă-pŏl-lÿ-on.

12 One woe is past; *and,* behold, there come two woes more hereafter.

Demons Released From Hell to Torture Wicked Men

What do demons look like? They are "unclean spirits" and spirits do not have bodies except as they assume them or enter into the bodies of others. We suppose that here we have a picture in striking language, perhaps some of it symbolic, like parables, to reveal spiritual truths. We do not doubt that the "locusts" (because locusts are a destructive plague) are here demons. There was a plague of literal locusts in Egypt that ate up the crops, but these are not literal insects. They are released out of the pit of Hell. The message is spiritual and these locusts eat not the grass, the trees, or any green thing, but come to torture only "those men which have not the seal of God in their foreheads."

Tortured and tormented by these "locusts," these demons from Hell, ". . .*shall men seek death, and shall not find it; and shall desire to die, and death shall flee from them"* (vs. 6). We remember that Job wished to die in such trouble of heart and pain of body and misunderstanding of friends: "Oh that I might have my request; and that God would grant me the thing that I long for! Even that it would please God to destroy me; that he would let loose his hand, and cut me off!" (Job 6:8, 9). Again we are reminded of the torment of mind which God promised Israel would come if they forsook the Lord. In Deuteronomy 28 is a moving passage. Verses 65 to 67 say:

"And among these nations shalt thou find no ease, neither shall the sole of thy foot have rest: but the Lord shall give thee there a trembling heart, and failing of eyes, and sorrow of mind: And thy life shall hang in doubt before thee; and thou shalt fear day and night, and shalt have none assurance of thy life: In the morning thou shalt say, Would God it were even! and at even thou shalt say, Would God it were morning! for the fear of thine heart wherewith thou shalt fear, and for the sight of thine eyes which thou shalt see."

I think the torment mentioned here is spiritual torment with a troubled, agonized mind. Here is something like that that came on Judas when he said, "I have betrayed the innocent blood" (Matt. 27:4) and went and hanged himself.

The picture of these locusts is fantastic, like a terrible dream, like a summing up of all the fears and troubles and heartbreaks of men put in poetic language. For *"their teeth were as the teeth of lions"* (vs. 8), but they do not tear the bodies of men; rather, they torment the soul. Their *"tails like unto scorpions"* (vs. 10) hurt men, but their hurt is not simply or only physical pain but torment of soul.

The *"king over them"* (vs. 11) is that fallen angel or archangel *"of the bottomless pit, whose name in the Hebrew tongue is Abaddon, but in the Greek tongue hath his name Appollyon."* Both mean "the destroyer." You will note that this trouble is for unsaved men, *"Those men which have not the seal of God in their foreheads"* (vs. 4). And they do not kill lost people but torment them (vs. 5). Can you imagine the awful ruin of soul when men are turned over to evil spirits!

During World War I, one time I did guard duty over some criminally insane in a hospital. One poor, troubled, demented man would put his thumbs in his eyes and try to put them out, and we frantically pulled his hands away. He would pull out his hair by handfuls until his head was partly bald. At the midnight hour I sat near his cot with an Enfield rifle, on guard duty. He whispered to me, "Leave your gun there for just a little bit and go out in the hall. Go for a drink of water. I promise I won't hurt anybody else but myself. Oh, give me a chance to kill myself!" He pleaded with me that I might shoot him, he was in such torment.

Who can understand the torment of a man who has passed forever out of the realm of mercy, passed the time when he could ever decide for Christ or want to decide for Christ and yet controlled and tormented by evil spirits! So it will be with these men and women on the earth toward the close of the tribulation time.

This then is the first "woe." *"One woe is past; and, behold, there come two woes more hereafter"* (vs. 12).

VERSES 13—19:

13 And the sixth angel sounded, and I heard a voice from the four horns of the golden altar which is before God,

14 Saying to the sixth angel which had the trumpet, Loose the four angels which are bound in the great river Eû-phrā-́tês.

15 And the four angels were loosed, which were prepared for an hour, and a day, and a month, and a year, for to slay the third part of men.

16 And the number of the army of the horsemen *were* two hundred thousand thousand: and I heard the number of them.

17 And thus I saw the horses in the vision, and them that sat on them, having breastplates of fire, and of jacinth, and brimstone: and the heads of the horses *were* as the heads of lions; and out of their mouths issued fire and smoke and brimstone.

18 By these three was the third part of men killed, by the fire, and by the smoke, and by the brimstone, which issued out of their mouths.

19 For their power is in their mouth, and in their tails: for their tails *were* like unto serpents, and had heads, and with them they do hurt.

Sixth Trumpet

The sixth trumpet follows with literal death to wicked men; follows the spiritual torments announced under the fifth trumpet. Here is a suggestion that the armies of the Antichrist begin to assemble. A heavenly voice commands the sixth angel, *"Loose the four angels which are bound in the great river Euphrates"* (vs. 14). They are already there but cannot act until permission is given, and then these four angels which have set themselves for the particular hour, the day, the month and the year, are to *"slay the third part of men"* (vs. 15).

The place of their loosing, the Euphrates, was the location of ancient Babylon, Unger reminds us. "The very hour of their release is determined as well as the extent of their destruction— vs. 15. The number of the cavalrymen is 200,000,000, as John heard it—vs. 16."

Why in the great River Euphrates? In chapter 16 we have the seven vials or bowls of the wrath of God and again there is a "sixth angel," and verse 12 says, "And the sixth angel poured out his vial upon the great river Euphrates; and the water thereof was dried up, that the way of the kings of the east might be prepared."

Dr. Ironside's comments on verse 14 are: "These angels are evidently at the present time restraining the great Asiatic hordes from pouring themselves upon the Land of Palestine and Europe. The Euphrates formed the eastern limit of the Roman Empire, and thus was the barrier, as it were, between the East and West."

Oh, not only the armies of restored Roman empire, but here come the hordes from China, Japan, Indonesia and, perhaps, India and, perhaps, Manchuria and other Asiatic nations! For God has planned that the armies of all the wicked in the world will be gathered to the Valley of Armageddon and there the millions will die with the sword that goes from the mouth of Christ when He returns to reign on the earth!" (19:1-21).

In verse 7 we learned that *"the shapes of the locusts were like unto horses prepared unto battle."* And those fantastic beings represented spiritual monsters. That is not the same as the army of literal horsemen, two hundred million (vs. 16), that are being gathered here. Remember that here it is planned that one-third of the population of the whole earth shall die (vs. 15), by the fire, by the smoke, by the brimstone which issue from their mouths.

How would you describe the weapons of war in a modern army, the tanks, the cannon, the flame throwers, the poison gas, the aerial bombs and rockets? The names of such things are not even in existence when this was written. Yet here we have pictured the awful destruction summing up the supernatural wrath of God and man's wicked rebellion against the Christ Himself.

Note the *"fire, and smoke and brimstone"* that comes from the horses (vs. 18), which no doubt are symbols of the weapons of destruction in the battle of Armageddon to come. It pictures tanks with *"power. . .in their mouth"* (vs. 18), and the cannon before *"and in their tails: for their tails were like unto serpents"* (vs. 19), and, perhaps, the machine guns and the flame throwers could be so pictured.

VERSES 20,21:

20 And the rest of the men which were not killed by these plagues yet repented not of the works of their hands, that they should not worship devils, and idols of gold, and silver, and brass, and stone, and of wood: which neither can see, nor hear, nor walk:

21 Neither repented they of their murders, nor of their sorceries, nor of their fornication, nor of their thefts.

Wicked Men Past Repentance and So Past Saving

Here we see wicked men who have gone beyond mercy and have passed over the line into the unpardonable sin. Will you notice that nothing here indicates God does not love them or that God would not forgive them. No, only we are told that they have become so incurably wicked they cannot turn, they do not want to turn, for they *"yet repented not of the works of their hands, that they should not worship devils, and idols of gold, and silver, and brass, and stone, and of wood."* They did not repent of *"their murders, nor of their sorceries, nor of their fornication, nor of their thefts."*

That does not mean that now the promises of God no longer stand. They do stand. It is still true that if any one of those would draw nigh to God, he would find God would draw nigh to him. It is still true that as Jesus said, "Him that cometh to me I will in no wise cast out" (John 6:37). It is still true that "Whosoever shall call upon the name of the Lord shall be saved" (Rom. 10:13).

But these wicked men do not want to call on God, do not want to leave their sins, do not repent of their idolatries, their wickedness, their murders, their worship of devils. This is a story of lost men, lost forever because of their own hardening of heart and permanent rejection of Christ.

We remind you again that those who worship the Antichrist and his image have gone so far that they cannot turn to Christ and be saved. Again, Revelation 14:9-11 says:

"And the third angel followed them, saying with a loud voice, If any man worship the beast and his image, and receive his mark in his forehead, or in his hand, The same shall drink of the wine of the wrath of God, which is poured out without mixture into the cup of his indignation; and he shall be tormented with fire and brimstone in the presence of the holy angels, and in the presence of the Lamb: And the smoke of their torment ascendeth up for ever and ever: and they have no rest day nor night who worship the beast and his image, and whosoever receiveth the mark of his name."

Even down in Hell the rich man in Luke 16 says, "Father Abraham, have mercy on me," but did not ask God for mercy. He knew he was in Hell because he did not repent and so he wanted his lost brothers to repent, but in Hell he did not repent. God says, "My spirit shall not always strive with man" (Gen. 6:3). But God's Spirit quits striving because man has already forever sealed his mind against the call of God. I think that in Hell men who must confess that Christ is Lord will do it knowing they could have been saved, and still they will hate Christ instead of loving Him, will despise Him instead of holding to Him, as Matthew 6:24 says.

Let us conclude this chapter with the solemn words of Dr. Ironside:

> Both here, and later in this same book, we find that the heaviest judgments of God, falling on guilty men, do not soften the stony, rebellious hearts; but that rather men become hardened in their sins and are more blasphemous and God-defiant when judgment is poured out upon them than before.
>
> In eternity, God will not permit open defiance of His will. Our Lord Jesus tells us that in Hell there will be not only "weeping" because of suffering, but "gnashing of teeth," which expresses not manifest opposition but the angry defiance of the heart of man, which will be filled with hatred to God but be powerless to openly oppose His government. If the cross of Christ, with its marvelous exhibition of holy love, will not reconcile men to God, punishment will never avail to win their hearts."

Chapter 10

VERSES 1—4:

AND I saw another mighty angel come down from heaven, clothed with a cloud: and a rainbow *was* upon his head, and his face *was* as it were the sun, and his feet as pillars of fire:

2 And he had in his hand a little book open: and he set his right foot upon the sea, and *his* left *foot* on the earth,

3 And cried with a loud voice, as *when* a lion roareth: and when he had cried, seven thunders uttered their voices.

4 And when the seven thunders had uttered their voices, I was about to write: and I heard a voice from heaven saying unto me, Seal up those things which the seven thunders uttered, and write them not.

A Mighty Angel and Seven Thunders

Here begins a parenthetical passage, down to chapter 11, verse 12. The sixth trumpet has sounded and its plagues are recorded. The orderly story of the plagues does not resume until chapter 11, verse 15, when the seventh trumpet shall sound. A most impressive angel is this mighty one clothed with a cloud, a rainbow on his head, his face as the sun, his feet as pillars of fire. Dr. Ironside, and Dr. W. B. Riley, following Scott, believed that the mighty angel is the Lord Jesus. Walvoord, J. B. Smith and others think not. It is true that Christ is sometimes called "an angel," "a messenger from God." He is once called "an apostle" (Heb. 3:1). But we think here the angel is not the Lord Jesus Christ, for Christ is not scheduled to return to the earth during the tribulation time. But a climax of the ages approaches. All the majesty of God goes with His announcement.

Note the stance: one foot on the sea, one on the land. So God has "all power. . .in heaven and in earth," on land and sea. The whole planet is involved in what he will announce; his voice is *"as when a lion roareth."*

Seven thunders are uttered—what do they say? John heard and understood but was forbidden to write it down. Surely that means there are other great plans for God's dealing with mankind in this earth, but they are to be after the great climax we will find now approaching. We are not to be concerned with them here.

The angel has a little book in his hand. Dr. Ironside says this book "could be no other than the very book we have had before us heretofore. It is the title-deed to the earth, the seals of which have been broken, one after the other, until the entire scroll is seen unrolled. The Lord descends with all the evidences of divine majesty, and with this title-deed in His hand, He sets His right foot upon the sea and His left foot upon the earth, as indicative of taking possession of His own inheritance—that inheritance which, as Man on earth, He had redeemed with His own precious blood."

VERSES 5—7:

5 And the angel which I saw stand upon the sea and upon the earth lifted up his hand to heaven,

6 And sware by him that liveth for ever and ever, who created heaven, and the things that therein are, and the earth, and the things that therein are, and the sea, and the things which are therein, that there should be time no longer:

7 But in the days of the voice of the seventh angel, when he shall begin to sound, the mystery of God should be finished, as he hath declared to his servants the prophets.

"There Should Be Time No Longer"

Strange announcement! But the real meaning is not that there will be no more time measured in days and months and years. God promised in Genesis 8:22, "While the earth remaineth, seedtime and harvest, and cold and heat, and summer and winter, and day and night shall not cease." A thousand years' reign of Christ on earth is particularly prophesied (Rev. 20). So there will yet be measured time. But the angel here is saying there will be no more delay before the fulfillment of God's great plan! In other words, no more intervening time before the mystery of God is finished.

What is the mystery that *"he hath declared to his servants the prophets"*? (vs. 7). It is the long expected "day of the Lord," including the reign of Christ on earth and foretold all through the Old Testament. That millennial earth is pictured in the Garden of Eden, which indicates that redeemed and resurrected men will dwell with God on a cleansed earth. The promises to Abraham, to David, to Israel have long awaited fulfillment. Now, "No more delay," says the mighty angel, until these principal prophecies will be rapidly fulfilled. Christ is to come from Heaven with saints and angels, the kingdoms of the earth are to become the kingdoms of Christ. The battle of Armageddon will take place. Israel will be regathered and saved. The Gentiles living then are to be gathered before the throne and judged (Matt. 25:31-46). There is no more time of delay before these great things occur.

Christ has delayed His coming. Second Peter 3:9 says, "The Lord is not slack concerning his promise, as some men count slackness; but is longsuffering to us-ward, not willing that any should perish, but that all should come to repentance." Men have been given every chance to repent. Now the "mystery" foretold by the prophets is to be finished.

"True as the life of God—certain as the Divine eternity-- unfailing as the Power which made the worlds—immutable as the oath of Jesus—the great consummating day will come, when the whole mystery of God shall be fulfilled. Unbelief, away! Misgiving, be thou buried in the depths of the sea! Doubt, be shamed into everlasting confusion!" (Seiss).

VERSES 8—11:

8 And the voice which I heard from heaven spake unto me again, and said, Go *and* take the little book which is open in the hand of the angel which standeth upon the sea and upon the earth.

9 And I went unto the angel, and said unto him, Give me the little book. And he said unto me, Take *it,* and eat it up; and it shall make thy belly bitter, but it shall be in thy mouth sweet as honey.

10 And I took the little book out of the angel's hand, and ate it up; and it was in my mouth sweet as honey: and as soon as I had eaten it, my belly was bitter.

11 And he said unto me, Thou must prophesy again before many peoples, and nations, and tongues, and kings.

The Little Book Sweet and Bitter

This is not the seven-sealed book of Revelation 5:1-4. That is large; this is small. That is sealed; this is opened. That had revealed the judgments of God in great tribulation times. Christ prevailed to open the seals of that book in Revelation 5. John is to eat this book and did. It relates to preaching the Gospel for then John "must prophesy again before many peoples, and nations, and tongues, and kings," as verse 11 says.

The Gospel—how sweet it is to the believing sinner! But afterward the message of God means damnation to all who reject it. One who, like John, gives himself gladly to getting out the Gospel will find it means sorrow for a lost world. "They that sow in tears shall reap in joy. He that goeth forth and weepeth, bearing precious seed, shall doubtless come again with rejoicing, bringing his sheaves with him" (Ps. 126:5, 6). We are glad for salvation. We weep for those still unsaved. Christians are not only to "rejoice with them that do rejoice," but to "weep with them that weep" (Rom. 12:15).

John could rejoice in the sweetness of sins forgiven. He must find the plagues and judgment here foretold very bitter to his soul. And through this book of Revelation and his Gospel and epistles John would still "prophesy again before many peoples, and nations, and tongues, and kings."

Chapter 11

AND there was given me a reed like unto a rod: and the angel stood, saying, Rise, and measure the temple of God, and the altar, and them that worship therein.

2 But the court which is without the temple leave out, and measure it not; for it is given unto the Gentiles: and the holy city shall they tread under foot forty *and* two months.

New Temple Measured

The temple here mentioned is to be, no doubt, the temple which will be built after the rapture of saints, when the newly risen dictator, taking power among the nations remaining out of the old Roman Empire, makes a treaty with a remnant group of Jews then to be in Palestine to restore their worship.

"And he shall confirm the covenant with many for one week: and in the midst of the week he shall cause the sacrifice and the oblation to cease, and for the overspreading of abominations he shall make it desolate, even until the consummation, and that determined shall be poured upon the desolate."—Dan. 9:27.

That covenant or treaty will be for seven or a "week" of years. So there will be a temple, a priesthood with sacrifices and Israel, as a nation, offering sacrifices and worshiping God and subjecting themselves to the ceremonies of the Mosaic law. Then, in the midst of that week of treaty, after three and a half years, the worship will be interrupted by the Man of Sin, the Antichrist. The world dictator will assume absolute dictatorship and claim to be God (II Thess. 2:3, 4). And then the last three and a half years or forty-two months (30 days to the month), the last 1,260 days of the Great Tribulation will begin. This is the tribulation temple.

The court without the temple is given to the Gentiles to tread it down throughout the tribulation time. And the sacrifice in the temple itself, we would think, must, during this time, stop and none be offered but to this "son of perdition" (II Thess. 2:3) claiming to be God. Luke 21:24 speaks of the "times of the Gentiles." Dr. Ironside says: "The expression, 'the times of the Gentiles,' refers to the entire period of Gentile supremacy, beginning with the day when God gave Judah into the hand of Nebuchadnezzar, king of Babylon, and continuing on to the time when the Stone from Heaven shall smite the image on its feet; that is, when the Lord Jesus Christ, at His second coming in judgment, shall destroy all Gentile dominion, and His own kingdom shall supersede every other."

The measuring reed, about ten feet long (Scofield says) will be used to measure "the temple. . .the altar" and also the people. Does it not mean that Christ here is saying to John and to us that God has all these things and people in His hands, will bring out justice, will bring righteousness out of sinfulness, order out of chaos, and will honor Himself in judgment as well as in salvation? Men measured? Then men are proven to be too short for the measure. No man is as tall as this rod. Isaiah 28:15-20 says:

"Because ye have said, We have made a covenant with death, and with hell are we at agreement; when the overflowing scourge shall pass through, it shall not come unto us: for we have made lies our refuge, and under falsehood have we hid ourselves: Therefore thus saith the Lord God, Behold, I lay in Zion for a foundation a stone, a tried stone, a precious corner stone, a sure foundation: he that believeth shall not make haste. Judgment also will I lay to the line, and righteousness to the plummet: and the hail shall sweep away the refuge of lies, and the waters shall overflow the hiding place. And your covenant with death shall be disannulled, and your agreement with hell shall not stand; when the overflowing scourge shall pass through, then ye shall be trodden down by it. From the time that it goeth forth it shall take you: for morning by morning shall it pass over, by day and by night: and it shall be vexation only to understand the report. For the bed is shorter than that a man can stretch himself on it: and the covering narrower than

that he can wrap himself in it."

Ezekiel, chapters 40 to 43, tell of measurements and the description of the temple that was to be built. Was it to be rebuilt as Israel was regathered in the days of Ezra and Nehemiah? Or the temple that will be built during the kingdom age? Most premillennialists think it pictures the temple of the kingdom age.

VERSES 3—6:

3 And I will give *power* unto my two witnesses, and they shall prophesy a thousand two hundred *and* threescore days, clothed in sackcloth.

4 These are the two olive trees, and the two candlesticks standing before the God of the earth.

5 And if any man will hurt them, fire proceedeth out of their mouth, and devoureth their enemies: and if any man will hurt them, he must in this manner be killed.

6 These have power to shut heaven, that it rain not in the days of their prophecy: and have power over waters to turn them to blood, and to smite the earth with all plagues, as often as they will.

Two Witnesses

We believe they are two literal men, Spirit-filled prophets, to witness for the Lord Jesus in the tribulation time, the 1,260 days.

In his discussion on this passage, Seiss says:

"The work of these witnesses is. . .a merciful work. Though they appear in judgment times, and evince the severity of the judgment spirit, dealing out plague and fire, lashing and harassing the impious Beast from the abyss, tormenting them that dwell on the earth, killing all who venture to harm them, and causing all nations to feel the disturbing effect of their presence, they are still messengers of mercy on an errand of good and grace. . . . But for these supernatural messengers the whole race would yield to the Antichrist, and perish with him."

Zechariah 4:1-7 prophesies of these witnesses:

"And the angel that talked with me came again, and waked me, as a man that is wakened out of his sleep, And said unto me, What seest thou? And I said, I have looked, and behold a candlestick all of gold, with a bowl upon the top of it, and his

*seven lamps thereon, and seven pipes to the seven lamps,
which are upon the top thereof: And two olive trees by it, one
upon the right side of the bowl, and the other upon the left
side thereof. So I answered and spake to the angel that talked
with me, saying, What are these, my Lord? Then the angel that
talked with me answered and said unto me, Knowest thou not
what these be? And I said, No, my lord. Then he answered and
spake unto me, saying, This is the word of the Lord unto Zerubbabel, saying, Not by might, nor by power, but by my spirit,
saith the Lord of hosts. Who art thou, O great mountain? before
Zerubbabel thou shalt become a plain: and he shall bring forth
the headstone thereof with shoutings, crying, Grace, grace
unto it."*

There, after the captivity, Israel was rebuilding a temple.
Now, Revelation 11:3, 4 tells us these two prophets of God are
"the two olive trees, and the two candlesticks" which Zechariah
foretold.

Who will these men be? Some think they will be Moses and
Elijah representing the law and the prophets of the Old Testament. Malachi 4:4, 5 tells us:

*"Remember ye the law of Moses my servant, which I com-
manded unto him in Horeb for all Israel, with the statutes and
judgments. Behold, I will send you Elijah the prophet before
the coming of the great and dreadful day of the Lord."*

So we think one of these will be Elijah. It is true that John the
Baptist came "in the spirit and power of Elias" (Luke 1:17), but
that should not avoid the literal fulfillment of prophecy. Elijah
must come before the Second Coming.

We remember that Moses and Elijah met with Jesus on the
Mount of Transfiguration, and that was a prefiguration of
Christ's coming in glory, as Luke 9:27 and the other Gospels, and
II Peter 1:16-18 tell us. Thus we tend to believe that the two will
be Moses and Elijah.

Some think the two will be Enoch and Elijah because those
two alone of all mankind, as far as we know, went to Heaven
alive without dying. And Hebrews 9:27 says, "And as it is ap-

pointed unto men once to die, but after this the judgment." I do not think, however, that that Scripture would necessarily apply here, to mean Moses could not die again. These two witnesses are to die and Moses has already died. Would he die again? And it is so obviously true that when Christ comes for His saints at the rapture, many living will never die. So it would be wrong to insist that Hebrews 9:27 was a prophecy that every man must die once and must die only once. We do not believe that is the meaning. It is appointed generally for men once to die and then come to judgment.

I do not think it should affect necessarily the decision of who are to be these two witnesses. They probably will be Moses and Elijah.

Note the power of God on these two men. They have power to have fire proceed out of their mouths to devour their enemies. So did Elijah in II Kings, chapter 1. They have power to "shut heaven, that it rain not in the days of their prophecy." So did Elijah in I Kings 17 and James 5:17. And Moses seemed to have had more intimate association with God than any other prophet who ever lived. It would not be unfitting, then, for these two men to come back and be used of God for a time on the earth again.

These men have power to turn the waters to blood as Moses had God's power to do in Egypt and to smite the earth with all the plagues like those that tormented Egypt when Israel was delivered.

VERSES 7—12:

7 And when they shall have finished their testimony, the beast that ascendeth out of the bottomless pit shall make war against them, and shall overcome them, and kill them.

8 And their dead bodies *shall lie* in the street of the great city, which spiritually is called Sodom and Egypt, where also our Lord was crucified.

9 And they of the people and kin- dreds and tongues and nations shall see their dead bodies three days and an half, and shall not suffer their dead bodies to be put in graves.

10 And they that dwell upon the earth shall rejoice over them, and make merry, and shall send gifts one to another; because these two prophets tormented them that dwelt on the earth.

11 And after three days and an half

the spirit of life from God entered into them, and they stood upon their feet; and great fear fell upon them which saw them.

12 And they heard a great voice from heaven saying unto them, Come up hither. And they ascended up to heaven in a cloud; and their enemies beheld them.

These Two Great Prophets Will Be Put to Death

Even though their bodies are to lay unburied for three days, and then they are to be resurrected and taken to Heaven, it seems fitting that along with powerful prophecy would come suffering and hatred of men. God does not change His plan. The mighty Paul must have shipwreck and beatings and imprisonment and beheading. And Stephen must be stoned to death. James the apostle was beheaded and Peter and John beaten in Acts, chapter 5.

It is part of God's plan that those who preach the Gospel should enter into the reproach of Christ and the sufferings of Christ. First Peter 2:21 says, "For even hereunto were ye called: because Christ also suffered for us, leaving us an example, that ye should follow his steps." And Jesus said, "If any man will come after me, let him deny himself, and take up his cross daily, and follow me" (Luke 9:23).

What city is that *"which spiritually is called Sodom and Egypt"* (vs. 8)? It is Jerusalem where our Lord was crucified!

I love the city of Jerusalem because of its past and because of God's promises for the future. I have been there at least fifteen times. We do well to note that in God's sight Jerusalem is still the city where Christ was crucified, and as long as Jews reject the Saviour and go on in their idolatry and sin, away from Christ, Jerusalem seems to God like Sodom and Egypt. And as long as Jews as a race reject the Saviour, the race is under the same curse for which God scattered them, first in the Babylonian captivity and then in A.D. 70 and the following years.

God has wonderful blessings through Abraham but they are not for just the fleshly seed. For one is not a Jew in God's sight who is only one outwardly: and circumcision of the flesh does not make one a favorite of God but circumcision in the heart. Romans 2:28, 29 says: "For he is not a Jew, which is one outwardly; neither is that circumcision, which is outward in the flesh: But he is a Jew, which is one inwardly; and circumcision is that of the heart, in the spirit, and not in the letter; whose praise is not of men, but of God." And "they which are of faith, the same are the children of Abraham" (Gal. 3:7).

Romans 9:6-9 explains:

"Not as though the word of God hath taken none effect. For they are not all Israel, which are of Israel: Neither, because they are the seed of Abraham, are they all children: but, In Isaac shall thy seed be called. That is, They which are the children of the flesh, these are not the children of God: but the children of the promise are counted for the seed. For this is the word of promise, At this time will I come, and Sarah shall have a son."

At this time, when we write these words, Israel as a nation has seized some of Palestine and the little nation Israel struggles for a place in the world. We have sympathy for them. We love them and wish them well. But we must remember that the regathering of Zionists who still reject the Saviour is not the regathering foretold in Deuteronomy 30:1-6 and Ezekiel 36:1-15, when the Lord Himself shall return, when Israel will be circumcised in heart, and as a nation will be saved. The curse on a Christ-rejecting nation is still there as it was when they were dispersed to all the world. And the troubles and heartache of the Jewish people can some way be connected to the cry of those Jews who would crucify Jesus. "His blood be on us, and on our children" (Matt. 27:25), as long as those children continue in the Christ-rejecting of those who crucified the Saviour. So He is crucified afresh day by day and Jerusalem is still spiritually Sodom and Egypt, until their people learn to trust the Saviour and love Him.

It is true the Jews wail at the wailing wall. But any seeking of God which involves hatred and crucifixion of the Lord Jesus is not acceptable seeking of God. Jesus said plainly, ". . .no man cometh unto the Father, but by me" (John 14:6).

Note the hatred of the masses of the people for these two witnesses (vss. 9, 10). It is the same people of whom we read that when Jesus comes "in the clouds of heaven with power and great

glory. . .all kindreds of the earth shall wail because of him"
(1:7). The people who hate the Lord Jesus Christ and will mourn
at His coming would rejoice at the death of His prophets here
and would want to gloat over these dead bodies, unburied, three
days and a half!

Seiss says about this that it is "so intense an outrage upon
common decency and humanity, that it is full of significance
here. Even to the worst of criminals the law awarded burial on
the same day of their execution (Deut. 21:22, 23); but all law and
right feeling is set at defiance with regard to these prophets of
God. The exposure of their dead bodies tells of a most extraor-
dinary malignity and spite. . . ."

It is necessarily involved that the world that hated Jesus
Christ must hate His true prophets. If the world crucified Jesus
Christ, then if we are enough like Him, surely they would be
troubled at our company and our message and would have a
degree of the same enmity toward us that they have toward
Christ.

But after three and a half days these two prophets will be
raised from the dead. Then let us all thus be reminded that "in
due season we shall reap, if we faint not" (Gal. 6:9), and that "if
we suffer, we shall also reign with him" (II Tim. 2:12).

The term, *"Come up hither"* (vs. 12), reminds us of the rapture of the saints. And their ascent in a cloud reminds us also of
the ascension of the Lord Jesus Christ in Acts 1:9. "People who
would not believe in the resurrection and ascension of Christ for
their hope and consolation, are now compelled to witness the
resurrection and ascension of His last witnesses, to their horror
and dismay" (Seiss).

These two witnesses, as well as the 144,000 of the twelve tribes
mentioned in Revelation 7, and saved people carrying out the
Great Commission at great cost, will get the Gospel to all the
world in the tribulation time and a multitude will be saved.

VERSES 13, 14:

13 And the same hour was there a great earthquake, and the tenth part of the city fell, and in the earthquake were slain of men seven thousand: and the remnant were affrighted, and gave glory to the God of heaven. 14 The second woe is past; *and*, behold, the third woe cometh quickly.

Second Woe

Revelation 8:13 announces three woes to come when three more trumpets sound. Chapter 9 tells the extended woes of satanic locust and an army of 200 million men and a third part of mankind is to be killed. In chapter 10 we have a parenthetical passage down to chapter 11, verse 12. All this happens during the tribulation time. Now, in the midst of the sixth trumpet sounding we take up the order of events again, marked by the same trumpet.

"The tenth part of the city fell." What city? Jerusalem (from verse 8, where Jesus was crucified). *"A great earthquake. . . ."* Now at the close of the tribulation period a tenth part of the city is to be destroyed. Probably more widespread will be the one mentioned in verse 19 than the one in Jerusalem in verse 13. Then when the Lord Jesus personally comes in glory, after the tribulation, we read:

"His feet shall stand in that day upon the mount of Olives, which is before Jerusalem on the east, and the mount of Olives shall cleave in the midst thereof toward the east and toward the west, and there shall be a very great valley; and half of the mountain shall remove toward the north, and half of it toward the south. And ye shall flee to the valley of the mountains; for the valley of the mountains shall reach unto Azal: yea, ye shall flee, like as ye fled from before the earthquake in the days of Uzziah king of Judah: and the Lord my God shall come, and all the saints with thee."—Zech. 14:4, 5.

Then such a convulsion of nature will be that rivers of water will flow from Jerusalem down to the Dead Sea and again to the Mediterranean Sea (Zech. 14:8).

Men who would not hear the Gospel must feel God's judgment

and be alarmed. Now woe number two has passed; the third comes.

VERSES 15—19:

15 And the seventh angel sounded; and there were great voices in heaven, saying, The kingdoms of this world are become *the kingdoms* of our Lord, and of his Christ; and he shall reign for ever and ever.

16 And the four and twenty elders, which sat before God on their seats, fell upon their faces, and worshipped God,

17 Saying, We give thee thanks, O Lord God Almighty, which art, and wast, and art to come; because thou hast taken to thee thy great power, and hast reigned.

18 And the nations were angry, and thy wrath is come, and the time of the dead, that they should be judged, and that thou shouldest give reward unto thy servants the prophets, and to the saints, and them that fear thy name, small and great; and shouldest destroy them which destroy the earth.

19 And the temple of God was opened in heaven, and there was seen in his temple the ark of his testament: and there were lightnings, and voices, and thunderings, and an earthquake, and great hail.

Understand "the Seventh Trumpet"

Some students confuse this "seventh trumpet" of the plagues during the tribulation with "the last trump" of I Corinthians 15:52. No, "the term last necessarily supposes trumpets anterior to this," says Godet. "The last trumpet is the one which concludes a series which have already been sounding. . . ," says Ellicott. But it could not refer to the seventh trumpet here in Revelation because the book of Revelation was not yet written, not yet revealed, and this series of trumpets had not been known. "The last trump" must be the last of a series given before.

As an illustration, in Joshua 6 we read that Israel compassed Jericho six days, with the priests blowing trumpets or rams horns. Then on the seventh day, "And it came to pass at the seventh time, when the priests blew with the trumpets, Joshua said unto the people, Shout; for the Lord hath given you the city" (Josh. 6:16). There was a series of trumpets and at the last of the series, a long blast, the walls fell down flat and Jericho was taken.

Israel was commanded to have a great jubilee each fifty years. Leviticus 25:8-10 says:

"And thou shalt number seven sabbaths of years unto thee, seven times seven years; and the space of the seven sabbaths of years shall be unto thee forty and nine years. Then shalt thou cause the trumpet of the jubile to sound on the tenth day of the seventh month, in the day of atonement shall ye make the trumpet sound throughout all your land. And ye shall hallow the fiftieth year, and proclaim liberty throughout all the land unto all the inhabitants thereof: it shall be a jubile unto you; and ye shall return every man unto his possession, and ye shall return every man unto his family."

This jubilee of fifty years, after seven sabbaths of years, each with its trumpet, is welcomed by a great sound of a trumpet. So our jubilee, our Sabbath in Heaven, should properly be announced also by "the last trump." There are similarities in the last trumpet of I Corinthians 15:52 and the seventh or last trumpet of Revelation, but they are not the same. In each case it is a fulfillment of a "mystery," that is, an event to be known only by revelation. Paul says, "I shew you a mystery," and tells of the trumpet sound at the rapture (I Cor. 15:51, 52). That is the glorious deliverance of Christians from the old body and death and the assembling with Christ in Heaven. But Revelation 10:7 says, "But in the days of the voice of the seventh angel, when he shall begin to sound, the mystery of God should be finished, as he hath declared to his servants the prophets." So this last trumpet of another series introduces the same joyful release of Christians but this time it is of those converted during the tribulation time. It announces the return of Christ with saints and angels to the glorious millennial reign.

"The temple of God was opened in heaven" (vs. 19). The temple on earth at Jerusalem at that time will have suffered "the abomination of desolation" by the Man of Sin, claiming to be God and causing the sacrifices to cease (Dan. 9:27; II Thess. 2:4). Though the earthly versions may fail, the heavenly pattern, temple, never. And though the tables of law on earth are sometimes broken and monstrously disobeyed, the "ark of his testament" in

Heaven abideth always. There were *"lightnings, and voices, and thunderings, and an earthquake, and great hail"* (vs. 19). These, on earth, we understand are a token that judgment on the earth and of sinful men is coming.

Chapter 12

God has already announced the end of the tribulation and Christ's assuming His kingdom in the closing verse of chapter 11. But the narrative must go back to more of the personalities and events before the reign of Christ is discussed more.

VERSES 1, 2:

AND there appeared a great wonder in heaven; a woman clothed with the sun, and the moon under her feet, and upon her head a crown of twelve stars:

2 And she being with child cried, travailing in birth, and pained to be delivered.

The Woman: Israel

What woman is this? It could not be Mary, for neither Mary nor any other literal woman is *"clothed with the sun, and the moon under her feet,"* etc. The woman is symbolic of Israel. The number twelve reminds us of twelve tribes, of twelve apostles who will judge Israel's twelve tribes (Matt. 19:27-29).

The child from Israel is the long prophesied Messiah, the Christ. It is true that "he is not a Jew, which is one outwardly; neither is that circumcision, which is outward in the flesh: But he is a Jew, which is one inwardly; and circumcision is that of the heart, in the spirit, and not in the letter; whose praise is not of men, but of God" (Rom. 2:28, 29). Yes, and Gentile Christians are to be blessed as Abraham's seed, for Galatians 3:29 says, "And if ye be Christ's, then are ye Abraham's seed, and heirs according to the promise."

But "God hath not cast away his people which he foreknew," that is, Israel (Rom. 11:2). To the Virgin Mary the angel said, "And the Lord God shall give unto him the throne of his father David: And he shall reign over the house of Jacob for ever." Not over spiritual Israel, but over literal Jacob, literally the descendants of Jacob, the Jews.

We do not believe the little nation of Zionist Jews, the Christ-rejecting Jews, is counted Israel in God's sight. As God cast out their fathers for unbelief and sin, so are these cast out until they repent. One is not a Jew who is only one physically and not spiritually; but God still will keep His promises to Abraham, and to David and to Israel. Jews are "beloved for the fathers' sakes" (Rom. 11:28). We are reminded that "unto them were committed the oracles of God" (Rom. 3:2). And from Israel Christ came, so it is written, "And so all Israel shall be saved: as it is written, There shall come out of Sion the Deliverer, and shall turn away ungodliness from Jacob" (Rom. 11:26). That will be the saved, believing remnant, true Jews. From Israel came the "man child" Jesus Christ.

VERSES 3, 4:

3 And there appeared another wonder in heaven; and behold a great red dragon, having seven heads and ten horns, and seven crowns upon his heads.

4 And his tail drew the third part of the stars of heaven, and did cast them to the earth: and the dragon stood before the woman which was ready to be delivered, for to devour her child as soon as it was born.

Satan Hates Israel for Christ's Sake

The *"great red dragon"* in Heaven with seven heads and ten horns is Satan. We see the beast with ten horns like the beast in Daniel 7:23-25 which pictures the Roman empire revived under the Antichrist in the tribulation time. Then Revelation 13:1 tells of a beast with seven heads and ten horns also, and that one comes out of the sea (that is from the mass of humanity). He is obviously the Antichrist, the world dictator.

Are these two the same, one in the heavens, the other from humanity? Well, they are pictured the same because Satan will incarnate himself in the Antichrist. As Christ and the Father are one, so Satan and his tool, his "son of perdition," are represented alike. And when, in the next chapter, we find the false prophet, we will see how Satan and the Antichrist and the false prophet, who works miracles, are a trinity, mocking God's Trinity with a false god, a false christ and a false spirit.

The great red dragon appears *"in heaven,"* but literally "in the heavens," not particularly in the Paradise of God.

"His tail drew the third part of the stars of heaven" (vs. 4). Does not this refer to the fall of Satan who was once an archangel (Ezek. 28:13-15; Isa. 14:12-15) and of the angels that fell with him (II Pet. 2:4)? Satan was once in Heaven, and, says Dr. Riley, "None other than the archangel Michael was required for his casting down; and, that he exercised wide influence in the celestial world is proven in that his tail drew the third part of the stars of heaven after him."

Satan tried to destroy the *"man child"* as soon as He was born. Herod's slaughter of the innocents was an effort to destroy Jesus at His birth. So were the efforts of the Jews in Nazareth who tried to push Jesus down the Hill of Precipitation to destroy Him (Luke 4:29, 30). So the angry Jews "took up stones. . .to stone him" (John 10:31), but God did not allow it.

VERSES 5, 6:

5 And she brought forth a man child, who was to rule all nations with a rod of iron: and her child was caught up unto God, and *to* his throne.
6 And the woman fled into the wilderness, where she hath a place prepared of God, that they should feed her there a thousand two hundred *and* threescore days.

The Man Child: Jesus Christ

Christ is *"to rule all nations with a rod of iron,"* but first He must return to Heaven and has, till the Second Coming. He came the first time to save; He is coming back the second time to rule.

Note that Satan's efforts to destroy or thwart Jesus were not only in His life on earth before but will extend even to the Great Tribulation period. So Satan will try to destroy the nation Israel. The Antichrist will break his covenant with Jews, will set out to kill all who do not "take the mark of the beast."

The persecution of Israel in the tribulation time was foretold by the Lord Jesus in Matthew 24:15-21:

"When ye therefore shall see the abomination of desolation, spoken of by Daniel the prophet, stand in the holy place, (whoso readeth, let him understand:) Then let them which be in Judaea flee into the mountains: Let him which is on the housetop not come down to take any thing out of his house: Neither let him which is in the field return back to take his clothes. And woe unto them that are with child, and to them that give suck in those days! But pray ye that your flight be not in the winter, neither on the sabbath day: For then shall be great tribulation, such as was not since the beginning of the world to this time, no, nor ever shall be."

Jesus said in Luke 21:20-24:

"And when ye shall see Jerusalem compassed with armies, then know that the desolation thereof is nigh. Then let them which are in Judaea flee to the mountains; and let them which are in the midst of it depart out; and let not them that are in the countries enter thereinto. For these be the days of vengeance, that all things which are written may be fulfilled. But woe unto them that are with child, and to them that give suck, in those days! for there shall be great distress in the land, and wrath upon this people. And they shall fall by the edge of the sword, and shall be led away captive into all nations: and Jerusalem shall be trodden down of the Gentiles, until the times of the Gentiles be fulfilled."

Zechariah 12:2 foretells it:

"Behold, I will make Jerusalem a cup of trembling unto all the people round about, when they shall be in the siege both against Judah and against Jerusalem."

Then Zechariah 14:1-3 tells of the siege of Jerusalem by all the armies of the Antichrist:

"Behold, the day of the Lord cometh, and thy spoil shall be

divided in the midst of thee. For I will gather all nations against Jerusalem to battle; and the city shall be taken, and the houses rifled, and the women ravished; and half of the city shall go forth into captivity, and the residue of the people shall not be cut off from the city. Then shall the Lord go forth, and fight against those nations, as when he fought in the day of battle."

Because of the determined effort of Satan to kill every Jew, God will prepare a place for the woman Israel *"in the wilderness"* to hide there all through the Great Tribulation, 1,260 days or 3½ years. Some Bible teachers assumed that would be Petra, the rose red city carved out of stone, in the country of the Edomites, now in Jordan, south of the Dead Sea. The late W. E. Blackstone, who wrote the very popular and valuable book, *Jesus Is Coming*, is said to have stored great boxes of Bibles in the cave-like houses there for Jews to read and hopefully to be saved. But Christ did not come so soon as Blackstone expected. Arabs have looted the stored Bibles, we suppose.

In Blackstone's day, no airplane had dropped bombs and Petra was thought almost impregnable. We do not know, of course, where God will hide fleeing Jews in the Great Tribulation time. It could be at Petra.

VERSES 7—12:

7 And there was war in heaven: Michael and his angels fought against the dragon; and the dragon fought and his angels,

8 And prevailed not; neither was their place found any more in heaven.

9 And the great dragon was cast out, that old serpent, called the Devil, and Satan, which deceiveth the whole world: he was cast out into the earth, and his angels were cast out with him.

10 And I heard a loud voice saying in heaven, Now is come salvation, and strength, and the kingdom of our God, and the power of his Christ: for the accuser of our brethren is cast down, which accused them before our God day and night.

11 And they overcame him by the blood of the Lamb, and by the word of their testimony; and they loved not their lives unto the death.

12 Therefore rejoice, *ye* heavens, and ye that dwell in them. Woe to the inhabiters of the earth and of the sea! for the devil is come down unto you, having great wrath, because he knoweth that he hath but a short time.

The Archangel and War in Heaven

The Angel Michael appears five times in Scripture: in Daniel 10:13; 10:21; 12:1; Jude 9; and here in Revelation 12:7. He is called "Michael your prince," in Daniel, so evidently he has special concern over Israel. Another angel named Gabriel appears in an announcement to Mary, to Zacharias and to Daniel. We suppose by the context that Michael was more God's agent in judgment and in war against the wicked, while Gabriel was usually a messenger. Michael, an archangel, will lead other angels in the war in Heaven or in the heavenlies. Now Satan is called the "prince of the power of the air" (Eph. 2:2) and "the prince of this world" (John 12:31; 14:30; 16:11).

It appears that Satan and his angels will be cast out of the upper air and must dwell on the earth in the closing days of the Great Tribulation before Satan (and we suppose his angels, also) are cast forever into the lake of fire. Dr. Unger says: "Michael is the special protector of Daniel's people the Jews (Dan. 12:1; cf. Dan. 10:13-21). He is involved in the war when Satan's expulsion from the heavenlies is at hand. Since his original rebellion, Satan and his hosts have been loose in the heavenlies (Job 1:6; 2:1; Gen. 3:1-10; Eph. 2:2; 6:10-12). In the middle of the Great Tribulation he and his angels will be expelled and cast on the earth (cf. Dan. 10:10-14)."

Now, how many titles and descriptions of Satan! He is the "great red dragon." He is "the serpent." He is "prince of the power of the air." He is "Abaddon" and "Apollyon," the destroyer. He is "Beelzebub." He is "father of liars." He is "accuser of the brethren," etc.

Satan's being cast out of the heavens with his demons is the beginning of the end for him. A. T. Robertson comments here that "the Devil's departure from his warfare in the heavens reveals to him that his time for doing harm to men is limited, and hence his great wrath" (the Greek word for wrath here is *thumon*, "boiling rage").

In the heavens he was allowed to approach God and to accuse Job. It was a constant effort, we may be sure, to "accuse the brethren," that is, all Christians. So great joy will be in Heaven when he is cast out, to accuse God's people no more. He will continue his wicked attacks on earth to hurt Christians, for he will have *"great wrath, because he knoweth that he hath but a short time"* (vs. 12).

But tempted and troubled Christians, then as now, can have victory over Satan. We are promised, "Resist the devil, and he will flee from you" (Jas. 4:7). In those tribulation times they will overcome him "by the blood of the Lamb, and by the word of their testimony; and they loved not their lives unto the death."

"The blood of the Lamb" gives eternal security, with sins all paid for, and knowledge of this and dependence on it gives peace and daily victory.

"The word of their testimony" (vs. 11) would overcome Satan by winning souls and witnessing. And martyrdom is great victory over Satan. "The blood of the martyrs is the seed of the church." So it is great blessing to be persecuted for Jesus. How precious is the heritage of our persecuted fathers!

> Faith of our fathers! living still
>   In spite of dungeon, fire, and sword:
> O how our hearts beat high with joy
>   Whene'er we hear that glorious word!
> Faith of our fathers! holy faith!
>   We will be true to thee till death!
>
> Our fathers, chained in prisons dark,
>   Were still in heart and conscience free:
> How sweet would be their children's fate,
>   If they, like them, could die for thee!
> Faith of our fathers! holy faith!
>   We will be true to thee till death!

But for a time there is woe to those on earth because Satan will be continually on earth among men after he is cast out of the heavens.

VERSES 13-16:

13 And when the dragon saw that he was cast unto the earth, he persecuted the woman which brought forth the man *child.*

14 And to the woman were given two wings of a great eagle, that she might fly into the wilderness, into her place, where she is nourished for

a time, and times, and half a time, from the face of the serpent.

15 And the serpent cast out of his mouth water as a flood after the woman, that he might cause her to be carried away of the flood.

16 And the earth helped the woman, and the earth opened her mouth, and swallowed up the flood which the dragon cast out of his mouth.

Satan Persecutes Israel in Tribulation

Israel will be persecuted more during the tribulation time. Satan knows they will be turning to God. The spiritual blindness now affecting Israel (Rom. 11:25) will begin to lift. It may be the awful troubles of that time will have much to do with turning Israel back to God. It often happened in the book of Judges and again in the Babylonian captivity.

"Two wings of a great eagle" (vs. 14). Some supernatural influences are here pictured—we do not know what. We quote Dr. Unger again: "The eagle wings given to the woman to escape to the wilderness recall how the Lord delivered Israel from Egypt and bore her 'on eagles' wings' (Exod. 19:4; Deut. 32: 11, 12; Isa. 26:20; 27:1)."

Again, the exile of Israel is said to be *"a time"* (one year) *"and times"* (two years) *"and half a time"* (that is half a year)—3½ years, the same 1,260 days of verse 6 above.

What is the *"water as a flood"* (vs. 15) which Satan will send out? We do not know. Will it be like Pharaoh or like Herod trying to have people kill all boy babies? Or like Haman the Agagite in the book of Esther, in the time of Mordecai and Esther who would have tricked the king to have all Jews killed? God, who protected His favored ones in those times, will protect them again. Satan and the Antichrist can go only as far as God allows. Nature or people or circumstances will be used to protect the fleeing, hiding Israelites.

VERSE 17:

17 And the dragon was wroth with the woman, and went to make war with the remnant of her seed, which keep the commandments of God, and have the testimony of Jesus Christ.

Jewish Remnant Turning to Christ

We have been told of 144,000 from the 12 tribes of Israel who
will turn to Christ. So here *"the remnant of her seed,"* not all but
some Jews, will learn to trust Christ and serve Him.
Deuteronomy 30:1-6 tells of the regathering of Israel and their
conversion to God. And there is indication that some Jews are
turning to God before they are regathered. Deuteronomy 30:1-3
says:

*"And it shall come to pass, when all these things are come
upon thee, the blessing and the curse, which I have set before
thee, and thou shalt call them to mind among all the nations,
whither the Lord thy God hath driven thee, And shalt return
unto the Lord thy God, and shalt obey his voice according to all
that I command thee this day, thou and thy children, with all
thine heart, and with all thy soul; That then the Lord thy God
will turn thy captivity, and have compassion upon thee, and will
return and gather thee from all the nations, whither the Lord
thy God hath scattered thee."*

Note the deliverance of Israel will be in answer to their seeking
God. Christ will return after many turn to God with all their
hearts.

Zechariah 12:10 says: "And I will pour upon the house of
David, and upon the inhabitants of Jerusalem, the spirit of grace
and of supplications: and they shall look upon me whom they
have pierced, and they shall mourn for him, as one mourneth for
his only son, and shall be in bitterness for him, as one that is in
bitterness for his firstborn."

And Zechariah 13:6 indicates that Jews will be startled and
awakened to learn who Jesus is and that Jews put these wounds
in His hands and feet! They will see that the crucifixion was at
the will of the Jews, so in the tribulation time some Jews will
"keep the commandments of God, and have the testimony of
Jesus Christ."

Chapter 13

AND I stood upon the sand of the sea, and saw a beast rise up out of the sea, having seven heads and ten horns, and upon his horns ten crowns, and upon his heads the name of blasphemy.

2 And the beast which I saw was like unto a leopard, and his feet were as *the feet* of a bear, and his mouth as the mouth of a lion: and the dragon gave him his power, and his seat, and great authority.

3 And I saw one of his heads as it were wounded to death; and his deadly wound was healed: and all the world wondered after the beast.

Roman Empire to Be Restored

Here we find the same kind of beast that represented Rome, the fourth world empire as pictured in Daniel 7:3-7:

"And four great beasts came up from the sea, diverse one from another. The first was like a lion, and had eagle's wings: I beheld till the wings thereof were plucked, and it was lifted up from the earth, and made stand upon the feet as a man, and a man's heart was given to it. And behold another beast, a second, like to a bear, and it raised up itself on one side, and it had three ribs in the mouth of it between the teeth of it: and they said thus unto it, Arise, devour much flesh. After this I beheld, and lo another, like a leopard, which had upon the back of it four wings of a fowl; the beast had also four heads; and dominion was given to it. After this I saw in the night visions, and behold a fourth beast, dreadful and terrible, and strong exceedingly; and it had great iron teeth: it devoured and brake in pieces, and stamped the residue with the feet of it: and it was diverse from all the beasts that were before it; and it had ten horns."

But the ten horns of that fourth beast picture ten nations or kingdoms that were left of the Roman Empire when it dissolved. Among those ten horns, God's prophecy here says, will come up another little horn, a king, who will violently take over three of the ten kingdoms and form a federation with the others. He, we will find, is to be the Antichrist or world dictator. Daniel 7 continues, in verses 8 to 11, as follows:

"I considered the horns, and, behold, there came up among them another little horn, before whom there were three of the first horns plucked up by the roots: and, behold, in this horn were eyes like the eyes of man, and a mouth speaking great things. I beheld till the thrones were cast down, and the Ancient of days did sit, whose garment was white as snow, and the hair of his head like the pure wool: his throne was like the fiery flame, and his wheels as burning fire. A fiery stream issued and came forth from before him: thousand thousands ministered unto him, and ten thousand times ten thousand stood before him: the judgment was set, and the books were opened. I beheld then because of the voice of the great words which the horn spake: I beheld even till the beast was slain, and his body destroyed, and given to the burning flame."

Here is prophecy for the future, not ending in past history for that violent king or dictator is to be cast down when "the Ancient of days" comes and brings all to judgment. Note the characteristics of the leopard, bear and lion, as Revelation 13:2 tells us. So this kingdom will have the characteristics of the world empires before, Babylon, Media-Persia and Greece, as pictured in Daniel 7:4-6.

"And upon his heads the name of blasphemy," we are told in verse 1, so we call this dictator "Antichrist."

"And the dragon," that is, Satan, *"gave him his power, and his seat, and great authority"* (vs. 2). So the man is Satan empowered, Satan incarnate.

One of his heads is *"wounded to death,"* says verse 3. Dr. Scofield says:

> Fragments of the ancient Roman empire have never ceased to exist as separate kingdoms. It was the imperial form of government which ceased; the one head wounded to death. What we have prophetically in Rev. 13:3 is the restoration of the imperial form as such, though over a federated empire of ten kingdoms; the

"head" is "healed," i.e. restored; there is an emperor again—the Beast.

So the Roman Empire is to be restored.

"And all the world wondered" (vs. 3), because this violent man seizes power worldwide. After he has seized and conquered three of the ten kingdoms of the Roman Empire, he will form a federation with the other nations, fragments of the old Roman Empire. Then he will set out to conquer the world.

VERSES 4—10:

4 And they worshipped the dragon which gave power unto the beast: and they worshipped the beast, saying, Who *is* like unto the beast? who is able to make war with him?

5 And there was given unto him a mouth speaking great things and blasphemies; and power was given unto him to continue forty *and* two months.

6 And he opened his mouth in blasphemy against God, to blaspheme his name, and his tabernacle, and them that dwell in heaven.

7 And it was given unto him to make war with the saints, and to overcome them: and power was given him over all kindreds, and tongues, and nations.

8 And all that dwell upon the earth shall worship him, whose names are not written in the book of life of the Lamb slain from the foundation of the world.

9 If any man have an ear, let him hear.

10 He that leadeth into captivity shall go into captivity: he that killeth with the sword must be killed with the sword. Here is the patience and the faith of the saints.

Worldwide Rule of Beast, Worshiped as God

"And they worshipped the dragon," that is, Satan. So some do now, but some worship Satan under another description. All humanism that rejects God exalts Satan. All enemies of Christ are friends of Satan. To the Christ-rejecting Pharisees Jesus said, "Ye are of your father the devil" (John 8:44). Jesus said, "He that is not with me is against me; and he that gathereth not with me scattereth abroad" (Matt. 12:30).

Those who chose Barabbas instead of Christ (Matt. 27:21) were choosing Satan instead of God. Judas died and went "to his own place" (Acts 1:25), so his identity with Satan as the "son of perdition" ended in Satan's place as his own place. That is,

Satan will be cast into Hell forever, as will Judas.

Most unconverted people claim some righteousness and would never admit, even to themselves, that they worship and follow Satan, but they do, whether consciously or not.

First Corinthians 10:19-21 says:

"What say I then? that the idol is any thing, or that which is offered in sacrifice to idols is any thing? But I say, that the things which the Gentiles sacrifice, they sacrifice to devils, and not to God: and I would not that ye should have fellowship with devils. Ye cannot drink the cup of the Lord, and the cup of devils: ye cannot be partakers of the Lord's table, and of the table of devils."

"And they worshipped the beast" as well as Satan, says verse 4. But those who worship Satan without understanding it worship men or systems of idolatry who represent Satan and do it consciously. Idolatry, whether worship of an image in a temple, or of Mary as mediatrix, or the Mass as a sacrifice on the altar to pay what Jesus paid or a religious system or hierarchy which they hope will save them, however unconsciously, yet men are worshiping Satan behind the idolatry. The sacrifices of the Gentiles are to devils, Paul said.

Satan has long sought to get men to worship a pope as infallible religiously, or a priest claiming to forgive sins, or Mohammed as God's one prophet, or one's own righteousness, as the Jews in Romans 10:3 who go about seeking to establish their own righteousness. "For they being ignorant of God's righteousness, and going about to establish their own righteousness, have not submitted themselves unto the righteousness of God." Or some are idolators like lodge members who trust their morality to get them into "Elysian Fields," accepted by "the Grand Architect of the Universe." At the last the Antichrist, as Satan incarnate, will demand and receive worship as God.

His blasphemies and rule will continue 42 months worldwide. That is the 3½ years of the Great Tribulation.

He will be allowed to *"make war with the saints"* (vs. 7), that is, with the saved people, that great host named in Revelation 7:9-14, converted during the tribulation time and with converted Jews who want to worship God.

Note his worldwide power *"over all kindreds, and tongues, and nations"* (vs. 7). The lines will be drawn so strongly that one cannot buy nor sell without the mark of the beast (see vss. 16, 17). Note that every living person shall worship this Antichrist *"whose names are not written in the book of life"* (vs. 8). And according to Revelation 14:9, 10, those who take the mark of the beast and worship him are thus committing the unpardonable sin. The line is so closely drawn that one may tell Christians by those who do not take the mark of the beast, those who oppose him.

The doom of the Antichrist is near. Dr. W. B. Riley says:

> It is of the mercy of God that while Christ is to reign on earth for a thousand years, and at the end of that time, His peaceful sovereignty is to be transferred to the Father, to continue forever; the bloody reign of His great antagonist, the Antichrist, shall be cut short in three and a half seasons, and this usurper shall meet his doom (Rev. 20:1-3). It has been so from the first! When Satan triumphed in the Garden of Eden, almost instantly his Conqueror came; while Haman sat at the king's table, the scaffold was building; when Belshazzar exalted himself to Heaven, that night he was slain; while Herod was listening to the huzzahs of the people who were proclaiming him god, he was smitten of worms and died; and right at the time when this Antichrist shall have clutched the scepter of universal sovereignty, the hand of might and power shall touch him, his kingdom shall be overthrown, and he himself cast down to chains and imprisonment to be followed by eternal torment, for John's vision was not ended. He says in Revelation 19:19, 20:

> *"And I saw the beast, and the kings of the earth, and their armies, gathered together to make war against him that sat on the horse, and against his army. And the beast was taken, and with him the false prophet that wrought miracles before him, with which he deceived them that had received the mark of the beast, and them that worshipped his image. These both were cast alive into a lake of fire burning with brimstone."*

This Explains Judgment of Living Gentiles of Matthew 25

When Christ returns to the earth to reign after the battle of Armageddon is over, Matthew 25:31-33 tells us:

"When the Son of man shall come in his glory, and all the holy angels with him, then shall he sit upon the throne of his glory: And before him shall be gathered all nations: and he shall separate them one from another, as a shepherd divideth his sheep from the goats: And he shall set the sheep on his right hand, but the goats on the left."

The term there "all nations" should represent the Gentiles, the heathen world, those Gentiles left alive after the battle of Armageddon. And this judgment seems at first glance to be based on good works. To those on his right hand the King will say:

"Come, ye blessed of my Father, inherit the kingdom prepared for you from the foundation of the world: For I was an hungred, and ye gave me meat: I was thirsty, and ye gave me drink: I was a stranger, and ye took me in: Naked, and ye clothed me: I was sick, and ye visited me: I was in prison, and ye came unto me."

Then these startled saved people will be told, "Inasmuch as ye have done it unto one of the least of these my brethren, ye have done it unto me."

And those on the left hand are told, "Depart from me, ye cursed, into everlasting fire, prepared for the devil and his angels," and of this judgment is said: "For I was an hungred, and ye gave me no meat: I was thirsty, and ye gave me no drink: I was a stranger, and ye took me not in: naked, and ye clothed me not: sick, and in prison, and ye visited me not" (Matt. 25:42, 43).

Again, these likewise will ask, When did they refuse to visit and feed and defend the Lord Jesus? "Then shall he answer them, saying, Verily I say unto you, Inasmuch as ye did it not to one of the least of these, ye did it not to me."

I say that seems, at first glance, that people will be saved by their good works, but that is not so. If you get the lesson here in Revelation, you will see that in the tribulation time every single person who takes the mark of the beast and defends him thus commits an unpardonable sin and will go to Hell forever. And those who resist the Antichrist and take the part of those he hates, take the part of those he abuses and persecutes and kills, are the saved people. So they will enter into Christ's kingdom, not because they did good works but they did good works because they decided for Christ against the Antichrist; they trusted Christ and are saved. And in this case they are the only people left in the world who are against the Antichrist and for the saved. That proves they are saved, that they belong to Christ, since they prove it by risking death to support Christians and oppose the Antichrist.

And those who take the mark of the beast will be told to depart into Hell, because that very fact shows that they rejected Christ and worshiped Satan so they did not take the part of those persecuted and killed by the Antichrist.

That passage in Matthew 25:31-46 does not teach that people will be saved by their good works. It teaches there that these who have already been clearly marked as saved or lost can be recognized by whether they take the mark of the beast and worship the Antichrist or whether they resist the Antichrist, will not take his mark and will take the part of the saved.

God has the lines drawn very closely now, but they are not as clearly visible as they will be then. In the days of the Antichrist, every single person who is unsaved will take the mark of the beast. Every single person who is saved will resist him and side with the Christians who are persecuted and killed. So they will be easily identified when the Lord Jesus judges the Gentile remnant left after the battle of Armageddon, after the tribulation time.

You will note that that passage is about "the nations," that is, the Gentiles. The judgment of Israel will be a different matter. Angels will gather every Jew left in the world (Matt. 24:31). They will be brought to the wilderness of wanderings and the rebels will be purged out (Ezek. 20:33-38). Then Christ will make Himself known to these other Jews who are seeking God and they will repent and trust Him and then that remnant that is left— ". . .all Israel shall be saved" (Rom. 11:26).

But here is sweet comfort in verse 10. The Man of Sin will come to judgment. He who imprisons Christians, he who kills

with the sword, must be killed. God give Christians patience to
abide temptation and trust that God always does right. "The
Lord executeth righteousness and judgment for all that are oppressed" (Ps. 103:6.)

All of us should learn the warning of Psalm 37:1-11:

*"Fret not thyself because of evildoers, neither be thou en-
vious against the workers of iniquity. For they shall soon be cut
down like the grass, and wither as the green herb. Trust in the
Lord, and do good; so shalt thou dwell in the land, and verily
thou shalt be fed. Delight thyself also in the Lord; and he shall
give thee the desires of thine heart. Commit thy way unto the
Lord; trust also in him; and he shall bring it to pass. And he shall
bring forth thy righteousness as the light, and thy judgment as
the noonday. Rest in the Lord, and wait patiently for him: fret
not thyself because of him who prospereth in his way, because
of the man who bringeth wicked devices to pass. Cease from
anger, and forsake wrath: fret not thyself in any wise to do evil.
For evildoers shall be cut off: but those that wait upon the Lord,
they shall inherit the earth. For yet a little while, and the wicked
shall not be: yea, thou shalt diligently consider his place, and it
shall not be. But the meek shall inherit the earth; and shall
delight themselves in the abundance of peace."*

Some persecution, some trouble is inevitable for all who live
godly in Christ Jesus. And those who are so persecuted and some
put to death in the tribulation time have sweet comfort that God
will bring judgment on the Antichrist, too. And in due time "the
meek shall inherit the earth" and "the way of the ungodly shall
perish."

VERSES 11—15:

11 And I beheld another beast
coming up out of the earth; and he
had two horns like a lamb, and he
spake as a dragon.

12 And he exerciseth all the power
of the first beast before him, and

causeth the earth and them which
dwell therein to worship the first
beast, whose deadly wound was
healed.

13 And he doeth great wonders, so
that he maketh fire come down from

heaven on the earth in the sight of men,

14 And deceiveth them that dwell on the earth by *the means of* those miracles which he had power to do in the sight of the beast; saying to them that dwell on the earth, that they should make an image to the beast, which had the wound by a sword, and did live.

15 And he had power to give life unto the image of the beast, that the image of the beast should both speak, and cause that as many as would not worship the image of the beast should be killed.

Rise of False Prophet: Priest of Antichrist

Satan tries to imitate God and act as God. Christ, who is God incarnate, came into the world and so Satan puts forth the Man of Sin, Satan incarnate. The Holy Spirit of God comes to dwell in Christians and give miraculous power and comfort and help day by day. So the Antichrist must have a false prophet and evil spiritual power, too. As Seiss says, "There is a supernatural power which is *against* God and truth, as well as one *for* God and truth. A miracle, simply as a work of wonder, is not necessarily of God. There has always been a devilish supernaturalism in the world, running alongside of the supernaturalism of divine grace and salvation."

We remember that down in Egypt when Aaron cast down his rod before Pharaoh and it became a serpent, "then Pharaoh also called the wise men and the sorcerers: now the magicians of Egypt, they also did in like manner with their enchantments. For they cast down every man his rod, and they became serpents: but Aaron's rod swallowed up their rods" (Exod. 7:11,12).

When Moses, with the rod of God, turned water to blood in the rivers and lakes, then "the magicians of Egypt did so with their enchantments: and Pharaoh's heart was hardened, neither did he hearken unto them; as the Lord had said" (Exod. 7:22).

When Moses brought a plague of frogs from the rivers and ponds over Egypt, then "the magicians did so with their enchantments, and brought up frogs upon the land of Egypt" (Exod. 8:7). After that the magicians of Pharaoh were not able to equal the miracles in the plagues that Moses brought from God.

But it is noteworthy that satanic power is more than human power. Satan cannot go beyond what God will allow him to do, but Satan can and sometimes does work miracles. He did with the magicians in Egypt. False prophets may be allowed to work miracles. In Deuteronomy 13:1-3 God gave this instruction:

"If there arise among you a prophet, or a dreamer of dreams, and giveth thee a sign or a wonder, And the sign or the wonder come to pass, whereof he spake unto thee, saying, Let us go after other gods, which thou hast not known, and let us serve them; Thou shalt not hearken unto the words of that prophet, or that dreamer of dreams: for the Lord your God proveth you, to know whether ye love the Lord your God with all your heart and with all your soul."

No miracle is to take the place of the Word of God.

Let us beware, then, for Satan goes about "as a roaring lion. . . seeking whom he may devour" (I Pet. 5:8). And he has more than human power. A spiritist, a fortuneteller, may be allowed to reveal some hidden matter, in a miraculous way.

In my boyhood, my cousin had a horse stolen in North Texas. He went to see a fortuneteller. The fortuneteller told him that a man with a certain appearance stole the horse, that he had taken it north into Oklahoma to Ardmore. My cousin went there, found the horse and recovered him. It was a secret thing which Satan revealed to a fortuneteller. No doubt many a person has thus been tempted by Satan to listen to spiritists and Devil-possessed teachers because God allowed some satanic miracle. But always we are to remember that anything that is not according to the Scriptures is still wicked and wrong.

Here we have, then, a false prophet of the Antichrist with miraculous powers. This false prophet will have *"two horns like a lamb"* (vs. 11), appearing to be peaceful and good *"and he spake as a dragon"* (vs. 11), that is, he spoke for the Devil, Satan. And just as secular kings and government in the Dark and Middle Ages put all their power behind the Roman church in its wicked Spanish Inquisition and the persecution and murder of Christian martyrs who would not follow the Roman church, so the powers of the Antichrist will be given to this false prophet that he can teach people to worship the Antichrist, dictator of the restored Roman empire whose emperorship is restored.

Note verse 13. This false prophet will make fire come down from Heaven. And he will deceive people by these miracles (vs. 14). He will teach people to worship an image of the Antichrist. He will make this idol live and speak and set out to kill every person who will not worship it.

Let every Christian beware then, for Satan is back of false religions. He deceives people. He sometimes works miracles to deceive. And his way will be more plain than ever in the tribulation time when the false prophet, with all the power of the Antichrist, works miracles and insists that everybody worship the Antichrist and his image or die.

VERSES 16—18:

16 And he causeth all, both small and great, rich and poor, free and bond, to receive a mark in their right hand, or in their foreheads:

17 And that no man might buy or sell, save he that had the mark, or the name of the beast, or the number of his name.

18 Here is wisdom. Let him that hath understanding count the ¹number of the beast: for it is the number of a man; and his number *is* Six hundred threescore *and* six.

Mark of the Beast: 666

Shallow preachers and sensation-mongers have made a great to-do about the number 666. Some have added up the Roman numerals represented by the letters used in the titles and by stretching a point made them come out 666, trying to prove that the pope is the Antichrist, or will be. Others have tried to find the number 666 in the nations of the European Common Market agreement.

Some sightseeing buses in Israel have the numbers in their license number include 666. Oh, in the minds of some, that must have meaning, that the coming of Christ is near, the Antichrist is about to appear, etc. All this is foolish. It is not good exposition of the Scriptures.

Note carefully the following facts.

1. The Man of Sin cannot appear until after the rapture. If he

were alive today, nobody in the world would know it, and he himself would not know it.

2. The Man of Sin must first rise up after the rapture and assume some power in one of the nations that was in the old Roman Empire. The Bible does not say how long it will be after the rapture until he appears. It is an indefinite time.

3. He will not be made known as the Antichrist even at the beginning of the seven years. He will overcome three nations of the old Roman Empire. Which ones we do not know. Then he will form a federation of the other nations of the Roman Empire and come into world prominence, and only then can he be recognized as having some authority over Palestine and the world; only then can he make a treaty with a remnant that will then be in Palestine, allowing them to have a temple and priesthood and animal sacrifices and begin the ancient Jewish worship, and Israel will be a nation. Note, it will not simply be that Jews will be allowed in Palestine, but it will be that the Jewish worship of the true God will be begun in Jerusalem in some temple that Jews will then prepare and with the priesthood and sacrifices. Until that covenant of seven years is made with Israel, nobody could possibly know who the Man of Sin is. That is the first identifying mark.

4. Even then, he will not begin his awful reign, manifest with the Antichrist and claim to be God on earth, until the midst of the seven years. After three and a half years he will break that covenant. He will have agreed with Jews that they will have seven years of such worship but he will break that treaty and enter into the temple, commit the abomination of desolation, and claim to be God on earth, etc.

You can see, then, that if the rapture should come today it would be some indefinite time—how long we do not know—before the Man of Sin would take over one of the nations that once helped form the Roman Empire, then violently take over a total of three, then have a federation of the other nations and, in a sense, re-form the Roman Empire. That cannot happen until some time after the rapture.

The Man of Sin is not known now and could not be known. It is a false and careless study of Scripture to pretend that anybody knows the time of the rapture or a later time when the Man of Sin will appear. He cannot be identified now, and cannot be definitely identified until he reaches worldwide power enough to make a treaty with the remnant of Jews who will be in Jerusalem, to build a temple, have priests and sacrifices and restore Israel as a nation under God in their land again, that is, a nation worshiping God and keeping the ceremonies and practices of the Mosaic law.

Seventy weeks were determined on Daniel's people. One week, the last of the weeks of seven years, is postponed. That meant seven years with the temple, with sacrifices, with priesthood and people trying to carry out the Mosaic law as the people of God. And that time will come, the week's treaty with the Jews, made by the Antichrist when he gets some worldwide power.

Why the number 666? Six in the Bible is in some sense man's number. First, remember that seven has a divine connotation. God made the earth in six days and the seventh day He rested. And thus the seventh day came to be a type of Heaven. Jews were commanded in the Ten Commandments to work six days and then keep a Sabbath, picturing Heaven. If one perfectly served God and did everything right, he would earn salvation. Of course, the sad fact is that sin came in and nobody ever does everything right. So God had to have a passover lamb and the feast of unleavened bread and people enter into a Sabbath of rest the very first day, on the merits of the shed blood and not on their works.

Seven, then, is often used for perfection. It appears in the cycles of life in many ways. A woman's menstrual periods ordinarily come every four weeks. Chickens hatch out in three weeks. Turkeys in four weeks. Some birds in two weeks. Seven is engrained in nature and thus represents God.

But man comes short of God, and so six represents a man's number. And here 666 would mean that the highest any man could reach toward seven and toward perfection the Antichrist will reach, but he cannot reach the seven. It is 666 but not 7.

Chapter 14

VERSES 1—5:

AND I looked, and, lo, a Lamb stood on the mount Sion, and with him an hundred forty *and* four thousand, having his Father's name written in their foreheads.

2 And I heard a voice from heaven, as the voice of many waters, and as the voice of a great thunder: and I heard the voice of harpers harping with their harps:

3 And they sung as it were a new song before the throne, and before the four beasts, and the elders: and no man could learn that song but the hundred *and* forty *and* four thousand, which were redeemed from the earth.

4 These are they which were not defiled with women; for they are virgins. These are they which follow the Lamb whithersoever he goeth. These were redeemed from among men, *being* the firstfruits unto God and to the Lamb.

5 And in their mouth was found no guile: for they are without fault before the throne of God.

The Lamb and the 144,000

In this chapter we have parenthetical material without chronological connection. Here are six scenes, separate snapshots, picturing facts and events around and after the tribulation period.

"A Lamb." It is Jesus. In Revelation 5:5 He is "the Lion of the tribe of Juda," who was worthy to open the seven-sealed book. But again there He was called "the Lamb."

"Mount Sion": at Jerusalem, on earth, as it will be after the tribulation time again. *"An hundred forty and four thousand"*— the same group from the twelve tribes of Israel saved during the tribulation time, mentioned in chapter 7.

"Having his Father's name written in their foreheads." The Jews have an inheritance from Old Testament Israelites who worship the God of Mount Sinai, the God of the prophets. The host of Christians will have been taken to Heaven in the rapture and possibly these Jews have not had the intimate contact of the New Testament narratives of the life of Christ as we have. They are saved and are with Christ, the Lamb, but their emphasis, I

suppose, is that of Old Testament prophets.

During the last half of Daniel's seventieth week, the Old Testament sacrifices and ceremonies will have been in force. The Old Testament Christians trusted in the coming Messiah. These trusted in the Messiah who has come but probably with more Old Testament influence than we. After nineteen hundred years of Gentile Christian culture and the New Testament in daily life, we may know Jesus better than the Father. But these have the name of the Heavenly Father in their foreheads.

We may not realize how little about Christ and the life and death and teachings is a part of Jewish life now. Persecuted by nominal Christians for centuries, hated as "Christ killers," with Jewish massacres in Poland and Russia, Hitler in Germany killing six million. Zechariah 10:10-13 and 13:6 tells of Jews first seeing Christ after His return. They are naive, shocked, amazed that He had been killed by His own people. And Gentiles of Christian background have a wealth of tradition and a culture that leads to Christ. These seem to find Christ through the prophets and types and then to know God.

The house of David and the nation Israel are to be restored. They are the days of Isaiah 32:1, 2 which says:

"Behold, a king shall reign in righteousness, and princes shall rule in judgment. And a man shall be as an hiding place from the wind, and a covert from the tempest; as rivers of water in a dry place, as the shadow of a great rock in a weary land."

They are the days of Isaiah 35:1, 2, 5, 6:

"The wilderness and the solitary place shall be glad for them; and the desert shall rejoice, and blossom as the rose. It shall blossom abundantly, and rejoice even with joy and singing: the glory of Lebanon shall be given unto it, the excellency of Carmel and Sharon, they shall see the glory of the Lord, and the excellency of our God. . .Then the eyes of the blind shall be opened, and the ears of the deaf shall be unstopped. Then shall the lame man leap as an hart, and the tongue of the dumb sing: for in the wilderness shall waters break out, and streams in the desert."

Isaiah 42:10 and Psalm 33:3 both tell us of *"a new song"* (vs. 3). The 144,000 have a new song no one else can learn. It must be that the song will tell of experiences no one else had, tell praises to God for individual blessings others have never known. Possibly others could learn the words but not the heart meaning.

These blessed 144,000 are *"virgins,"* never having been *"defiled with women"* (vs. 4). It is no sin to be married, and have the normal sex life of husband and wife, for "marriage is honourable in all, and the bed undefiled" (Heb. 13:4). First Corinthians 7:28 says, "But and if thou marry, thou hast not sinned; and if a virgin marry, she hath not sinned. Nevertheless such shall have trouble in the flesh: but I spare you." God Himself said of Adam, "It is not good that the man should be alone" (Gen. 2:18).

Dr. Ironside calls them a "virgin band, who have kept themselves from the uncleanness everywhere prevailing in those fearful days." He further says: "The blessing of Psalm 32 pronounced upon the man in whom is no guile, the blessing that our Lord pronounced upon Nathanael, is the portion of this special company. A guileless man is not a sinless man; he is one who has nothing to hide. When sin is all confessed and judged in the presence of God, guile is absent. And so this guileless company are described as without fault before the throne of God . . . ." But there have been great sacrifices in voluntarily giving up normal life and love, wife and children, to serve God. Paul gave up all these to serve God without hindrance. The Nazarites, we learn in Numbers 6, took vows not to drink grape juice, not even to eat grapes or raisins. He was not to defile or make himself unclean because of grieving at the death of a loved one. It is good for Christians to voluntarily give up some things, even good things, so they may serve God better. You remember that Moses forsook Egypt and the royal family and all the treasures of Egypt to bear the reproach of Christ and a race of slaves (Heb. 11:23-29).

So sometimes we who seek earnestly to have the power of God, may leave off eating or stay awake in the night watches while others sleep, in order to pray and better do God's will and have

His power. Some of us have spent a total of long years of our lives away from family and dear ones in evangelism. So do others for the foreign mission field.

So these devoted Israelites *"follow the Lamb withersoever he goeth"* (vs. 4). They were redeemed *"being the firstfruits unto God"* (vs. 4), we are told, that is, they are firstfruits of that wave of conversions that will follow: they begin the turning of the nation Israel to God. Others will have been saved before them and even a scattering of Jews down through the years, but, in the sense of turning the nation Israel back to God, they are the "firstfruits." It may be that as they are named before the great multitude reported saved in tribulation time in chapter 7, that they are specially the firstfruits of the tribulation. How sweet they are to stay near the Saviour in His millennial reign and be counted without fault or guile!

VERSES 6, 7:

6 And I saw another angel fly in the midst of heaven, having the everlasting gospel to preach unto them that dwell on the earth, and to every nation, and kindred, and tongue, and people,

7 Saying with a loud voice, Fear God, and give glory to him; for the hour of his judgment is come: and worship him that made heaven, and earth, and the sea, and the fountains of waters.

The Angel and the Everlasting Gospel

Dr. Scofield, in notes on these two verse, says, "Four forms of the Gospel are to be distinguished." And he names them:

1. The Gospel of the kingdom.
2. The Gospel of the grace of God.
3. The everlasting Gospel
4. That which Paul calls, "my Gospel."

That seems to me very unfortunate and making a distinction God did not intend. I believe there is but one true Gospel. The Gospel Paul preached to Galatians was not one of four kinds of Gospels but the only true Gospel. Paul says, "But though we, or an angel from heaven, preach any other gospel unto you than that which we have preached unto you, let him be accursed. As we said before, so say I now again, If any man preach any other gospel unto you than that ye have received, let him be accursed" (Gal. 1:8, 9).

Paul said, "But I certify you, brethren, that the gospel which was preached of me is not after man. For I neither received it of man, neither was I taught it, but by the revelation of Jesus Christ" (Gal. 1:11, 12).

So there is only one true God-given Gospel.

Paul gave the inspired definition of the Gospel he preached and by which people are saved in I Corinthians 15:1-4:

"Moreover, brethren, I declare unto you the gospel which I preached unto you, which also ye have received, and wherein ye stand; By which also ye are saved, if ye keep in memory what I preached unto you, unless ye have believed in vain. For I delivered unto you first of all that which I also received, how that Christ died for our sins according to the scriptures; And that he was buried, and that he rose again the third day according to the scriptures."

Paul wrote to Rome, "So, as much as in me is, I am ready to preach the gospel to you that are at Rome also" (Rom. 1:15). One Gospel, the only one, the same one.

It was that one same Gospel "which was preached to every creature which is under heaven" (Col. 1:23).

Paul was inspired to say "my gospel" (Rom. 2:15) and "our gospel" (II Cor. 4:3). He meant simply the true Gospel as he preached it.

Christ will come "in flaming fire taking vengeance on them that know not God, and that obey not the gospel of our Lord Jesus Christ" (II Thess. 1:8).

There is only one Gospel—the saving Gospel.

In different connotations and circumstances the Gospel is related to different ideas. When Peter preached the Gospel to the Jews, it was called "the gospel of the circumcision," but when he preached the same Gospel to Gentiles, it was "the gospel of the uncircumcision," says Galatians 2:7. When Jesus preached the

Gospel saying, "Repent ye: for the kingdom of heaven is at hand" (Matt. 3:2), it was the same Gospel, though it was called the Gospel of the kingdom.

Thus the modern idea that there is a Gospel that Christ died for sinners and another "social gospel" is wrong and unscriptural. There is only one Gospel, just as in all ages, Old Testament and New Testament, there has been but one plan of salvation preached by all the prophets (Acts 10:43).

The liberals who insist on the "social gospel" have been sometimes ignorant, sometimes actively dishonest in pretending that fundamental, Bible-believing Christians, soul winners, were unconcerned with benevolence and human welfare. The truth simply is that it is fundamental Christianity that builds rescue missions, helps the poor, cares for orphans, builds charity hospitals. No liberal ever so loved the poor and did so much for the ignorant and unfortunate as did John Wesley, George Muller, General Booth, D. L. Moody, Mel Trotter and other Christian soul winners. The simple truth is that the liberals who go away from the true Gospel bring infidelity, drunkenness, dishonesty and crime in the wake of their "gospel."

So the *"everlasting gospel"* (vs. 6) as preached by the angel here in these verses will surely be the same Gospel of salvation. The prophecy that "this gospel of the kingdom shall be preached in all the world for a witness unto all nations; and then shall the end come" (Matt. 24:14), may refer to this angel's preaching; it certainly refers to the end of the tribulation, not to the rapture before it.

This angel preached that sinners should *"fear God, and give glory to him; for the hour of his judgment is come"* (vs. 7). Yes, and so have honest preachers preached down through the years, warning of the judgment to come and demanding that men repent. But that is a part of the saving Gospel that people should repent and believe on Christ.

———————————

VERSE 8:

8 And there followed another angel, saying, Babylon is fallen, is fallen, that great city, because she made all nations drink of the wine of the wrath of her fornication.

Restored Rome, Here Called Babylon, Falls

In Revelation 11:8 Jerusalem is symbolically called "Sodom and Egypt." Here Rome is called Babylon. It must be Rome, because in Daniel 9:26 we are told, ". . .and the people of the prince that shall come shall destroy the city and the sanctuary." That speaks of the destruction of Jerusalem in A.D. 70, after the crucifixion of Jesus. That destruction was by the Roman army under Titus. So Antichrist is to be of Rome and that is his capital city. Revelation 16:19 says, "And the great city was divided into three parts," referring to the seat of the Antichrist. Revelation 17:9 tells us of the false religion of the Antichrist centered in the city of the seven hills, which is Rome.

Why call it Babylon? Because it is the culmination of world empires from Babylon, Media-Persia, Greece and Rome, then of Rome restored. It symbolizes all the Gentile world power to be destroyed at Christ's second coming, to reign after the tribulation time. From the time of Babel until the Antichrist, mankind has tried to develop a world rule without God. Even now "the mystery of iniquity doth already work: only he who now letteth will let, until he be taken out of the way. And then shall that Wicked be revealed, whom the Lord shall consume with the spirit of his mouth, and shall destroy with the brightness of his coming: Even him, whose coming is after the working of Satan with all power and signs and lying wonders" (II Thess. 2:7-9). It is Satan's plan and all of it is symbolized by the term Babylon.

Note carefully in the preceding part of the New Testament that Rome is never called Babylon. It was to the dispersed of Israel in the literal country of Babylon to whom Peter preached and from which he sent greetings in II Peter 5:13. Peter was never at Rome. He was not mentioned in the twenty-eight persons and families Paul addressed in Romans 16. He did not meet with Paul there when Paul came in Acts 28. He was not there when

Paul wrote his farewell in II Timothy 4 and said, "Only Luke is with me."

But here in Revelation, Rome is the revived culmination of world rule by Satan and is symbolically called Babylon.

Why is the city to be destroyed? Because it will have become the center of idolatry and spiritual fornication. This will be mentioned again in Revelation 17:1, 2 where the kings are said to have committed fornication with the false religion of Rome.

VERSES 9—12:

9 And the third angel followed them, saying with a loud voice, If any man worship the beast and his image, and receive *his* mark in his forehead, or in his hand,

10 The same shall drink of the wine of the wrath of God, which is poured out without mixture into the cup of his indignation; and he shall be tormented with fire and brimstone in the presence of the holy angels, and in the presence of the Lamb:

11 And the smoke of their torment ascendeth up for ever and ever: and they have no rest day nor night, who worship the beast and his image, and whosoever receiveth the mark of his name.

12 Here is the patience of the saints: here *are* they that keep the commandments of God, and the faith of Jesus.

All Who Worship Beast Go to Eternal Hell

The "beast," the "son of perdition," the world dictator, the Antichrist will have claimed to be God, demanding worship as God (II Thess. 2:4). Then an image or idol representing him will be miraculously made alive by the false prophet. All who will not worship the beast and his image will be put to death. They must take the mark of the beast as beast worshipers in order to be allowed to buy or sell, but all who do so (worship the beast) are to go to Hell forever.

Verses 10 and 11 are significant: they speak of Hell as eternal torment. Some may say the fire in Hell will be figurative. Will the smoke be figurative also? And the brimstone? And are the worms that "dieth not," as Jesus said in Mark 9:44, 46, 49—are they figurative too? Is the water the rich man in Hell cried for figurative too? And is his thirst figurative? We feel compelled to take it at face value, when Christ so many times mentioned the fire in Hell.

How would the fire torment and not annihilate and destroy any physical bodies in Hell? I do not know. When we ignorant, frail mortals step, like fools, into eternal things, we do not know it all. I do not know how the three Hebrew children in Daniel 3 were unharmed in the fiery furnace, so hot that it killed others who cast them in. But that story is obviously true. When God says that Hell is a lake of fire and brimstone and it goes on forever, who is so wise to explain it away? Clear it is that all who worship the beast turn forever away from God's offer of salvation through Christ. Their sin thus becomes unpardonable.

VERSE 13:

13 And I heard a voice from heaven saying unto me, Write, Blessed *are* the dead which die in the Lord from henceforth: Yea, saith the Spirit, that they may rest from their labours; and their works do follow them.

God's Blessed Dead

How sweetly God speaks of the Christian dead. They are called "them. . .which sleep in Jesus" (I Thess. 4:14). Strange that any born-again one should dread it.

> Asleep in Jesus! blessed sleep,
> From which none ever wakes to weep!
> A calm and undisturbed repose,
> Unbroken by the last of foes.

> Asleep in Jesus! O how sweet
> To be for such a slumber meet!
> With holy confidence to sing,
> That death hath lost his venomed sting.

> Asleep in Jesus! peaceful rest,
> Whose waking is supremely blest!
> No fear, no woe, shall dim that hour
> That manifests the Saviour's pow'r.

> Asleep in Jesus! O for me
> May such a blissful refuge be!
> Securely shall my ashes lie,
> Waiting the summons from on high.

We say good-by but not for long. Do we weep that they will have God wipe away all their tears? Are we sad that they enter into eternal happiness?

Ira D. Sankey wrote that sweet little farewell hymn,

> Sleep on, beloved, sleep, and take thy rest;
> Lay down thy head upon thy Savior's breast;
> We love thee well, but Jesus loves thee best—
>   Good-night! Good-night! Good-night!
>
> Calm is thy slumber as an infant's sleep;
> But thou shalt wake no more to toil and weep:
> Thine is a perfect rest, secure and deep—
>   Good-night! Good-night! Good-night!
>
> Until eternal glory lights the skies,
> Until the dead in Jesus shall arise,
> And He shall come, but not in lowly guise—
>   Good-night! Good-night! Good-night!
>
> Only "Good-night," beloved—not "Farewell!"
> A little while, and all His saints shall dwell
> In hallowed union indivisible—
>   Good-night! Good-night! Good-night!
>
> Until we meet again before His throne,
> Clothed in the spotless robe He gives His own,
> Until we know even as we are known—
>   Good-night! Good-night! Good-night!

Blind Fanny Crosby died rejoicing that the first face those long-blinded eyes would see would be that of Jesus! My mother, dying, raised her frail hands as we sang at her request, "How firm a foundation," at her bedside. And she said joyfully, "I can see Jesus and my baby now!" then fell asleep. So blessed are the dead who die in the Lord for they have sweet rest from their labors and their works follow them.

The word Sabbath means rest. And Heaven is pictured in the Sabbath in the Bible and in Hebrews 4:9 the Scripture says, "There remaineth therefore a rest to the people of God." Oh, thank God for the heavenly Sabbath to lay aside our burdens and rest!

It is true that the Scripture says, ". . .and his servants shall serve him" (22:3), but one can enter into sweet rest eternally, with all trouble gone, all tiredness and weariness gone forever, when we go to Heaven. So, "blessed are the dead which die in the Lord."

"Their works do follow them." Oh, how important it is when we come to the judgment seat of Christ that some already are going on serving the Lord whom we won to Christ.

Today in the airport a young man stopped me, told me his name and reminded me that years ago in a revival in Springfield, Missouri when I preached he was saved. Their works follow on.

And the Scripture says about those who obey His commandments and keep His covenant that "the mercy of the Lord is from everlasting to everlasting. . .and his righteousness unto children's children" (Ps. 103:17). Good works follow!

We must leave this scene shortly; what kind of works are going to follow you? Dr. Ironside makes this earnest appeal:

> If saved, what have you been doing for the Lord? If unsaved, oh, then, I beg you remember, your sins will follow after you—those sins you have been trying to forget; those sins from which you have fled; those sins for which, in your folly, you thought you could atone by effort of your own. When you stand up, at last, poor and naked and miserable, before the great white throne, you will find all your sins there, and they will fasten upon you like the hellhounds that they really are, and drag you down to the lake of fire. Do not, I beseech you, turn away from this solemn truth.

VERSES 14—20:

14 And I looked, and behold a white cloud, and upon the cloud *one* sat like unto the Son of man, having on his head a golden crown, and in his hand a sharp sickle.

15 And another angel came out of the temple, crying with a loud voice to him that sat on the cloud, Thrust in thy sickle, and reap: for the time is come for thee to reap; for the harvest of the earth is ripe.

16 And he that sat on the cloud thrust in his sickle on the earth; and the earth was reaped.

17 And another angel came out of the temple which is in heaven, he also having a sharp sickle.

18 And another angel came out from the altar, which had power over fire; and cried with a loud cry to him that had the sharp sickle, saying, Thrust in thy sharp sickle, and gather the clusters of the vine of the earth; for her grapes are fully ripe.

19 And the angel thrust in his sickle into the earth, and gathered the vine of the earth, and cast *it* into the great winepress of the wrath of God.

20 And the winepress was trodden without the city, and blood came out of the winepress, even unto the horse bridles, by the space of a thousand *and* six hundred furlongs.

Picture of Armageddon

In Revelation 19:11-20 we have a picture as on earth of Christ's coming with armies of angels to fight and destroy the Antichrist. Here we have an angel's view of the wickedness that demands judgment.

Here the battle is pictured as a reaping. In Isaiah 63:1-5 the same battle is pictured as a treading of the winepress.

"The harvest of the earth is ripe" (vs. 15). We are reminded that God told Abraham, "The iniquity of the Amorites is not yet full" (Gen. 15:16), and so they were not yet to be destroyed. Later they were to be utterly destroyed (Deut. 20:17; Josh. 3:10). Before the flood, sin so abounded that at last mercy scorned became judgment. So here in the reign of Antichrist a race of sinners must be destroyed.

Notice it is Christ Himself who will reap the harvest, who will punish sin. So it is Christ Himself who will say to the unsaved, "And then will I profess unto them, I never knew you: depart from me, ye that work iniquity" (Matt. 7:23). It is Christ Himself who will sit on the throne of His kingdom and will say, "Depart from me, ye cursed, into everlasting fire, prepared for the devil and his angels" (Matt. 25:41).

Says Dr. H. A. Ironside:

> We need to remember that the Jews brought their judgment upon their own heads by refusing the Prince of Peace when He came in grace to deliver them. In Pilate's judgment hall they cried, "His blood be on us and on our children." How dreadfully has this fearful imprecation been answered by a just God, the centuries bear witness. . . .
>
> Immanuel's land, once stained with His own precious blood, will be red with the gore of those who reject Him. . .Of old, they chose Barabbas in place of Jesus which is called Christ. Unchanged in spirit to the very end, they will prefer the "son of perdition" to the Son of God, and thus bring upon themselves swift destruction.

Chapter 15

VERSE 1:

AND I saw another sign in heaven, great and marvellous, seven angels having the seven last plagues; for in them is filled up the wrath of God.

Seven Last Plagues Announced

Says Dr. Riley: "This Book of the Apocalypse has been called the Book of the Sevens. There are seven visions, seven Spirits of God, seven candlesticks, the seven stars, seven lamps of fire, seven seals, seven horns and seven eyes of the Lamb, seven angels with seven trumpets, seven thunders, seven heads of the beast with seven crowns upon the heads, the seven plagues, seven vials, seven mountains and seven regencies." Jacob Seiss says, "All this is because the Apocalypse is the Book of the fulness of everything of which it treats!"

This chapter is preliminary: the next chapter will discuss the seven plagues. Here God is justified in the great plagues He sends on the earth. These plagues express God's judgment against sin.

"The wrath of God." Tribulation time is the time of wrath, the time of "the day of the Lord" (Isa. 13:9; 34:8), the whole matter of judgment for the death of thousands slain by the Antichrist, the wickedness of men who worship him, the judgment of the great world empires—Babylon, Media-Persia, Greece, Rome— God's law of sowing and reaping must be fulfilled. "The way of transgressors is hard." "Be sure your sin will find you out." "For they have sown the wind, and they shall reap the whirlwind."

Here also must be punished openly, publicly and officially, the wickedness of the false church (see chap. 17). Individuals have been punished and are being punished in Hell, we believe, for the Spanish Inquisition, the burning at the stake, the breaking on the rack of those who were called heretics by Rome through the

Middle and Medieval Ages. Here is the official, public answer of
God to Hitler's massacre of thousands, the oppression and killing
of Christians by communists in Russia, China, Romania,
Albania, Vietnam, etc. It is a climax of the ages in the plagues on
sin.

Remember that God's mercy restrains, rebukes, pleads, bless-
es and at last gives way to wrath. Jesus, after long, loving offers
of mercy, rebuking the Pharisees and Sadducees, at last said
that the guilt of the slaying of God's prophets, killed in all ages,
from the murder of Abel down to Christ's rejection and crucifixion would be required of that generation. In Luke 11:47-50 Jesus
says,

*"Woe unto you! for ye build the sepulchres of the prophets,
and your fathers killed them. Truly ye bear witness that ye allow
the deeds of your fathers: for they indeed killed them, and ye
build their sepulchres. Therefore also said the wisdom of God, I
will send them prophets and apostles, and some of them they
shall slay and persecute: That the blood of all the prophets,
which was shed from the foundation of the world, may be required of this generation."*

The punishment, public and national, of those who persecuted
God's prophets of all the years was shown in the utter destruction
of Jerusalem, the violent death or slavery or expulsion of all Jews
from Palestine. So here in Revelation 15 we find God's last
plagues announced, somewhat justifying God for the punishment of all the sins of the ages.

"The wrath of God." The wickedness of men is to hate and dis-
claim and deny the wrath of God. A generation that stops the
death penalty for murder, that sheds all its compassion on the
criminal instead of those killed or mugged or raped or victimized
by the criminals, does not know a God who hates sin. An age that
calls spanking children "child abuse," though the Bible plainly
commands it (Prov. 13:24; 19:18; 20:30; 22:15; 23:24), will not
agree to "the wrath of God." How many dodges, how many dishonest perversions of Scripture the left-wingers, the religious
liberals, the mushy-minded religionists make to avoid the truth

that God hates sin and must punish it! Some say the Old Testament speaks of God's wrath but the New Testament corrects it, telling of a loving, merciful Saviour who would never send sinners to Hell. No, the fact is the Lord Jesus said more about Hell and eternal punishment than any prophet before or since.

The plain teaching of all Scriptures bears out the teaching that "God is angry with the wicked every day" (Ps. 7:11), that "he that believeth not the Son shall not see life; but THE WRATH OF GOD abideth on him" (John 3:36). In the midst of God's awful punishment of Israel by the Babylonian captivity, two different godly prophets at different times prayed for God's mercy on Israel that a remnant might return. They alike admitted God's righteousness in judgment.

Nehemiah prayed, "O Lord God of heaven, the great and terrible God. . ." (Neh. 1:5).

Daniel prayed in the same spirit and awe of a righteous God's wrath who punished sin and offers mercy: "And I prayed unto the Lord my God, and made my confession, and said, O Lord, the great and dreadful God. . ." (Dan. 9:4).

Both appealed to His mercy.

God is "the great and terrible God."

He is "the great and dreadful God."

1. His curse of death on mankind for Adam's sin and His curse on all nature was terrible!

2. The plagues of Egypt were terrible in the death of multitudes.

3. The Babylonian captivity of Israel, with Jerusalem destroyed, thousands slain, women raped, many enslaved, was terrible.

4. The destruction of Jerusalem by Titus in A.D. 70, with the whole nation scattered "to all the world" and strangely hated in all nations, as Jews have been, was terrible.

5. Sending Christ-rejecting sinners to eternal torment in a lake of fire and brimstone is the most terrible fact of all human life in history. It is true but terrible.

6. That Christ was given to pay for man's sin, to suffer the torments of the damned, to have bloody sweat, a traitor's kiss, to be

scourged, have beard plucked out, a crown of thorns, be nailed to
a cross amid pitiless hate, mocked for six hours while He hung
between God and man, when the Father turned His face away to
let Jesus die like a sinner—how terrible!

Oh, but God's love is as great as His righteousness. If God
would be merciful to guilty sinners, He must let just and holy
wrath fall on our Substitute, "the Lamb of God, which taketh
away the sin of the world" (John 1:29).

We do not wonder that the whole of chapter 15 prepares us for
the seven last plagues.

VERSES 2—4:

2 And I saw as it were a sea of glass
mingled with fire: and them that had
gotten the victory over the beast, and
over his image, and over his mark,
and over the number of his name,
stand on the sea of glass, having the
harps of God.

3 And they sing the song of Moses
the servant of God, and the song of
the Lamb, saying, Great and marvellous *are* thy works, Lord God Almighty; just and true *are* thy ways,
thou King of saints.

4 Who shall not fear thee, O Lord,
and glorify thy name? for *thou* only
art holy: for all nations shall come
and worship before thee; for thy
judgments are made manifest.

For Sake of Those Who Suffered, Plagues Must Come

Among modern religionists, left-wingers, it is counted very
pious to have great sympathy for criminals and ignore their victims. So they would do away with the death penalty; they scoff
at the idea of prohibition of infamous liquor traffic; they would
blot out laws against marijuana. They insist that the homosexuals, whom God names as most vile sinners, be accepted in
society without reproach. They even want to ordain homosexuals
as ministers! They want no preaching of Hell and judgment, no
"puritanical" moral standards. They ignore all the victims of
murder and liquor and dope and extramarital sex, but God does
not. He must see that the victims of the Antichrist who stand
against his blasphemies and for God are justified and vindicated.

So here we see the rejoicing that eventually was to come to
those who "had gotten the victory over the beast" in all his

persecution. Oh, how they will praise God for His deliverance, and the eventual, eternal triumph of God and Christ over the Antichrist, over Satan and the wicked, when all nations will come to bow down to Christ at last in a millennial reign.

Ah, God must punish sin! The very ground that received the blood of murdered Abel cried out to God for vengeance (Gen. 4:10). The tears of a neglected or forsaken wife 'cover the altar' and make it so God will not regard the offering any more, says Malachi 2:13-16, by the God who "hateth putting away" or divorce of a wife. He says then, "Be sure your sin will find you out" (Num. 32:23) and "they have sown the wind, and they shall reap the whirlwind" (Hosea 8:7). "Vengeance is mine; I will repay, saith the Lord" (Rom. 12:19).

Song of Moses and the Lamb

The reference in verse 3 is, we think, to the inspired song of Moses and Israel in Exodus 15 after Pharaoh's army of chariots and horsemen had been drowned in the Red Sea, after Israel passed through on dry ground. But it is *"the song of the Lamb"* also. As Pharaoh was a type of the Antichrist; so the destruction of his army is a type of the destruction of the army of the Antichrist when his millions of soldiers (9:16) will be killed by the sword from the mouth of Christ (10:15, 21) when the blood will mount "even unto the horse bridles" (14:20).

Note the things alike about the plagues of Egypt in Exodus compared with the tribulation and its plagues.

1. Here an all-powerful ruler oppresses the Jews.

2. Pharaoh's false prophets worked miracles; so does the false prophet of the Man of Sin.

3. Plagues of water turned to blood, of hail, of earthquakes, of locusts have similarities in both cases.

4. In both cases, wicked rulers opposed God openly, blasphemously, and must be destroyed.

5. In each case, Israel is brought back to God, brought into Palestine. In the case in Exodus it ends 430 years of sojourning from Abraham to the day they came out (Exod. 12:40, 41). But when God promised deliverance to Abraham after 400 years

(Gen. 15:13), we suppose he had already sojourned away from his home in Ur of the Chaldees 30 years (Heb. 11:8, 9). In Revelation Israel will have fled into a wilderness, hiding out for protection (12:14), will be regathered (Matt. 24:31; Deut. 30:1-6; Jer. 23:3-6; Ezek. 36:24-28). And after the rebels are purged out (Ezek. 20:33-38) they will be saved (Zech. 12:10-14; 13:1; Rom. 11:26).

VERSES 5—8:

5 And after that I looked, and, behold, the temple of the tabernacle of the testimony in heaven was opened:

6 And the seven angels came out of the temple, having the seven plagues, clothed in pure and white linen, and having their breasts girded with golden girdles.

7 And one of the four beasts gave unto the seven angels seven golden vials full of the wrath of God, who liveth for ever and ever.

8 And the temple was filled with smoke from the glory of God, and from his power; and no man was able to enter into the temple, till the seven plagues of the seven angels were fulfilled.

All Heaven Approves, Awaits These Last Plagues

Seven angels are here to announce the seven last plagues. They represent all angels. Seven means all, complete, perfect, so all the angelic hosts agree with God about the punishment of sin on the earth. When Christ came to earth to die for sinners, God commanded all the angels of Heaven to worship Him (Heb. 1:6). So the Heaven was filled with "a multitude of the heavenly host" when the angel announced the birth of Christ to the shepherds (Luke 2:13). Now the seven angels are also glad to see Christ's judgment. And when Christ comes to fight the battle of Armageddon against the millions of the Antichrist and the kings of the East (19:11-16), He will be followed by 'the armies of heaven,' all the angels of God.

And the four living creatures, heavenly beings, besides the angels, joined in the announcing, in the approval. Yes, and eventually, praise God, every knee in Heaven and earth and Hell will bow to Christ and every tongue confess that He is God, Creator and Lord (Phil. 2:10,11).

We note too *"the glory of God"* (vs. 8) that filled the heavenly temple. For Christ is glorified in the due and proper punishment of sin, the vindication of His righteousness. "What if God, willing to shew his wrath, and to make his power known, endured with much longsuffering the vessels of wrath fitted to destruction: And that he might make known the riches of his glory on the vessels of mercy, which he had afore prepared unto glory" (Rom. 9:22, 23).

God, whose mercy would be glorified in the repentance and salvation of sinners, will have His righteousness glorified in their just punishment if they refuse mercy.

The seven plagues or vials or bowls of wrath are told in the next chapter. Dr. W. B. Riley outlines them as follows in *The Bible of the Expositor and the Evangelist:*

> The *first vial* caused a noisome and grievous sore upon the men which had the mark of the beast, and which worshiped his image.
>
> The *second vial* "turned the sea into clotted blood, as of dead men, and every living soul, even the things which were in the sea died."
>
> The *third vial* touched the fountain of waters, the very source from which they flowed, and changed it unto blood so that those who had taken the blood of saints and prophets had nought else now to drink than blood.
>
> The *fourth vial* affected the sun so that it scorched men with fire.
>
> The *fifth vial* brought the beast and his kingdom into darkness, so that they gnawed their tongues with pain.
>
> The *sixth vial* dried up the great river Euphrates and cut off the highway for kings.
>
> The *seventh vial* charged the air with the thunder bolts of death, and shook the earth with such an earthquake as it has never seen since man came upon it, dividing cities, submerging islands and mangling men, bringing in a condition of confusion before the terror of which nothing was heard than the blasphemy of the followers of the beast.

Now we confess that we see no way of interpreting these symbols save to receive them for what the Word says. . . .

> There was a time when Egypt was smitten with every one of these plagues, because she oppressed God's people. If we accept that record as real, why not accept this as imminent, and look for the last of it to be fulfilled. . .Why should we expect less colossal

things to characterize the end of the age? Why should we believe
that God whelmed Egypt with plagues because they had oppressed His people and shall deal less gently with Satan himself, and
his accessories, seeing that they have been oppressors from the
beginning?. . . .

Every judgment of the past has in some measure voiced God's
feeling toward sin; but the fulness of His wrath will be reserved for
the last day, and expressed in the outpouring of the seven plagues.
O men! Let me beg you not to treat sin lightly, as if it were an indifferent thing!

Chapter 16

AND I heard a great voice out of the temple saying to the seven angels, Go your ways, and pour out the vials of the wrath of God upon the earth.

2 And the first went, and poured out his vial upon the earth; and there fell a noisome and grievous sore upon the men which had the mark of the beast, and *upon* them which worshipped his image.

First Vial (Bowl) of God's Wrath

"Bowls" is better than "vials," the Greek word designating that which is broad rather than deep, more like the vessels used in the Temple below.

A *"grievous sore upon the men which had the mark of the beast."* Note, as in Egypt, the Jews were exempted from some of the plagues in Egypt. God said, "And I will put a division between my people and thy people: to morrow shall this sign be" (Exod. 8:23). So when all the rest of Egypt was plagued with swarms of flies, there were none in Goshen where the Jews lived (Exod. 8:22). Israelite cattle were exempted from the murrain of cattle (Exod. 9:6,7). And Israelites also were saved from the killing hail that fell upon the Egyptians and their cattle (Exod. 9:26).

The plagues came partly as a natural result of sin. The drinker may have sclerosis of the liver and weakened lungs besides the accidents, fights and crimes and broken homes that liquor brings. Tobacco brings lung cancer and heart trouble. Sex sin tends to lead to venereal disease, aside from the unease, the death of married happiness, the shame involved and the company of the wicked. Covetousness, unbelief and striving to be rich—all bring unrest, heart trouble, nerves, indigestion and misery. Sin brings trouble.

But aside from the natural results of sin comes the hand of God. How many of the heart attacks, the automobile wrecks, the unexplained murders, the wayward children, the broken health, the failure in business, the breakup of homes, is a direct punishment of God for sin? Even Christians who sinned about the Lord's Supper at Corinth were sick or died for it (I Cor. 11:29-32). Ananias and Sapphira were struck dead for lying to the Holy Ghost (Acts 5:1-11). Eighteen people were killed when the wall of Siloam fell on them because of sin (Luke 13:3). And the punishment by government is God's punishment (Luke 13:1, 2; Rom. 13:1-4).

VERSES 3—7:

3 And the second angel poured out his vial upon the sea; and it became as the blood of a dead *man:* and every living soul died in the sea.

4 And the third angel poured out his vial upon the rivers and fountains of waters; and they became blood.

5 And I heard the angel of the waters say, Thou art righteous, O Lord, which art, and wast, and shalt be, because thou hast judged thus.

6 For they have shed the blood of saints and prophets, and thou hast given them blood to drink; for they are worthy.

7 And I heard another out of the altar say, Even so, Lord God Almighty, true and righteous *are* thy judgments.

Second and Third Vials

The sea turned to blood! We do not know what chemical added makes the sea like blood or whether it actually is blood, like in animals and human bodies. But every living soul died in the sea. That is, literally, everything that had life. So we suppose every fish. Does it mean that even persons on shipboard would die? In Egypt the River Nile became blood for a short time. They dug wells then for water. Here the plague is greater: first, all the sea, then every river and spring, we understood, is turned to blood. And whether this is blood of plasma and corpuscles or chemical blood, it is intended to recompense the violent blood shed by wicked men. Let them drink blood for they are bloodthirsty, said the angel! A righteous God will recompense.

Innocent Naboth's blood was shed in his vineyard, seized to please King Ahab. So Ahab's blood would be licked by the same dogs at the same place and Jezebel would be eaten by dogs (I Kings 21:17-19; 22:37, 38; II Kings 9:30-37). Let every reader repeat the words of "another out of the altar" that "Even so, Lord God Almighty, true and righteous are thy judgments." We take sides with God.

VERSES 8, 9:

8 And the fourth angel poured out his vial upon the sun; and power was given unto him to scorch men with fire.

9 And men were scorched with great heat, and blasphemed the name of God, which hath power over these plagues: and they repented not to give him glory.

Fourth Vial: Sun Cursed

Unbelieving scientists think of the earth as a small planet revolving around the sun, one of millions of heavenly bodies and not more significant than many others. They think all came by accident, not by a miracle. They think that possibly other planets by evolutionary processes and without God, are peopled with beings like humans and possibly, many think, farther advanced in evolution than the human race!

Such so-called scientists are not scientifically sensible in their persistent unbelief to think of creation without a Creator, of intricate plans without a Planner, of benevolences without a personal God. How foolish, how wicked are such ideas by blinded men. Such unbelievers ignore the teaching of Scripture that God made the earth the center of His creation, made it for man, made the sun, moon and stars as corrollaries of the earth, to serve the earth.

Sure the sun is larger than the earth, some stars indescribably larger even than the sun. But one man is more important than a mountain, and an immortal soul is more important than a planet of stone and dirt and chemicals. God made the sun to give light by day and the moon to give light by night (Gen 1:14-18). Plants and animals were made for man. The proportions of land and water on the earth's surface, the depths of air above are all made for climate and living space suitable for man.

So the sun will here be cursed for man's sake for a time, to scorch men with fire. How easy for God to control the elements He made and daily sustains (Col. 1:16, 17)! And we need not be surprised, then, that after the millennium, when the planet will be purged by fire and the "first earth" as we know it has passed away, there will be a new heavens, that is, the universe of stars, suns and planets will be made over (21:1, 2). And the heavenly city that will come down from God will have no need of sun and moon, since "the glory of God did lighten it, and the Lamb is the light thereof" (21:23). So the new earth, not having its light from the sun and so having no night caused by the earth's revolution, will have no night nor need any (21:25).

Remember, sun, moon and stars are all under God's control, useful and then made a curse on sin or abandoned when God is through with them.

And in the midst of obvious punishment from God the worshipers of the Man of Sin will still blaspheme God in their pain, set forever in their rejection of Christ.

VERSES 10, 11:

10 And the fifth angel poured out his vial upon the seat of the beast; and his kingdom was full of darkness; and they gnawed their tongues for pain, 11 And blasphemed the God of heaven because of their pains and their sores, and repented not of their deeds.

Fifth Vial: Darkness on Kingdom of "the Beast"

This curse is particularly on the "kingdom" of the beast and on his seat, we think Rome, the symbolic Babylon, the center of the restored Roman Empire. This is the city of the seven hills of Revelation 17:9, "That great city, which reigneth over the kings of the earth" (17:18). Remember that when John wrote the book of Revelation, Rome actually did reign then. It will reign again over the part it once covered.

Here, as in Egypt, God makes a distinction between His own

and the people of the Antichrist.

What "sores" and "pains" are these which make people *"gnaw their tongues with pain"* and blaspheme God? Is it like the "very grievous murrain" that came on the animals of the Egyptians in Exodus 9:1-7? Or did it come like the plague of boils and blains on men and beasts in the same chapter? We are reminded of the curse God promised on Israel if they should go into idolatry and forsake His commandments:

"The Lord shall send upon thee cursing, vexation, and rebuke, in all that thou settest thine hand unto for to do, until thou be destroyed, and until thou perish quickly; because of the wickedness of thy doings, whereby thou hast forsaken me. The Lord shall make the pestilence cleave unto thee, until he have consumed thee from off the land, whither thou goest to possess it. The Lord shall smite thee with a consumption, and with a fever, and with an inflammation, and with extreme burning, and with the sword, and with blasting and with mildew; and they shall pursue thee until thou perish. And thy heaven that is over thy head shall be brass, and the earth that is under thee shall be iron. The Lord shall make the rain of thy land powder and dust: from heaven shall it come down upon thee, until thou be destroyed."—Deut. 28:20-24.

But still there is no repentance.

VERSES 12-16:

12 And the sixth angel poured out his vial upon the great river Eû-phrā́-tēŝ; and the water thereof was dried up, that the ʰway of the kings of the east might be prepared.

13 And I saw ·three unclean spirits like frogs *come* out of the mouth of the dragon, and out of the mouth of the beast, and out of the mouth of the false prophet.

14 For they are the spirits of devils, working miracles, *which* go forth unto the kings of the earth and of the whole world, to gather them to the battle of that great day of God Almighty.

15 Behold, I come as a thief. Blessed *is* he that watcheth, and keepeth his garments, lest he walk naked, and they see his shame.

16 And he gathered them together into a place called in the Hebrew tongue Ăr-mă-gĕd́-dŏn.

Sixth Vial: Kings of East With Others
Come to Armageddon

The armies of the Antichrist will assemble, numbering 200 million (Rev. 9:16). The transportation of millions of soldiers from China, India and the rest of Asia will be a problem. And God will have had four angels on guard reserved in the River Euphrates for this same purpose, "to slay the third part of men," when the army assembled (9:14, 15). They are part of God's provision for a set time and hour. Now the sixth angel will pour the vial of wrath on the river to dry it up ready for the hordes to cross and come to their doom at Armageddon.

Here evil spirits are allowed to work—to do God's will. An "evil spirit from God" made King Saul melancholy (I Sam. 18:10). God put a lying spirit in the mouth of Ahab's prophets to entice Ahab to his death (I Kings 22:19-23). God permitted Satan to try Job but always limited as God chose.

Dr. Walvoord reminds us that "the river Euphrates, here called 'the great' is one of the prominent rivers of the world and forms the eastern boundary of the ancient Roman Empire as well as the prophesied eastern boundary of the land which God promised to the seed of Abraham (Gen. 15:18; Deut. 1:7; 11:24; Josh. 1:4)."

The above references also call it "the great river, the river Euphrates." So Dr. Walvoord comments wisely, "These references seem to establish unmistakably the geographic usage in this passage."

Dr. Merrill Unger, commenting on verse 12, says:

> The drying up of the Euphrates River, 1,780 miles in length, the largest stream in western Asia, symbolizes the removal of every barrier for the advance of "the kings from the east" to Armageddon. This great river formed the eastern boundary of the Roman Empire and is stipulated as the eastern limit of enlarged Palestine (Gen. 15:18). It was a natural barrier in antiquity to invading armies from the east. No longer shall it be a barrier when the Lord gathers the hosts to Armageddon or when He gathers Israel back into the kingdom (Isa. 11:15, 16). The kings from the east are the rulers of powers east of the Euphrates.

I quote again from Dr. Unger:

> "Frogs" in verse 13 symbolize the demons who will be the spiritual dynamic behind Armageddon (I Kings 22:20-28). The dragon (Satan), the beast (the Antichrist), and the false prophet symbolize the Satanic trinity of evil, the source of "the spirits of demons," (vs. 14), i.e., demon spirits. These demons form the delusive means of persuading the nations to gather for the supreme folly of Armageddon—man's insensate fight against God and Christ's sovereignty over the earth. Armageddon, "Hill of Megiddo," is the ancient battlefield and site of several decisive battles in Israel's history (Judges 5:19; II Kings 9:27; II Chron. 35:22). It symbolizes the place of the gathering of the nations, as the valley of Jehoshaphat (Joel 3:2, 12) symbolizes the place of slaughter in the final age-end battle. This battle decides the governmental question of the sovereignty of the earth.

The *"great day of God Almighty"* (vs. 14) will be the day of battle, called the Battle of Armageddon. It is to be the great day ending the "times of the Gentiles" (Luke 21:24) and beginning "the day of the Lord," when the Lord Jesus takes over the kingdoms of the earth. Armageddon, "mount of slaughter," will be in the valley of Megiddo where a tel or mound of an ancient fortress and town are now excavated. There Solomon had stables for many horses and chariots. The valley of Megiddo or Jezreel or Esdraelon, is a lovely valley the normal route of any invading army to Israel from the north and east. The "Fertile Crescent" goes in a half moon above the Arabian desert so enemies would naturally come north by the Sea of Galilee and then southwest. Here the Crusaders fought the Arabs. In this mountainous country of Israel no other way from the north and east would be convenient for great armies but by the wide fertile valley. Hence, Solomon and other kings of Judah and Israel fortified Megiddo to defend the valley against approaching armies.

Scripture speaks here of *"the battle of that great day of God Almighty,"* but this battle, it appears, is only part of a mighty war over all of Palestine. Daniel 11:42, 43 says, about the Antichrist:

"He shall stretch forth his hand also upon the countries: and the land of Egypt shall not escape. But he shall have power over

the treasures of gold and of silver, and over all the precious things of Egypt: and the Libyans and the Ethiopians shall be at his steps."

We have already read that "he shall speak great words against the most High, and shall wear out the saints of the most High, and think to change times and laws: and they shall be given into his hand until a time and times and the dividing of time" (Dan. 7:25). So the Antichrist will surely have troops controlling Palestine. Zechariah 14:1-3 says:

"Behold, the day of the Lord cometh, and thy spoil shall be divided in the midst of thee. For I will gather all nations against Jerusalem to battle; and the city shall be taken, and the houses rifled, and the women ravished; and half of the city shall go forth into captivity, and the residue of the people shall not be cut off from the city. Then shall the Lord go forth, and fight against those nations, as when he fought in the day of battle."

Zechariah 12:2, speaking of that time, says, "Behold, I will make Jerusalem a cup of trembling unto all the people round about, when they shall be in the siege both against Judah and against Jerusalem."

Then Zechariah 12:8, 9 says:

"In that day shall the Lord defend the inhabitants of Jerusalem; and he that is feeble among them at that day shall be as David; and the house of David shall be as God, as the angel of the Lord before them. And it shall come to pass in that day, that I will seek to destroy all the nations that come against Jerusalem."

Ezekiel, chapters 38 and 39, tells of the rising of Gog, prince of Magog, who will bring great armies against Israel and evidently lined up with him "Persia, Ethiopia, and Libya with them; all of them with shield and helmet: Gomer, and all his bands; the house of Togarmah of the north quarters, and all his bands: and many people with thee" (Ezek. 38:5, 6). Dr. Scofield says, "That the primary reference is to the northern (European) powers, headed up by Russia, all agree." He continues: "Russia and the northern powers have been the latest persecutors of dispersed Israel, and it is congruous both with divine justice and with the covenants (e.g. Gen. 15:18, note; Deut. 30:3, note) that destruction should fall at the climax of the last mad attempt to exterminate the remnant of Israel in Jerusalem."

A good many expositors think that these other nations are rising against the Antichrist. But at any rate they are going to be combined against Israel and in one mad war they are all combined against Christ and His people and will be blotted out in that terrible war of which the key battle is called Armageddon.

Ezekiel 39:4 says about the tremendous armies of Gog, "Thou shalt fall upon the mountains of Israel, thou, and all thy bands, and the people that is with thee: I will give thee unto the ravenous birds of every sort, and to the beasts of the field to be devoured."

Then Ezekiel 39:12-15 says:

"And seven months shall the house of Israel be burying of them, that they may cleanse the land. Yea, all the people of the land shall bury them; and it shall be to them a renown the day that I shall be glorified, saith the Lord God. And they shall sever out men of continual employment, passing through the land to bury with the passengers those that remain upon the face of the earth, to cleanse it: after the end of seven months shall they search. And the passengers that pass through the land, when any seeth a man's bone, then shall he set up a sign by it, till the buriers have buried it in the valley of Hamongog."

Note then all the armies of the kingdoms of the world join together with the Antichrist against Christ and His heavenly armies.

Does it seem unreasonable that men should blindly assault God Himself? No more than that Satan, when an archangel in "Eden, the garden of God," should have decided to rebel against God or that the Antichrist should "claim to be God," so decided and indwelt by Satan "shewing himself that he is God" (II Thess. 2:4). No more strange, we think, than that wicked sinners should defy God and hate Him and think to prevail against His plain warnings!

This final battle will involve *"the kings of the earth and of the whole world"* (vs. 14). So the prophecies in Ezekiel about Gog and Magog must be included here, we think.

VERSES 17-21:

17 And the seventh angel poured out his vial into the air; and there came a great voice out of the temple of heaven, from the throne, saying, It is done.

18 And there were voices, and thunders, and lightnings; and there was a great earthquake, such as was not since men were upon the earth, so mighty an earthquake, *and* so great.

19 And the great city was divided into three parts, and the cities of the nations fell: and great Babylon came in remembrance before God, to give unto her the cup of the wine of the fierceness of his wrath.

20 And every island fled away, and the mountains were not found.

21 And there fell upon men a great hail out of heaven, *every stone* about the weight of a talent: and men blasphemed God because of the plague of the hail; for the plague thereof was exceeding great.

Seventh Vial

The plagues of this chapter, revealed as the seven vials of the wrath of God, are:

1. On unsaved men.

2. On the sea and all life in the sea.

3. Rivers and fountains on earth turned to blood.

4. On the sun itself, the physical source of light, making it a curse to men.

5. On the city of Rome and particularly the kingdom of the Antichrist.

6. On the River Euphrates, particularly releasing to destruction the invading armies of the kings of the East, led by evil spirits to their doom.

7. Now the curse is poured into the air. Air is everywhere. Perhaps that means, too, that every breath of all the people is cursed, that all nature around them is cursed. The curse is moral and spiritual as well as physical.

Satan is called "the prince of the power of the air" (Eph. 2:2) and, cast out of Paradise, his influence is still everywhere in the air, so we suppose this special curse is on his realm.

On verse 17 we quote from Dr. Unger: " 'It is done!' announces the completion of the wrath of God upon those who have refused the cry from the cross, 'It is finished!' God's voice from both temple and throne is heard. His judicial action symbolized by voices, thunders and lightnings, precedes the great earthquake (vs. 18). This earthquake is a physical reality, for in no other way could there result the complete overthrow of which all previous judgments have been precursors. Other prophecies foretell such an earthquake (Zech. 14:4, 5), and indicate results which only a literal cataclysm could effect."

The earthquake at this time will be the greatest ever to shake the earth. *"And the great city was divided into three parts"* (vs. 19) by this earthquake, *"and the cities of the nations fell."* All the great cities of the world? Yes, the Scriptures indicate. Such a convulsion of nature has never been known in nature. The time of the flood with tidal waves, with ocean bottoms sinking to hold the great waters, with mountains rising, with volcanoes erupting, as we now know—that convulsion at the time of the flood was next in violence to this great earthquake that will come. But the flood itself killed the people and not the earthquake and volcanic action of the time.

In this earthquake every island is misplaced, and mountains disappear. What an end to an age and what an introduction preceding the reign of Christ on earth!

Hailstones about the weight of a talent. Biederwolf says "the weight of a talent" in verse 21 is fifty-seven pounds Attic, or ninety-six pounds Hebrew; sixty times heavier than ever known before. It will be a greater plague than the hail in Egypt that killed men and beasts.

"And great Babylon came in remembrance before God, to give unto her the cup of the wine of the fierceness of his wrath."—Vs. 19.

The rebellion of men against God, which began after the flood with the building of the tower of Babel, went on to build Babylon, a world empire, then Media-Persia, Greece and Rome and now the restored Rome which has all of the marks of Babylon and earthly government to ignore God and against God: that human government is to be destroyed. We believe that this restored Roman Empire and the city of Rome are here symbolically called Babylon.

Chapter 17

AND there came one of the seven angels which had the seven vials, and talked with me, saying unto me, Come hither; I will shew unto thee the judgment of the great whore that sitteth upon many waters:

2 With whom the kings of the earth have committed fornication, and the inhabitants of the earth have been made drunk with the wine of her fornication.

3 So he carried me away in the spirit into the wilderness: and I saw a woman sit upon a scarlet coloured beast, full of names of blasphemy, having seven heads and ten horns.

4 And the woman was arrayed in purple and scarlet colour, and decked with gold and precious stones and pearls, having a golden cup in her hand full of abominations and filthiness of her fornication:

5 And upon her forehead *was* a name written, MYSTERY, BABYLON THE GREAT, THE MOTHER OF HARLOTS AND ABOMINATIONS OF THE EARTH.

6 And I saw the woman drunken with the blood of the saints, and with the blood of the martyrs of Jesus: and when I saw her, I wondered with great admiration.

7 And the angel said unto me, Wherefore didst thou marvel? I will tell thee the mystery of the woman, and of the beast that carrieth her, which hath the seven heads and ten horns.

Apostate State Church of Antichrist

Dr. Ironside calls attention to the fact that "chronologically the 19th chapter immediately follows chapter 16, and before going on with the direct order of events, John is taken aside as it were to see this remarkable vision of the false church, ere he beholds the union of the true church with the Lamb in the glory."

Now another picture, a phase of the reign of the Antichrist, not described in the chronological narrative before, narratives of the seven angels with the seven vials of the wrath of God.

Dr. Walvoord thinks the "great whore" as pictured will reign religiously in the first half of Daniel's seventieth week of years, before the Great Tribulation of the last three and a half years. That is probable though not clearly stated. Verses 16 and 17 below indicate the destruction of this false religion before the close of the tribulation time.

The *"whore"* (vs. 1) or harlot represents a false religion professing to be Christianity. When Israel in the Old Testament went into idolatry, it was called adultery. Israel was then pictured as the adulterous wife of Jehovah, untrue to Him. See examples in Jeremiah 13:27 and Ezekiel 23:43,44.

James 4:4 says: "Ye adulterers and adulteresses, know ye not that the friendship of the world is enmity with God? whosoever therefore will be a friend of the world is the enemy of God."

So here the harlot woman pictures an apostate Christianity. She *"sitteth upon many waters"* (vs. 1). Verse 15 below says, "And he saith unto me, The waters which thou sawest, where the whore sitteth, are peoples, and multitudes, and nations, and tongues."

The Antichrist also came from the sea (13:1). Daniel 7:3 shows that the great world empires before (Babylon, Media-Persia, Greece and Rome) came "out of the sea," so, out of the multitudes of people. So the world dictator and the false church all come from the mass of people and have their support. Dictators become oppressors and the enslaving of the people may become hateful to them, but at the first a Hitler, a Mussolini, a Stalin or Franklin Roosevelt in America, or multiplying Federal control have the support and come to power by the people. So will the Antichrist come and so comes this false apostate religion.

Even now millions accept the rule of the pope as infallible, as the vicegerent of God on earth, where he speaks officially. So they accept the human tradition that invalidates the Scripture. The sinful heart of mankind is easily turned to perverted religion, the substitute for the real.

"With whom the kings of the earth have committed fornication. . ." (vs. 2). Who is the harlot woman? She is a state church supported by the Antichrist and his government. The *"names of blasphemy"* (vs. 3) mean that the Antichrist is a hater of God and the harlot woman has only a form of godliness, no true love for God, no Gospel, no saving message.

". . .arrayed in purple and scarlet colour" (vs. 4). Note the colors of the robes of cardinals and popes. Note the *"precious stones and pearls"* (vs. 4) and think of the untold wealth owned

by the Roman Church. It amounts to many billions of dollars, not only in Italy but around the world.

The *"golden cup. . .full of abominations and filthiness of her fornication"* (vs. 4) must refer to the falsity of teaching a salvation by the church and by church rites. How God must hate the mass where priests claim to offer a fresh sacrifice of Christ and His blood for sins every day! "It is finished," said Jesus in John 19:30. And "there remaineth no more sacrifice for sins" (Heb. 10:26). Any dependence on anything to save sinners but the atonement of Jesus, which is already paid, is abominable to God and is spiritual fornication.

She is *"THE MOTHER OF HARLOTS"* (vs. 5), that is, the mother of false religions. She taught the Anglicans and Episcopal churches to have "priests" instead of preachers. She taught all the Pedobaptists to take babies into the church, to sprinkle them and call it baptism instead of the immersion of a believer on profession of faith, as the Bible teaches. She taught Baptists and "Church of Christ" people to boast of a chain of human organizations, a kind of "apostolic succession," to call themselves the true church and to affirm the only right to baptize and to ordain, the only authority or authorized way to get out the Gospel!

She taught them that the human organization or its pastors are the ones who must tell you where you must give your money. This harlot woman taught others that the church is synonymous with a beautiful building, that you must have reverence for that house. She taught many to rule by coercion and to punish by law.

"The Mother of Harlots and Abominations!"

"The blood of the martyrs" (vs. 6). How many millions in every Catholic country have died as martyrs! *Foxe's Book of Martyrs* is recommended reading. The Spanish Inquisition! The Saint Bartholomew's Massacre! "Bloody Mary!" The persecution by Christians in heathen lands never caused as many innocent deaths as the Catholic Church. The Orthodox Catholics have not been as worldwide and aggressive but possibly as rigidly against any independent Christian teaching and practice.

But we must say the harlot woman represents only the un-converted part of the Roman Church. Multitudes of Catholics, we believe, have trusted in Christ, have seen through the forms and ceremonies, the misleading traditions, and looked to Jesus Christ and trusted Him. We know that Jesus said, "Him that cometh to me I will in no wise cast out," so those who come even in ignorance, only with a little light, are not rejected. And the Scripture says, "Draw nigh to God, and he will draw nigh to you." So this harlot woman does not represent all the Catholic Church but only the unsaved part that will be left here at the rapture, when born-again Christians are taken to Heaven with the Saviour.

And this harlot woman surely will represent many who are nominally Protestants, nominally Christians but unconverted, great numbers of them from all religious groups who will be left here when Jesus comes for His own. Then, no doubt, the worldly trend of the present to have all unite will then make one mammoth world church. We suppose liberal, unconverted leaders (there are many such) in the World Council of Churches will then join with Catholics, as many want to do now. We suppose some Baptists, Methodists, Presbyterians, Lutherans and many others who are left behind at the rapture because they have never been converted, will be ready to join the "big church." It will be supported by the state, and will be popular.

So although the trapping and the place (the city of the seven hills, vs. 9); the connection with past murders of the saints and the spiritual adultery with the kings, all point to Rome, we may be sure this false state church will represent unsaved Christianity in name, those left from other groups besides Rome.

I quote from *Halley's Bible Handbook* here:

> The harlot woman, in alliance with the beast, called Babylon, is on a throne of world government, reigning over kings of the earth
>
> . . . .
>
> Two women—the harlot and the true bride of Christ. Two cities—Babylon and the New Jerusalem. The harlot church and the true church, thus, in antithesis, are set the one over against the other. The one seated, in power, on a throne of worldly splendor, driving the other underground by persecution. This all seems

to identify Babylon the harlot of this chapter, with the leopard-lamb-beast of chapter 13.

VERSE 8:

8 The beast that thou sawest was, and is not; and shall ascend out of the bottomless pit, and go into perdition: and they that dwell on the earth shall wonder, whose names were not written in the book of life from the foundation of the world, when they behold the beast that was, and is not, and yet is.

"The Beast That Was, and Is Not, and Yet Is"

Note here these facts about the Antichrist:

1. He *"was."* The Roman Empire was the fourth world empire ruling in John's time.

2. It, for a time, *"is not."* At this moment there is no Roman Empire, no emperor of Rome.

3. Yet it *"shall ascend out of the bottomless pit."* He shall be Satan incarnate. He will be "the son of perdition" (II Thess. 2:3).

4. One of the heads or thrones of this Roman Empire was "wounded to death." The empire died. But at tribulation time John saw the "deadly wound was healed," and so it will happen, the dictatorship will be restored.

5. The whole world will wonder after this beast who restores the Roman Empire, claims to be God, whose false prophet works miracles, who has an image come to life to be worshiped. All will wonder and will be impressed, will worship him, all except those whose names are "in the book of life."

VERSE 9:

9 And here *is* the mind which hath wisdom. The seven heads are seven mountains, on which the woman sitteth.

City of Seven Hills, Rome

The Greek term here translated mountains is very general and could mean small hills, as I think it does here, though through the centuries Rome has been famous as situated on seven hills: Palatine, Aventine, Caelian, Esquiline, Viminal, Quirinal, and Capitoline.

This seems clearly to place the state church at Rome, a continuation of the Catholic Church becoming a state church supported by the government of the Antichrist, as Catholicism was once in many countries, is now supported in some.

VERSES 10—14:

10 And there are seven kings: five are fallen, and one is, *and* the other is not yet come; and when he cometh, he must continue a short space.

11 And the beast that was, and is not, even he is the eighth, and is of the seven, and goeth into perdition.

12 And the ten horns which thou sawest are ten kings, which have received no kingdom as yet; but receive power as kings one hour with the beast.

13 These have one mind, and shall give their power and strength unto the beast.

14 These shall make war with the Lamb, and the Lamb shall overcome them: for he is Lord of lords, and King of kings: and they that are with him *are* called, and chosen, and faithful.

Kings Who Follow and Serve With Antichrist

The beast, the dictator, a man of sin, Antichrist, is pictured by a beast with seven heads and ten horns. The ten horns picture the ten nations that formed the Roman Empire and were left when the emperorship was dissolved. See Daniel 7:24 which says, "And the ten horns out of this kingdom are ten kings that shall arise: and another shall rise after them; and he shall be diverse from the first, and he shall subdue three kings."

They are pictured also by the ten toes of the great image of Nebuchadnezzar's dream in Daniel 2. The little horn is the rise of the Antichrist. He will pluck up or conquer three horns, that is, three kingdoms or nations that once formed the Roman Empire. Now the seven nations left of the old Roman Empire join with the Antichrist and "give their power and strength unto the beast" (vs. 13). That makes eight, with the seven and the Antichrist, the beast, ruling the others. These united kings under dominance of the world dictator Antichrist made "war with the

Lamb" (vs. 14). They will come to the Battle of Armageddon to oppose Christ in the most insane folly and, of course, will be destroyed.

VERSE 15—18:

15 And he saith unto me, The waters which thou sawest, where the whore sitteth, are peoples, and multitudes, and nations, and tongues.

16 And the ten horns which thou sawest upon the beast, these shall hate the whore, and shall make her desolate and naked, and shall eat her flesh, and burn her with fire.

17 For God hath put in their hearts to fulfil his will, and to agree, and give their kingdom unto the beast, until the words of God shall be fulfilled.

18 And the woman which thou sawest is that great city, which reigneth over the kings of the earth.

Great Harlot to Be Destroyed

The woman came from the world's people, like the beast and like the four world empires before it, Babylon, Media-Persia and Greece and the old Rome. Do you not see that the Tower of Babel was built in rebellion against God? The world empires carry on this determination for a human government without God, a religion without Christ as virgin-born Son of God.

Nebuchadnezzar had a great image in the plain of Dura, demanding that all worship it. Belshazzar and his lords and concubines worshiped and praised gods of gold and silver and stone, bringing vessels that were taken from the Temple of God at Jerusalem for their wine (Dan. 5). Darius the Median passed the decree making it a capital crime to pray to any god for thirty days but to himself (Dan. 6).

Rome, as head of the "Holy Roman Empire" had assumed a religious dictatorship, too. Here the element of Babylon's self-will, rule and religion without God appears in the Antichrist, at first with the apostate church of liberal unbelievers, then with the worship of the Antichrist himself and his image.

On verses 16 to 18, Dr. Ironside says:

> There is no mistaking her identity. Pagan Rome was the lineal successor of Babylon.

Papal Rome absorbed the Babylonian mysteries; and the Rome of the Beast in the last days will be the seat of the revived satanic system that began with Nimrod and his infamous consort Semiramis, which has from that day to this been opposed to everything that is of God; and which changed the truth of God into a lie, worshiping and serving the creature more than the Creator.

Babylon of old, as we have seen, was the mother of idolatry. In Jeremiah 50:38 we read, "It is the land of graven images; they are mad upon their idols." It was she who taught the nations to substitute idolatry for spiritual worship, and today one third of Christendom has followed her in the adoration of images, and another third worships ikons, or pictures. There can be no question as to the Babylonish origin of these abominations. Nothing of the kind was known in the churches of God until the heathen mysteries were grafted unto Christianity. The images of the mother and child that are enshrined in Rome's temples are only different in name to the images worshiped in the groves and temples of Semiramis, Ashtoreth, Isis, and other so-called "queens of heaven." In many instances the old idols were simply renamed and adored as before. There is in one place in southern Europe a statue of Apollo, the sun-god, identical with Tammuz and Baal, which is worshiped by deluded Romanists as St. Apollos; and the S is carved upon the pedestal by a later hand than the original name!

Do you see why the harlot woman is an integral part of the heritage of Babylon, religious confusion? She is "Babylon the great" religiously, and the city politically in the kingdom of the Antichrist or Babylon politically, as discussed in the next chapter.

The *"ten horns"* (vs. 16), the rulers who have given their power to the beast, are nominally kings while he has actual dictatorial powers with their consent. They hate the apostate state church. They seize the property and kill the power of this great heirarchy, the harlot woman. This must be about the beginning of the three and one half years of the Great Tribulation. At first the beast allowed Jews to have a Temple, a priesthood and sacrifices. Then in the midst of the seven years he breaks that treaty, comes into the Temple, commits the abomination of desolation, claims to be God on earth and demands to be worshiped. So, during this same time when Jews are allowed to worship, we think the harlot woman, a state church, will be supported by and backing the Antichrist. But when he claims to be God and demands death for all who will not worship him and his image, then these sub-kings will want to destroy the pseudo-Christian harlotry to stop all religion but the worship of the beast. So we agree with Dr. Walvoord that the harlot state church will probably prosper only in the first three and one half years of Daniel's seventieth week when the Antichrist allows Jews and others some freedom of worship.

"The woman. . .is that great city, which reigneth over the kings of the earth" (vs. 18). So as the emperor will rule politically, a kind of Vatican City within the Empire of Rome will rule religiously until she is destroyed and the man of sin shall claim to be and be supported as the only god to be worshiped.

Chapter 18

VERSES 1—3:

AND after these things I saw another angel come down from heaven, having great power; and the earth was lightened with his glory.

2 And he cried mightily with a strong voice, saying, ·Babylon the great is fallen, is fallen, and is become the habitation of devils, and the hold of every foul spirit, and a cage of every unclean and hateful bird.

3 For all nations have drunk of the wine of the wrath of her fornication, and the kings of the earth have committed fornication with her, and the merchants of the earth are waxed rich through the abundance of her delicacies.

The City, Spiritual Babylon, Falls

There are some things similar between "the great whore" who is called "Babylon the great" in 17:3, and *"Babylon the great"* here in 18:2. But they are not the same. The "judgment of the great whore" was announced by "one of the seven angels" (17:1). This judgment is announced by *"another angel,"* not the same, nor is the time the same. The great whore will be hated by kings who "shall make her desolate and naked, and shall eat her flesh, and burn her with fire" at about the beginning of the Great Tribulation proper, that is, we understand, when these kings determine to see that all worship goes to the Antichrist. That is a spiritual rebellion, a putting down of this false apostate Christianity.

But now in this chapter 18 we see, three and a half years later, the fall, the desolation of a city, "the seat of the beast," the "great city divided into three parts" as we read in Revelation 16:19. This is Babylon the wicked city: the great whore was Babylon spiritually.

This great city of Rome, spiritually called Babylon, will have *"become the habitation of devils, and the hold of every foul spirit, and a cage of every unclean and hateful bird"* (vs. 2), yes, and again like with the great whore *"the kings of the earth have committed fornication with her"* (vs. 3). That is spiritual fornication. A false religion. For the worship of the Antichrist and his image will have superceded the worship of the state church, the apostate harlot religion!

In the first half of the seven years we understand the false religion of this false church will corrupt men, and kings will sell out to that. But after "the great whore" is destroyed, three and one half years gone when Rome will be the seat of the vilest idolatry, worship of the beast and his image, and to gain favor and please the Antichrist, kings will join the idolatry.

Notice the intimation of the growth of idolatry through the whole earth, but centered, with more demons, more wicked manifestations, in Rome itself. Why not—with a false prophet with power to make an image of the Antichrist to live and to talk? Why not—with his power to work miracles and bring down fire from Heaven? It is centered now at that city as you see in Revelation 13:11-15.

"Another parable put he forth unto them, saying, The kingdom of heaven is like to a grain of mustard seed, which a man took, and sowed in his field: Which indeed is the least of all seeds: but when it is grown, it is the greatest among herbs, and becometh a tree, so that the birds of the air come and lodge in the branches thereof."

The Gospel work starts out sowing seed, preaching the Gospel. Satan and our fleshly, sinful natures change the work of churches and Christians and preachers to growing trees! The tree is the symbol of an organized institution and primarily of a kingdom. See Nebuchadnezzar's tree (Dan. 4) and Christ as a Branch or Sprout of the kingly tree of David (Isa. 11:1) and Israel as an olive tree (Rom. 11:6-21). So the decay, the backsliding from soul winning to building denominations and institutions. And the end of that declension is papal Rome, then the religion of the Antichrist.

As the Christian work grows into a tree, "the birds of the air come and lodge in the branches thereof," Jesus said. The emphasis changes from soul winning to a scholarship, from fidelity to the Word of God to a humanistic philosophy, and from the next world to this world. So liberals, unbelievers, take refuge in the denominations, infidels teach in their colleges and seminaries. Unbelieving bishops get the honor and support there. And, as here, the trees become "the habitation of devils, and the hold of every foul spirit, and a cage of every unclean and hateful bird." So the tendency is always, as denominations grow and get popular and strong and build many institutions, to let modernism come in and take over. So that ends in the papal Rome now and eventually in the religion of the Antichrist.

VERSE 4:

4 And I heard another voice from heaven, saying, Come out of her, my people, that ye be not partakers of her sins, and that ye receive not of her plagues.

"Come Out of Her, My People"

These chapters say so much about the Antichrist, the false prophet, the adulterous state church, that we may forget that God will have a great multitude of saints on earth at this time, all saved since His coming into the air to receive His own when the Christian living will be changed and the Christian dead will be raised.

Dr. Ironside says:

The call of verse 4 is. . .not merely a warning to saints in a coming day who may be in danger of being deceived by her, but it is a message for all who even now discern her true character: *"I heard another voice from heaven, saying, Come out of her, my people, that ye be not partakers of her sins, and that ye receive not of her plagues."* Separation from evil is imperative for all who would have the Lord's approval. This was the call heard by the reformers of the 16th century. But, alas, alas, many who are supposed to be their successors have returned in spirit to that which their fathers left behind, and there is many a Babylonish garment today hidden in Protestant tents, or even displayed upon Protestant shoulders. . . ."

There will have been some time between the rapture of saints and the beginning of Daniel's seventieth week of Jewish history as a nation with temple, priest and sacrifices. Time must be allowed for Antichrist to appear, to seize power enough and authority in Palestine so he can guarantee Jews a seven-year treaty to have a temple, priests and sacrifices.

It may be in that interval between the rapture and the seven-year treaty that in Israel there will come about a majority and power of devoted Jews seeking God who will want to have the temple, sacrifice, priesthood and ceremonial law restored. At this writing only a minority in Israel so desire it. The mass of people in Israel today are Jews nationally, not religiously. They are not only unsaved but are often infidels, sometimes communists. We find Jews in Israel much harder to win than the Arabs we see in every trip to the Middle East.

So there will be an interval between the rapture and the state of affairs in the beginning of Daniel's seventieth week as pictured in the Bible. And since the coming of Christ for His own is imminent, that is always possible, and since there can be no way to tell ahead of time, then these events in Israel and with the Man of Sin cannot occur until after the rapture. No events can come that show the approach of Christ's immediate return.

There will be a multitude saved in the tribulation time. Revelation 7:9 says, "After this I beheld, and, lo, a great multitude, which no man could number, of all nations, and kindreds, and people, and tongues, stood before the throne, and before the Lamb, clothed with white robes, and palms in their hands." Then verse 14 following says, "These are they which came out of great tribulation, and have washed their robes, and made them white in the blood of the Lamb."

There will be great persecutions and many will be put to death (see 6:9-11 again). But the Gospel will be preached with power by the 144,000 of Israel, by a flying angel who will preach the Gospel (14:6) and the testimony of amazing revivals led by the two witnesses (11:3-12). But such an amazing number of converts in the midst of such persecution pictures a powerful movement like that in Acts 8:4 when Christians "went every where preaching the word." Yes, they had such persecution in the book of Acts, too, but multitudes were saved. So it will be in the tribulation time.

So with his rule of no buying and selling without the mark of the beast and his effort to compel all to worship him and his image, the government of the Antichrist will no more be able to stop the Gospel than the chief priests, the Pharisees and King Herod were in the time of the apostles!

Christians imprisoned will be visited by Christians who help them. Christians who are hungry because they cannot buy or sell will be fed by other Christians, as Jesus will remind them later (Matt. 25:11-40). Hated, persecuted, imprisoned, Christians will yet multiply rapidly until there will be a multitude no man can number of all nations and tribes.

So before the utter destruction of the city of Rome, God's people are commanded, *"Come out of her, my people, that ye be not partakers of her sins, and that ye receive not of her plagues"* (vs. 4).

Here is a principle often taught in the Scripture. Israel was to come out of Egypt. Then going into the land occupied by heathen races they were commanded:

"Neither shalt thou make marriages with them; thy daughter thou shalt not give unto his son, nor his daughter shalt thou take unto thy son. For they will turn away thy son from following me, that they may serve other gods: so will the anger of the Lord be kindled against you, and destroy thee suddenly."— Deut. 7:3, 4.

It is clearly commanded that Christians are to come out of situations that involve giving Christian fellowship or Christian standing to the wicked, the unconverted.

Psalm 1:1 says, "Blessed is the man that walketh not in the counsel of the ungodly, nor standeth in the way of sinners, nor sitteth in the seat of the scornful." And Ephesians 5:11 commands us, "And have no fellowship with the unfruitful works of darkness, but rather reprove them." See also II Corinthians 6:14-18:

"Be ye not unequally yoked together with unbelievers: for

what fellowship hath righteousness with unrighteousness? and what communion hath light with darkness? And what concord hath Christ with Belial? or what part hath he that believeth with an infidel? And what agreement hath the temple of God with idols? for ye are the temple of the living God; as God hath said, I will dwell in them, and walk in them; and I will be their God, and they shall be my people. Wherefore come out from among them, and be ye separate, saith the Lord, and touch not the unclean thing; and I will receive you, And will be a Father unto you, and ye shall be my sons and daughters, saith the Lord Almighty."

Second John, verses 9 to 11, says:

"Whosoever transgresseth, and abideth not in the doctrine of Christ, hath not God. He that abideth in the doctrine of Christ, he hath both the Father and the Son. If there come any unto you, and bring not this doctrine, receive him not into your house, neither bid him God speed: For he that biddeth him God speed is partaker of his evil deeds."

It is clear that we are not to receive into our houses, into our churches, into our Christian colleges or seminaries, or into any Christian fellowship, those who abide not in the Bible doctrine about Jesus Christ. To do so is to be a partaker of the evil deeds. So the command of the Lord to these in the city of Rome when it is about to be destroyed is a command for us today also to leave the fellowship of the unsaved.

Among the millions of population who will then live in Rome, the capital city of the world at the close of the tribulation time, will be many saved people. They are commanded to come out. First, "be not partakers of her sins" (vs. 4). Sometimes for a person to remain in the presence of outright sin means a mild acceptance of it or neutrality toward it. It was so with Peter sitting for an hour or two or more by the fire of the soldiers who would crucify the Lord Jesus. It was so for Solomon to take the heathen wives.

Second, they should come out that they "receive not of her plagues" (vs. 4). So today those who remain in a secret order where it is taught that good works will guarantee entrance to "Elysian Fields" and acceptance by "the Grand Architect of the universe," are accounted as approving that false gospel, though they be ever so active in a Bible-believing church on Sunday. One who stays in a denominational system where his gifts support its infidel leaders in seminary, college and literature, is "partaker of his evil deeds" and must suffer for it.

One of the most devout, soul-winning, Bible-believing preachers I know stayed in a denomination controlled by liberal unbelievers. His children stayed in also. He is now in Heaven but his children who stayed in that environment are openly unbelievers, and one is an alcoholic. To stay in with unbelievers means to take the suffering that comes to unbelievers.

The principle now and in the tribulation time is the same. Christians should "come out of her, my people," come out from fellowship with wicked unbelief.

The city of Rome is about to fall. Christians must flee. But today many are in the same spiritual problem and should flee the influence and the curse of unbelief and wickedness.

VERSES 5—8:

5 For her sins have reached unto heaven, and God hath remembered her iniquities.

6 Reward her even as she rewarded you, and double unto her double according to her works: in the cup which she hath filled fill to her double.

7 How much she hath glorified herself, and lived deliciously, so much torment and sorrow give her: for she saith in her heart, I sit a queen, and am no widow, and shall see no sorrow.

8 Therefore shall her plagues come in one day, death, and mourning, and famine; and she shall be utterly burned with fire: for strong *is* the Lord God who judgeth her.

Rome Reaps as She Sowed

This prophesied Babylon of iniquity, seat of the Antichrist, center of the world empire, must now reap what she sowed, *"For her sins have reached unto heaven, and God hath remembered her iniquities"* (vs. 5).

Sin must have a reaping. "Be not deceived; God is not

mocked: for whatsoever a man soweth, that shall he also reap. For he that soweth to his flesh shall of the flesh reap corruption . . ." (Gal. 6:7, 8). Nobody gets by with sin. "The wages of sin is death."

Karl Marx tried to negate this truth. The motto of communism is that every man is to work as he is able, and every person is to receive according to his needs, whether he earns it or not. But it does not work out even in economics. No man works the same for an intangible government and for a dictator, who holds a gun over him, as one works for his own profit. The free enterprise system is right. It is based on essential principles that God Himself has put into mankind and human dealings.

The man whose pound gained ten pounds is to rule over ten cities, Jesus said. The man whose pound won five pounds is to rule over five cities (Luke 19:1-25). In giving, "He which soweth sparingly shall reap also sparingly; and he which soweth bountifully shall reap also bountifully" (II Cor. 9:6).

It is so in other matters. God told the men of the two and one half tribes who wanted to stay on the west side of Jordan that they must go ahead with their companions to fight the battles of Palestine, and He said, "But if ye will not do so, behold, ye have sinned against the Lord: and be sure your sin will find you out" (Num. 32:23). Oh, sin has a way of coming out! Sins come up to face God! God remembers iniquity.

Not only is judgment for sins inevitable but it is accelerated and multiplied judgment. *"Reward her even as she rewarded you, and double unto her double according to her works: in the cup which she hath filled fill to her double"* (vs. 6). Oh, yes, if she measured sin in a cup, measure her punishment in two cups.

"They have sown the wind, and they shall reap the whirlwind" (Hos. 8:7). David committed adultery and murder, but he must restore fourfold. His baby died. His beautiful daughter Tamar was raped. His son Amnon was murdered. Absalom then rebelled and would have killed his father the king, and died himself with many others. Oh, sin doesn't end easily!

God has this principle in Christian rewards, too. "He that soweth to the Spirit shall of the Spirit reap life everlasting," says

Galatians 6:8. One who gives will find when he is repaid it will be "good measure, pressed down, and shaken together, and running over, shall men give into your bosom" (Luke 6:38). So sin must pay back double and more.

A strong young man walked briskly down a sidewalk in a western town. By the walk sat a gray-headed man in a wheelchair. He stopped the young man and asked, "Can you solve a mathematic equation for me?"

The young man smiled and replied, "I will try. What is it?"

The old man said, "On one side of the equation is fifteen minutes' pleasure with a little Spanish girl on the Mexican border. On the other side of the equation is fifteen years in a wheelchair. Is it equal?"

"My God, no!" said the startled young man.

"Then be sure your sin will find you out," the victim of syphilis answered.

Her sins reached unto Heaven and God remembered her iniquities. Someone whispers, "Come on! Nobody will ever know!" But God knows and He will remember and bring every sin to judgment. God will open record books, people will be judged out of those books.

Sudden destruction after long warning will be the case here. It came to Sodom and Gomorrah. It came to Jersualem, destroyed by Titus in A. D. 70. So it will come to the city and kingdom of the Antichrist.

VERSES 9, 10:

9 And the kings of the earth, who have committed fornication and lived deliciously with her, shall bewail her, and lament for her, when they shall see the smoke of her burning,

10 Standing afar off for the fear of her torment, saying, Alas, alas that great city Babylon, that mighty city! for in one hour is thy judgment come.

Kings Lament Loss of All

How will the kings "have committed fornication" with this spiritual Babylon? They will have supported its Antichrist, his claim to be God, his idolatry, his murders, his obvious demon-possession!

What loyalty had they betrayed; what sacred vows and trusts have they violated to be called spiritually fornicators?

Do you think they will really have thought that the beast is the God he claims to be? Do they help him and give him all their powers as a matter of noble conviction? I do not think so. They will have sold their convictions to keep their position, their wealth and honor!

When men do wickedly, they are not blameless. They would know that they who had authority over people are those who must give account. When he first takes office, nearly every king, nearly every president, makes solemn vows to deal justly, and to serve his people well. And though such men often prove unfaithful, compromise holy convictions and sell the rights of the people, they probably in the high hour of accession of office mean to do well.

Remember Solomon's accession to the throne, his prayer, his intent to rule well his people. He did not then plan the idolatry, the insupportable burden of taxation that would spoil his son, split Israel and turn the face of God away in anger.

So these kings, then, will have been untrue to vows, to convictions, to oaths of office for power with the Antichrist. They will have endorsed his demonic course. They will have *"lived deliciously"* with this Babylon for a time and will now see the smoke of her destruction and torment in one hour and their own fall and eternal ruin!

VERSES 11—19:

11 And the merchants of the earth shall weep and mourn over her; for no man buyeth their merchandise any more:

12 The merchandise of gold, and silver, and precious stones, and of pearls, and fine linen, and purple, and silk, and scarlet, and all thyine wood, and all manner vessels of ivory, and all manner vessels of most precious wood, and of brass, and iron, and marble,

13 And cinnamon, and odours, and ointments, and frankincense, and wine, and oil, and fine flour, and wheat, and beasts, and sheep, and

horses, and chariots, and slaves, and souls of men.

14 And the fruits that thy soul lusted after are departed from thee, and all things which were dainty and goodly are departed from thee, and thou shalt find them no more at all.

15 The merchants of these things, which were made rich by her, shall stand afar off for the fear of her torment, weeping and wailing,

16 And saying, Alas, alas that great city, that was clothed in fine linen, and purple, and scarlet, and decked with gold, and precious stones, and pearls!

17 For in one hour so great riches is come to nought. And every shipmaster, and all the company in ships, and sailors, and as many as trade by sea, stood afar off,

18 And cried when they saw the smoke of her burning, saying, What *city is* like unto this great city!

19 And they cast dust on their heads, and cried, weeping and wailing, saying, Alas, alas that great city, wherein were made rich all that had ships in the sea by reason of her costliness! for in one hour is she made desolate.

Wail of Merchants Over Burning Babylon

If New York, London or Tokyo should suddenly be destroyed by earthquakes and burned to the ground, and if all the other cities that trade with them were suddenly destroyed, what a disruption of trade and commerce, what a loss of billions, what a destruction of livelihood and hope for millions of people!

What will happen to the commercial Babylon will be worse than bombed-out Berlin that destroyed Germany when Berlin surrendered and the European part of World War II closed. Who can imagine the utter panic Japan saw when the unimaginable ruin of the American atomic bomb was realized!

Hitler's reign was made possible by the gun makers, the airplane builders, the industrialists, the businessmen who profited under his favor. So in the wicked, prophetic Babylon, the Antichrist will have been kept in power by the greed of those who profit by the world trade, the affluence of a world capital. Now these merchants will weep and lament.

Note the wealth of the trade in verses 12 and 13. Merchants will not only have bought and sold the riches of world commerce, the chariots of war and horses, but also *"slaves, and souls of men"* (vs. 13). And those who will disregard even the souls of men to make their profit will come to judgment. God may well say to them as to the rich man in Luke, chapter 12, who laid up wealth with no thought of God or death or judgment, "Thou fool, this night thy soul shall be required of thee: then whose shall those things be, which thou hast provided?"

But the awful suddenness with which the end will come to this capital city and all the kingdom of the Antichrist is in one hour!

VERSES 20—24:

20 Rejoice over her, *thou* heaven, and *ye* holy apostles and prophets; for God hath avenged you on her.

21 And a mighty angel took up a stone like a great millstone, and cast *it* into the sea, saying, Thus with violence shall that great city Babylon be thrown down, and shall be found no more at all.

22 And the voice of harpers, and musicians, and of pipers, and trumpeters, shall be heard no more at all in thee; and no craftsman, of whatsoever craft *he be*, shall be found any more in thee; and the sound of a millstone shall be heard no more at all in thee;

23 And the light of a candle shall shine no more at all in thee; and the voice of the bridegroom and of the bride shall be heard no more at all in thee: for thy merchants were the great men of the earth; for by thy sorceries were all nations deceived.

24 And in her was found the blood of prophets, and of saints, and of all that were slain upon the earth.

God's People in Heaven and Earth Rejoice at Fall of This Babylon

"Rejoice over her, thou heaven" (vs. 20). Jesus said, "I say unto you, that likewise joy shall be in heaven over one sinner that repenteth, more than over ninety and nine just persons, which need no repentance" (Luke 15:7). Then again He said, "Likewise, I say unto you, there is joy in the presence of the angels of God over one sinner that repenteth" (Luke 15:10). In Heaven they rejoice over souls saved; but here they are to rejoice when sin is avenged and when the wicked are put down.

In Revelation 6:9-11 we read of the great concern of saints in Heaven after dying as martyrs:

"And when he had opened the fifth seal, I saw under the altar the souls of them that were slain for the word of God, and for the testimony which they held: And they cried with a loud voice, saying, How long, O Lord, holy and true, dost thou not judge and avenge our blood on them that dwell on the earth? And white robes were given unto every one of them; and it was

said unto them; that they should rest yet for a little season until their fellowservants also and their brethren, that should be killed as they were, should be fulfilled."

Now they will rejoice that their patience is rewarded, that their death is avenged!

Angels in Heaven must rejoice also with those who rejoice "in the presence of the angels." How their gladness peals out in that beautiful chant at the birth of Christ when the sky was filled with them! Angels are the guides and the servants, the protectors of Christians (Heb. 1:14; Matt. 18:10; Ps. 37:7; 91:11, 12). Will they not rejoice when those they love and serve rejoice? Holy beings as they are, will they not rejoice that sin is punished and God is vindicated?

So angels, with the apostles and prophets of all ages, will rejoice that sin is put down and in the destruction of that great city of sin, the spiritual Babylon of the tribulation time.

So the troubled saints on earth, at the approach of triumph and deliverance in those days, are to rejoice also. They may well rejoice as the psalmist did.

"The Lord is my light and my salvation; whom shall I fear? the Lord is the strength of my life; of whom shall I be afraid? When the wicked, even mine enemies and my foes, came upon me to eat up my flesh, they stumbled and fell. Though an host should encamp against me, my heart shall not fear: though war should rise against me, in this will I be confident."—Ps. 27:1-3.

Now in that great city there are no musicians, no night-club singers performing, no concerts playing, no housewives humming about the house, no men whistling at work. No wheels are turning in factories, no mills are making flour, no candles or other lights shine; now only the smoke ascending and the utter torment and destruction of the city. There are no weddings, no rejoicing; now only groans of torment, words of anguish, tears of loss and shame!

Babylon has had her sorceries, her wickedness, her flaunting of sin and the work of devils. No more! By satanic miracles and lies, wicked people have been willingly deceived. Now judgment is come.

Now, as if never before realized, we are told, *"And in her was found the blood of prophets, and of saints, and of all that were slain upon the earth"* (vs. 24).

As the sins against all the prophets and witnesses from Abel to Christ were required of the men of Christ's day (Luke 11:47-50), now here the piled up sins of the ages come to judgment, centered in the world powers that have fostered sin.

Now skeletons, hidden for centuries, come out of closets. Now Achan's stolen treasures, hidden in his tent, are exposed. God's books are open. Sin comes to judgment.

Chapter 19

AND after these things I heard a great voice of much people in heaven, saying, Alleluia; Salvation, and glory, and honour, and power, unto the Lord our God:

2 For true and righteous *are* his judgments: for he hath judged the great whore, which did corrupt the earth with her fornication, and hath avenged the blood of his servants at her hand.

3 And again they said, Alleluia. And her smoke rose up for ever and ever.

4 And the four and twenty elders and the four beasts fell down and worshipped God that sat on the throne, saying, Amen; Alleluia.

5 And a voice came out of the throne, saying, Praise our God, all ye his servants, and ye that fear him, both small and great.

6 And I heard as it were the voice of a great multitude, and as the voice of many waters, and as the voice of mighty thunderings, saying, Alleluia: for the Lord God omnipotent reigneth.

Alleluias of Saints and Angels Over God's Vengeance

Here are four "Alleluias." We read, *"I heard a great voice of much people in heaven"* (vs. 1). This is a response to the instruction in chapter 18, verse 20, when they were commanded, "Rejoice over her, thou heaven, and ye holy apostles and prophets; for God hath avenged you on her." Apostles, prophets and all in Heaven, whose oppression by spiritual Babylon deserved this vengeance, now rejoice.

We suppose that apostles and prophets of the past rejoice in this summing up of judgment on the world system that persecuted them. For all these years "the mystery of iniquity doth already work: only he who now letteth will let, until he be taken out of the way" (II Thess. 2:7). At last all the injustices, all the oppressions, all the violence and murders against the people of God and against the innocent, are to be brought to public, official judgment in the destruction of the spiritual Babylon.

Delayed Punishment for Sin

There are good reasons why sin is not always punished immediately. The Scripture says about alcoholic liquor, "At the last it biteth like a serpent, and stingeth like an adder" (Prov. 23:32). At the last, not at the first. At first wine seems to bring gaiety, fellowship. At the first it is not the sclerosis of the liver, the enslaving habit, the broken home, the accident, the poverty, the drunkard's grave. That comes later.

The Scripture says about the harlot and her companion, "Her end is bitter as wormwood, sharp as a twoedged sword. Her feet go down to death; her steps take hold on hell" (Prov. 5:4, 5). Not the beginning, but the end. Lust, excitement, pleasure at first, but disease, guilt and Hell at the end.

And of the God-fearing, good man Psalm 37:37 says, ". . .the end of that man is peace." Not always freedom from strife, but the end will turn out good for the godly man.

In Psalm 73 the inspired writer tells how at first he complained about the temporary prosperity of the wicked. But then by the Spirit of God he tells us, "Until I went into the sanctuary of God; then understood I their end. Surely thou didst set them in slippery places: thou castedst them down into destruction" (Ps. 73:17, 18). So is the end of the wicked.

Why is a reward for virtue and punishment for sin delayed? Why not immediately?

For one thing, God wants the natural result of good work, the natural result of sin to appear in due course. The law of sowing and reaping is built into nature. The faithful work of the farmer—plowing, planting, weeding—is rewarded only at the harvest. It is a part of righteousness to believe that it pays to do good, to believe that "in due season we shall reap, if we faint not" (Gal. 6:9). One should do right because he knows a holy God will do justly to reward or punish, to pay for the things we cannot see at once but expect because God's mercies fail not.

God's longsuffering mercy is a good reason for delay in punishment of sin. "The Lord is merciful and gracious, slow to anger, and plenteous in mercy. He will not always chide: neither will he keep his anger for ever. He hath not dealt with us after our sins; nor rewarded us according to our iniquities" (Ps. 103:8-10).

I am so glad God allows time for repentance and patiently waits so we may turn before judgment comes. We should learn, when sin seems to go unpunished so long, to "rest yet for a little season," as the souls of martyrs were ordered to do in Revelation 6:9-11.

God is honored. Here *"salvation, and glory, and honour, and power"* are ascribed to God in praises (vs. 1). That is, He is praised in salvation or deliverance of His own. Remember God's honor is at stake. He must punish sin. He must see that His own are protected and avenged when they are wronged and oppressed.

The wickedness, the worldwide spiritual fornication *"which did corrupt the earth"* (vs. 2), is of tremendous earth-shaking importance to God. The oppression will have reached and, even in our day, have wronged and deceived and persecuted millions of people.

The offence of Heaven is so monstrous that God emphasized again the rejoicing that justice is done and the *"great whore"* (vs. 2) and her city are judged and laid waste. Rejoice, then, all the redeemed in Heaven and all the apostles and prophets over God's righteousness in this!

"Alleluia." Shout it up and down the streets of gold and along the river of life in the Paradise of God. Again they said it, the great voice of many people in Heaven, "Alleluia."

"And her smoke rose up for ever and ever" (vs. 3). Surely, the, the burning of the city on seven hills, divided and fallen in a mighty earthquake, is continued in Hell. God puts this divine, supernatural destruction of this spiritual Babylon along with the fires of Hell. The destruction of the city physically will be accompanied by the torments of the damned and that burning is simply carried over into a literal burning Hell "where their worm dieth not, and the fire is not quenched" (Mark 9:44, 46, 48), where "the smoke of their torment ascendeth up for ever and ever" (14:11).

The destruction of the seat of the beast, then, will not be simply through natural causes but is the miraculous, literal act of God in wrath to destroy the wicked. So the smoke of burning Rome, the seat of the beast, the city of "seven mountains, on which the woman sitteth," is a smoke of eternal judgment, a bit of Hell starting on earth and continuing eternally in Hell. *"And her smoke rose up for ever and ever"* (vs. 3).

We remember that Sodom and Gomorrah are said to have suffered "the vengeance of eternal fire" (Jude 7). We might illustrate it by imagining that God took a double handful of the fire and brimstone of Hell and poured it out on those wicked, wicked cities and destroyed Sodom and Gomorrah along with Admah and Zeboim. It was "the vengeance of eternal fire." And the judgment of Hell is simply a continuation of judgment which sometimes begins on earth.

Perhaps Judas Iscariot already felt the torment of Hell when he brought back the bribe money, the thirty pieces of silver for which he had sold the Saviour, threw it on the stone floor and cried out, "I have betrayed the innocent blood," then in an agony of mind went and hanged himself!

Twenty-four elders who are to reign with Christ on earth (5:8-10) also join in shouting "Alleluia." The four heavenly creatures who represent God's holiness and proclaim it joined with the elders in their praise and adoration. How wonderful for the time to come when we of earth will be so orientated and adjusted to Heaven that, redeemed and forever purified, we can join with angels and heavenly creatures in praising God acceptably! And how wonderful that the judgment and rewards of sin which we may have thought so long delayed (and perhaps even doubted the certain justice of God)—how wonderful that we will know that judgment as well as angels. Then in God's appointed hour we will all see the judgment as perfectly as they, and so join in understanding with satisfied praise! Alleluia!

A voice from the throne comes again to admonish, *"Praise our God, all ye his servants, and ye that fear him, both small and great"* (vs. 5). The response of the multitude is like the roar of oceans and waterfalls and thunder that fills the sky! They will shout, *"Alleluia: for the Lord God omnipotent reigneth"* (vs. 6).

Handel's oratorio, *The Messiah,* closes with the "Hallelujah Chorus," built on this very verse. How often we have sung it and heard it with rejoicing of heart! Oh, what a glad time when Christ comes to reign on the earth and "the earth shall be filled with the knowledge of the glory of the Lord, as the waters cover the sea"!

VERSES 7, 8:

7 Let us be glad and rejoice, and give honour to him: for the marriage of the Lamb is come, and his wife hath made herself ready.

8 And to her was granted that she should be arrayed in fine linen, clean and white: for the fine linen is the righteousness of saints.

Lamb's Wife Prepared

Weddings are happy occasions. They mean that love matches love. They mean permanent union of the two beloved ones to each other. They mean a happy, long future together. So the time when all the saved will be gathered to Christ forever is likened unto a marriage. And here the saved are pictured as the bride.

Who is the Bridegroom? Christ. Seiss mentions that. . .

Christ represents Himself as the Bridegroom (Matt. 9:15). He speaks of the kingdom of heaven being "like unto a certain king, which made a marriage for his son," and those called by the Gospel as "bidden to the marriage" (Matt. 22:1-13). He speaks often of the judgment time as the coming of the Bridegroom for his Bride (Matt. 25:1-10). John the Baptist spoke of Christ as the Bridegroom, and of himself as "the friend of the bridegroom, which standeth and heareth him, and rejoiceth greatly because of the bridegroom's voice" (John 3:29). Paul speaks of those whom he begat in the Gospel as espoused to one husband, whom he desired to present as a chaste virgin to Christ (II Cor. 11:2). Earthly marriage is likewise spoken of as a mystery, significant of Christ's relation to His church (Eph. 5:23-32).

Dr. Riley tells this story, and makes a beautiful application:

In a city where I was pastor years ago, a young couple were to be married at the break of day, in a Catholic church. Out of personal friendship I attended. The sister of the bride had a beautiful voice, and just as the bride entered the church, and began her march to the marriage altar, this sister, located in the gallery, sang a sweet wedding song. "How beautiful!"

But oh, one day, when the blessed Bride shall go up to meet

God's only Son, throughout the heavens there will ring, not the
music of solitary voice but a chorus as *"the voice of many waters,
and as the voice of mighty thunderings, saying, Alleluia. . .for
the marriage of the Lamb is come, and His wife hath made herself
ready."*

There may be joy in the presence of the angels of God when one
sinner repenteth, but who can imagine the joy on the part of the
angels of God, when the whole redeemed who have made
themselves ready, shall be received by Him, who has waited long
for this response to His unspeakable affection?

But as one has said, "Parables are not made to walk on all
fours"; so the poetic, fitting and beautiful figure of a wedding is
not to be pressed literally in all details like a wedding of a man
and a woman who take each other bodily to their arms and marriage bed.

Jesus used the figure of a wedding in several ways. In the
parable of the ten virgins in Matthew 25 He pictured the Christians as *bridesmaids* waiting for the bridegroom; the wise virgins
who had the oil of salvation in their lamps as born-again Christians having the Holy Spirit dwelling within. *Bridesmaids?* Yes.
But in the parable of the king's marriage for his son, in Matthew
22, Christians are pictured as *guests* at the wedding! And in
Ephesians 5:21-33 the inspired apostle likens the whole body of
Christians to the *bride* of Christ. So Christians are like
bridesmaids or like guests at the heavenly wedding or are like the
bride. All three of the pictures are good ones for us.

And in Revelation 21:2, 9, 10 the "bride, the Lamb's wife" is
there the heavenly "Jerusalem, coming down from God out of
heaven."

Do not, then, make any doctrine out of this lovely picture of
the wedding more than is clearly given in the Scripture.

Some have made "the church" in Ephesians 5 mean their
denomination or the institution of the local church (of their own
kind, of course).

No, the bride never means a denomination, nor an earthly
organization or group of organizations. It does picture all Christians. It does picture the Heavenly Jerusalem.

But here we understand all the saved are pictured as the bride, *"for the fine linen is the righteousness of saints"* (vs. 8). And Isaiah 61:10 speaks of these "garments of salvation" with which God clothes His people. The garment of salvation is pictured in that garment provided for the king's wedding for his son in Matthew 22:11, 12. And the man who had not a wedding garment was cast outside, as anyone who does not claim the righteousness of Christ to cover his sins is kept out of Heaven.

"The righteousness of saints" is twofold. First, of course, is the imputed righteousness of Christ, credited to everyone who trusts in Him for salvation. Paul was inspired to say about the Jews:

"Brethren, my heart's desire and prayer to God for Israel is, that they might be saved. For I bear them record that they have a zeal of God, but not according to knowledge. For they being ignorant of God's righteousness, and going about to establish their own righteousness, have not submitted themselves unto the righteousness of God. For Christ is the end of the law for righteousness to every one that believeth."—Rom. 10:1-4.

"Abraham believed God, and it was counted unto him for righteousness" (Gen. 15:6; Rom. 4:3; Col 3:6).

Of the old natural man, every unconverted person, God says, "There is none righteous, no, not one" (Rom. 3:10). But God continues:

"But now the righteousness of God without the law is manifested, being witnessed by the law and the prophets; Even the righteousness of God which is by faith of Jesus Christ unto all and upon all them that believe: for there is no difference: For all have sinned, and come short of the glory of God; Being justified freely by his grace through the redemption that is in Christ Jesus: Whom God hath set forth to be a propitiation through faith in his blood, to declare his righteousness for the remission of sins that are past, through the forbearance of God; To declare, I say, at this time his righteousness: that he might be just, and the justifier of him which believeth in Jesus."—Rom. 3:21-26.

This imputed righteousness of Christ which God uses to cover the sinner and count him righteous is pictured by that seamless robe of Jesus taken off at the cross that He might die as a sinner and the robe carried away by a guilty soldier (John 19:23, 24).

But there is another teaching of *"the righteousness of saints,"* which is pictured here as a wedding dress. When we are saved, there is a new creature, "the new man" the Bible calls it, born of God, and it is this new creature of whom it is said in I John 3:9, "Whosoever is born of God doth not commit sin; for his seed remaineth in him: and he cannot sin, because he is born of God." And again I John 5:17 says, "All unrighteousness is sin: and there is a sin not unto death."

So, like Paul, we must say, "With the mind I myself serve the law of God; but with the flesh the law of sin" (Rom. 7:25). A born-again Christian has something inside that grieves over sin and has repented about sin. See the grief of sinning David in Psalm 51. Remember how Peter, after he had cursed and sworn and had denied Jesus Christ three times, "went out, and wept bitterly" (Matt. 26:75; Luke 22:62). Thus, as the settled fact of Christ's righteousness given us, and the imputed righteousness that makes us try to be good, it comes about "that the righteousness of the law might be fulfilled in us, who walk not after the flesh, but after the Spirit" (Rom. 8:4).

But now the Scripture says, *". . .and his wife hath made herself ready"* (vs. 7). No more in these resurrected saints, now made perfect, is there the struggle of the flesh against the Spirit, the contrast of what one does with what one would do. Now how gloriously white and clean and how fine are the "garments of salvation" with which He clothes His bride!

VERSES 9, 10:

9 And he saith unto me, Write, Blessed *are* they which are called unto the marriage supper of the Lamb. And he saith unto me, These are the true sayings of God.

10 And I fell at his feet to worship him. And he said unto me, See *thou do it* not: I am thy fellowservant, and of thy brethren that have the testimony of Jesus: worship God: for the testimony of Jesus is the spirit of prophecy.

Marriage Supper

When will the wedding supper take place? The indication here is that it will be after the tribulation time when the Christians, converted and slain by the Antichrist during the tribulation, will have glorified, resurrection bodies. *"Blessed are they which are called unto the marriage supper of the Lamb"* (vs. 9). And that indicates that all the saved will be there, and all the unconverted left out. So one great official ceremony, limited in time, as a wedding, would not leave out these who are rejoicing in God's judgment on their murderers.

Yet Ephesians 5 likens "the church" as the bride for which Christ died. "The church" is that "general assembly and church of the firstborn, which are written in heaven," Hebrews 12:23 says. The Greek word for church is *ekklesia*, meaning "a called-out assembly." The rapture of the saints will be the greatest assembly ever called out in this world.

Will the wedding supper be immediately after the rapture? Or several years later after the tribulation time? We would think that the wedding supper does not mean a brief ceremony time which is soon over; rather the wedding supper may stand for the marvelous reunion with Christ at both times, at the rapture and at the close of the tribulation with another group and those who were saved and went to Heaven in between. Surely all Christians—those taken up at the rapture and those who go to Heaven during the tribulation and after—have the joy of union with Christ and all His own, in whatever may be pictured by "the marriage supper."

The one who makes this announcement is the "voice" that "came out of the throne" in verse 5. But it is not from Christ, although out of the throne, but evidently is that of an angel or of a saint in Heaven, because John is forbidden to worship him, and the speaker says he is a *"fellowservant,"* one of John's brothers who gave his testimony for Christ.

"The testimony of Jesus is the spirit of prophecy" (vs. 10). Prophecy means to witness in the power of the Holy Spirit. The heart and the purpose of such witness, of course, is Jesus. The

double theme of all the prophets is stated in Acts 10:43, "To him give all the prophets witness, that through his name whosoever believeth in him shall receive remission of sins." Every prophet's witness to Jesus—the prophecy of Joel 2:28-32, as quoted by Peter in Acts 2:17, 18, was, "And it shall come to pass in the last days, saith God, I will pour out of my Spirit upon all flesh: and your sons and your daughters shall prophesy, and your young men shall see visions, and your old men shall dream dreams: And on my servants and on my handmaidens I will pour out in those days of my Spirit; and they shall prophesy." So preaching and witnessing empowered by the Holy Spirit is about Jesus and leads to Him.

VERSES 11-16:

11 And I saw heaven opened, and behold a white horse; and he that sat upon him *was* called Faithful and True, and in righteousness he doth judge and make war.

12 His eyes *were* as a flame of fire, and on his head *were* many crowns; and he had a name written, that no man knew, but he himself.

13 And he *was* clothed with a vesture dipped in blood: and his name is called The Word of God.

14 And the armies *which were* in heaven followed him upon white horses, clothed in fine linen, white and clean.

15 And out of his mouth goeth a sharp sword, that with it he should smite the nations: and he shall rule them with a rod of iron: and he treadeth the winepress of the fierceness and wrath of Almighty God.

16 And he hath on *his* vesture and on his thigh a name written, KING OF KINGS, AND LORD OF LORDS.

Christ's Armies Leave Heaven for Armageddon

"I saw heaven opened" (vs. 11). John saw it opened. When Jesus came up from the waters of baptism, "the heavens were open unto him," and the Spirit descended upon him, and a voice said, "This is my beloved Son, in whom I am well pleased" (Matt. 3:16).

When Stephen was martyred, he saw "the heavens opened, and the Son of man standing on the right hand of God" (Acts 7:56).

When Jesus was on earth He promised His disciples that they should see the Heaven opened (John 1:51).

At the beginning of these visions John beheld a door opened in the heaven, and through that opening he was called up, while all was closed to the general mass of men (Rev. 4:1).—J. A. Seiss.

Conquering generals and kings rode horses. So the picture of a rising dictatorship of the Man of Sin in Revelation 6:2 is of a man on a white horse. Then the great plagues of war and of famine and of death are pictured by a red horse, a black horse and a pale horse respectively. No doubt the Antichrist, who would imitate the Lord Jesus, appeared as if on a white horse. But we suppose the white horse here is figurative, as are those in Revelation 6; but this is the Lord Jesus leaving Heaven with the armies of Heaven following Him on white horses. He is to put down the Antichrist and topple all the kingdoms of this world. Dr. Ironside reminds us "that we read of a rider on a white horse when the first seal was broken: but that one did not come from Heaven. He went forth on the earth and was of the earth; and his plans were doomed to disappointment. This rider comes from Heaven and His plans shall never miscarry."

He rides upon a white horse. His little domestic animal—the ass—is exchanged for the martial charger.

"Faithful and True" (vs. 11) He is called. His war is a righteous war. He is "the Word" of God as Jesus is called in John, chapter 1.

Again on verse 13, Dr. Ironside says: "His garments are to be reddened with the blood of His enemies, as we are told by the Prophet Isaiah, but the vesture dipped in blood with which He is here seen clothed, is, I take it, like the rams' skins, dyed red, in the tabernacle, the sign of His consecration unto death. It is His own blood that is here in view, the price of our redemption."

"The armies . .in heaven" (vs. 14). One would think these are the armies of angels, and they may be, for both saints and angels will be with Jesus. Enoch, "the seventh from Adam," as quoted in Jude 14 and 15, "prophesied of these, saying, Behold, the Lord cometh with ten thousands of his saints, To execute judgment upon all, and to convince all that are ungodly among them of all their ungodly deeds which they have ungodly committed, and of

all their hard speeches which ungodly sinners have spoken against him."

But Jesus said, "Verily I say unto you, There be some standing here, which shall not taste of death, till they see the Son of man coming in his kingdom" (Matt. 16:28).

So both saints and angels will come with Jesus when He returns in glory to the earth. In Matthew 25:31 Jesus said, "When the Son of man shall come in his glory, and all the holy angels with him, then shall he sit upon the throne of his glory."

The death of the wicked as reported here will be from *"a sharp sword"* which goeth *"out of his mouth"* (vs. 15). Second Thessalonians 2:8 tells of the wicked one "whom the Lord shall consume with the spirit of his mouth, and shall destroy with the brightness of his coming."

This we understand is the climactic and final battle of the war when hosts shall have already set out to destroy Israel. Zechariah 12 tells of the siege of Jerusalem. There verse 8 says, "In that day shall the Lord defend the inhabitants of Jerusalem; and he that is feeble among them at that day shall be as David; and the house of David shall be as God, as the angel of the Lord before them." So, Christ, with the sword of His mouth, will bring to an end that war, will deliver Jerusalem and all Palestine, and will utterly destroy all who oppose Christians and devout Jews and the Lord Jesus Himself.

The battle is pictured here as a winepress, and the wine pressed out is the blood of millions here destroyed in a moment. The blood is suddenly released from these 200 million soldiers (9:16). It will make a flood to the bridles of the horses (14:20). This picture of Christ destroying those armies at the Second Coming in glory after the rapture and tribulation is used also in Isaiah 63:1-4. There again it is Christ treading the winepress:

"Who is this that cometh from Edom, with dyed garments from Bozrah? this that is glorious in his apparel, travelling in the greatness of his strength? I that speak in righteousness, mighty to save. Wherefore art thou red in thine apparel, and thy garments like him that treadeth in the winefat? I have trodden the winepress alone; and of the people there was none with me:

for I will tread them in mine anger, and trample them in my fury; and their blood shall be sprinkled upon my garments, and I will stain all my raiment. For the day of vengeance is in mine heart, and the year of my redeemed is come."

The blood of Jesus is prominent as poured out in loving sacrifice to serve sinners. Then here we find much prominence given to the blood of Christ's enemies. In the parable of the pounds the king says, "But those mine enemies, which would not that I should reign over them, bring hither, and slay them before me" (Luke 19:27).

His name? He is to us Messiah and Christ, the Hebrew and Greek words for "the anointed one." Ah, He comes as the Light of the world burning in the power of the Holy Spirit. He is our Saviour, and angels gladly announce that to the shepherds as an angel did to Joseph. He is all in all to Christians. He is called "Wonderful, Counsellor, The mighty God, The everlasting Father, The Prince of Peace." Oh, the names of Jesus!

Now He has come to the time to emphasize another name. At long last and with the literal reign on earth Jesus is to be *"KING OF KINGS, AND LORD OF LORDS"* (vs. 16). Here in omnipotence He is to reign! Zechariah 14:9 says of that time, "And the Lord shall be king over all the earth: in that day shall there be one Lord, and His name one."

VERSES 17, 18:

17 And I saw an angel standing in the sun; and he cried with a loud voice, saying to all the fowls that fly in the midst of heaven, Come and gather yourselves together unto the supper of the great God;
18 That ye may eat the flesh of kings, and the flesh of captains, and the flesh of mighty men, and the flesh of horses, and of them that sit on them, and the flesh of all *men, both* free and bond, both small and great.

Birds of World to Eat the Bodies of Slain

"We are to be occupied with two opposite scenes on this occasion: one of which is to take place very shortly in Heaven, and the other on earth. Both are called Suppers. The one is the Marriage Supper of the Lamb. The other is the Great Supper of God. The first is all joy and gladness. The second is a scene of deepest gloom and anguish.

The Marriage Supper of the Lamb ushers in the fulness of glory for the heavenly saints. The Great Supper of God concludes the series of judgments that are to fall upon the prophetic earth, and opens the way for the establishment of the long-waited-for kingdom of God" (H. A. Ironside).

Here in Revelation 19 the detailed description is more about the battle of Armageddon, the armies directly connected with the Antichrist and put to death by the word of the mouth of the Lord Jesus. But we must remember that Ezekiel has prophesied that Gog, a ruler of the north and probably Russia, will have brought his multitudes to attack Jerusalem and Israel. Ezekiel 39:1-9 tells us of the destruction of Gog and his army:

"Therefore, thou son of man, prophesy against Gog, and say, Thus saith the Lord God; Behold, I am against thee, O Gog, the chief prince of Meshech and Tubal: And I will turn thee back, and leave but the sixth part of thee, and will cause thee to come up from the north parts, and will bring thee upon the mountains of Israel: And I will smite thy bow out of thy left hand, and will cause thine arrows to fall out of thy right hand. Thou shalt fall upon the mountains of Israel, thou, and all thy bands, and the people that is with thee: I will give thee unto the ravenous birds of every sort, and to the beasts of the field to be devoured. Thou shalt fall upon the open field: for I have spoken it, saith the Lord God. And I will send a fire on Magog, and among them that dwell carelessly in the isles: and they shall know that I am the Lord. So will I make my holy name known in the midst of my people Israel; and I will not let them pollute my holy name any more: and the heathen shall know that I am the Lord, the Holy One in Israel. Behold, it is come, and it is done, saith the Lord God; this is the day whereof I have spoken. And they that dwell in the cities of Israel shall go forth, and shall set on fire and burn the weapons, both the shields and the bucklers, the bows and the arrows, and the handstaves, and the spears, and they shall burn them with fire seven years."

But the birds of the air are now called to a feast, to *"the supper of the great God"* (vs. 17). Not a few of the birds, not simply the carrion-eating vultures of that general area, but the call is *"to all the fowls that fly in the midst of heaven"* (vs. 17). For this is a worldwide catastrophe, a worldwide judgment, and the fowls of all the air around the world are called to have a part in it. Birds that eat seeds normally will now eat flesh. Birds that are the first to pick the cherries or currants from the tree when they can will now eat the flesh of men.

It is not surprising that God can have animals do His will. He had the animals before the flood come two and two to Noah in the ark. He had the hornets help drive the Canaanites from Palestine. He had a donkey witness to Balaam. He had a fish bring a coin to pay taxes for Peter and Jesus. He had the fishes stay out of the net of the backslidden disciples in John 21, then had them fill Peter's nets then, as He had the fish fill the nets before when Peter was called to preach. He had a rooster crow to remind Peter of his great sin in denying the Lord.

So now the Lord will have the birds of the air come to *"eat the flesh of kings, and the flesh of captains, and the flesh of mighty men, and the flesh of horses, and of them that sit on them, and the flesh of all men, both free and bond, both small and great"* (vs. 18).

The land would be poisoned and defiled with the death of these millions if God did not provide birds to eat their flesh.

And besides this great battle in the valley of Armageddon or the plain of Jezreel, or Esdraelon, there will be the dead scattered all over Palestine. And Ezekiel 39:11-15 tells us:

"And it shall come to pass in that day, that I will give unto Gog a place there of graves in Israel, the valley of the passengers on the east of the sea: and it shall stop the noses of the passengers: and there shall they bury Gog and all his multitude: and they shall call it The valley of Hamon-gog. And seven months shall the house of Israel be burying of them, that they may cleanse the land. Yea, all the people of the land shall bury them; and it shall be to them a renown the day that I shall be glorified, saith the Lord God. And they shall sever out men of

continual employment, passing through the land to bury with
the passengers those that remain upon the face of the earth, to
cleanse it: after the end of seven months shall they search. And
the passengers that pass through the land, when any seeth a
man's bone, then shall he set up a sign by it, till the buriers have
buried it in the valley of Hamon-gog."

And when the Lord calls all the birds of the whole heaven
together to help clean up the dead bodies after Armageddon, it
will be a part of the cleansing of the whole earth getting ready for
the kingdom age.

VERSES 19-21:

19 And I saw the beast, and the kings of the earth, and their armies, gathered together to make war against him that sat on the horse, and against his army.

20 And the beast was taken, and with him the false prophet that wrought miracles before him, with which he deceived them that had received the mark of the beast, and them that worshipped his image. These both were cast alive into a lake of fire burning with brimstone.

21 And the remnant were slain with the sword of him that sat upon the horse, which *sword* proceeded out of his mouth: and all the fowls were filled with their flesh.

Doom of Beast and His False Prophet

Note that in the midst of the battle the beast himself will be
captured and the false prophet and *"cast alive into a lake of fire
burning with brimstone"* (vs. 20). They are due some special
treatment, some special, vivid demonstration to men and angels
and demons of God's judgment on the Antichrist and his
wickedness.

But with these captured and sent alive to Hell, then the remnant are slain by the sword of Christ, the sword that went out of
His mouth. You remember from verse 19 that all these armies of
the kingdoms of the earth were *"gathered together to make war
against him that sat on the horse, and against his army."* It was a
direct assault on Jesus Christ. It was a war against God.

Here is the awful end of those who fight God. *". . .lake of fire
burning with brimstone"* (vs. 20). We do not agree with Dr.

Scofield and some others who teach that there are, or have been, two places of heavenly rest for departed saints and two different Hells. The note in the Scofield Reference Bible on Luke 16:23 is as follows:

"Gr. *Hades,* 'the unseen world,' is revealed as the place of departed human spirits between death and resurrection. The word occurs, Mt. 11.23; 16.18; Lk. 10.15; Acts 2.27, 31; Rev. 1.18; 6.8; 20:13, 14, and is the equivalent of the O.T. *sheol* (Hab. 2.5, note). The Septuagint invariably renders *sheol* by *hades.*

"Summary: (1) *Hades before the ascension of Christ.* The passages in which the word occurs make it clear that hades was formerly in two divisions, the abodes respectively of the saved and of the lost. The former was called 'paradise' and 'Abraham's bosom.' Both designations were Talmudic, but adopted by Christ in Luke 16.22; 23.43. The blessed dead were with Abraham, they were conscious and were 'comforted' (Lk. 16.25). The believing malefactor was to be, that day, with Christ in 'paradise.' The lost were separated from the saved by a 'great gulf fixed' (Lk. 16.26). The representative man of the lost who are now in hades is the rich man of Lk. 16.19-31. He was alive, conscious, in the full exercise of his faculties, memory, etc., and in torment.

"(2) *Hades since the ascension of Christ.* So far as the unsaved dead are concerned, no change of their place or condition is revealed in Scripture. At the judgment of the great white throne, hades will give them up, they will be judged, and will pass into the lake of fire (Rev. 20.13, 14). But a change has taken place which affects paradise. Paul was 'caught up to the third heaven. . .into paradise' (2 Cor. 12.1-4). Paradise, therefore, is now in the immediate presence of God. It is believed that Eph. 4.8-10 indicates the time of the change. 'When he ascended up on high he led a multitude of captives.' It is immediately added that He had previously 'descended first into the lower parts of the earth,' i.e. the paradise division of hades. During the present church-age the saved who died are 'absent from the body, at home with the Lord.' The wicked dead in hades, and the righteous dead 'at home with the Lord,' alike await the resurrection (Job 19.25; I Cor. 15.52). See Mt. 5.22, note."

We comment here. *Hades* and *sheol* in the New Testament and Old Testament respectively both mean "the unseen world" or "the realm of the dead." The Hebrew word *sheol* is many times translated as "the grave." As in Genesis 37:35 when Jacob said, "I will go down into the grave unto my son. . . ." And as in Psalm 6:5, ". . .in the grave who shall give thee thanks?" It never refers to a particular sepulchre but to the state of the dead, to the unseen world, life after death. So it is indefinite.

In I Corinthians 15:55 Paul was inspired to say, "O death, where is thy sting? O grave, where is thy victory?"

So *hades* and *sheol* do not identify a literal place divided into compartments. Both Heaven and Hell are literal places, but terms like "the realm of the dead" and "the unseen world" are symbolic of "the grave" and simply refer to life after death of people saved or lost. So when Psalm 16:10 has a prophetic statement as from Jesus, "Thou wilt not leave my soul in hell; neither wilt thou suffer thine Holy One to see corruption," it simply means God would not leave Jesus dead nor leave His body to decay.

Psalm 68:18, quoted in Ephesians 4:8-10, says: "Wherefore he saith, When he ascended up on high, he led captivity captive, and gave gifts unto men. (Now that he ascended, what is it but that he also descended first into the lower parts of the earth? He that descended is the same also that ascended up far above all heavens, that he might fill all things.)"

We believe that simply refers to the bodily resurrection of the Lord Jesus and the gifts He has given in His church since then. ". . .the lower parts of the earth" would be the grave into which Jesus went and then arose. On the cross Jesus said to the dying thief, "To day shalt thou be with me in paradise." Is not that the same "third heaven" and "paradise" mentioned by Paul in II Corinthians 12:2 and 4?

That lake burning with fire and brimstone into which the beast is cast and the Hell Jesus mentioned in Luke 16:19-31 must be the same place of torment in fire, and so is the place Jesus warned of "where their worm dieth not, and the fire is not quenched" (Mark 9:44, 46, 48).

Heaven and Hell have always been separate places. In the Old Testament Elijah went UP in a chariot of fire (II Kings 2:11). But wicked Korah, Dathan and Abiram, who led a rebellion against

Moses, went DOWN, not up. Numbers 16:32, 33 says:

"And the earth opened her mouth, and swallowed them up, and their houses, and all the men that appertained unto Korah, and all their goods. They, and all that appertained to them, went DOWN alive into the pit, and the earth closed upon them: and they perished from among the congregation."

Elijah went up to Heaven and the wicked went down to Hell. Heaven and Hell were not two compartments of a place, though they were both in the realm of the dead or in life after death.

In Luke 15:7 Jesus said, "I say unto you, that likewise joy shall be in heaven over one sinner that repenteth, more than over ninety and nine just persons, which need no repentance." Again in verse 10 He said, "Likewise, I say unto you, there is joy in the presence of the angels of God over one sinner that repenteth."

So the saved were even then with God in the presence of the angels in Heaven.

Chapter 20

AND I saw an angel come down from heaven, having the key of the bottomless pit and a great chain in his hand.

2 And he laid hold on the dragon, that old serpent, which is the Devil, and Satan, and bound him a thousand years,

3 And cast him into the bottomless pit, and shut him up, and set a seal upon him, that he should deceive the nations no more, till the thousand years should be fulfilled: and after that he must be loosed a little season.

Satan Bound a Thousand Years

He is called by four names: *the dragon, that old serpent, the Devil, and Satan* (vs. 2). We remember that in the Garden of Eden, Satan entered a serpent to deceive Eve, and serpents were cursed because of their use by Satan; so the term is a symbol of sin and rebellion against God. John the Baptist called the wicked Pharisees "a generation of vipers" (Matt. 3:7). Jesus called them, "Ye serpents, ye generation of vipers" (Matt. 23:33). And the Scripture says of the natural man, ". . .the poison of asps is under their lips" (Rom. 3:13).

Bottomless Pit

Is Hell temporary? No. The rich man in Hell, portrayed by the Lord Jesus in that moving but awful passage in Luke 16:19-31, could not get a drop of water to cool his tongue, could not go to Heaven, but he surely must be brought out of Hell for that last judgment of Revelation 20:11-15.

Then, with God vindicated and with every voice that would complain in Heaven or Hell, forever stopped, the wicked man will be cast "both soul and body in hell" (Matt. 10:28). So Hell now has souls tormented waiting judgment.

Now can we call the bottomless pit "the Abyss," where Satan will be bound? That depends on our choice of words, I think. When Korah, Abiram and their adherents were destroyed by God's hand for their rebellion, they "went down alive into the

pit." Was that not "the bottomless pit"? The Bible uses the term
"the pit" in Job 33:24; Psalm 28:1 and Psalm 143:7 as if it referred to Hell. But Satan in the bottomless pit was "bound," that
is, restrained, kept helpless, held in a helpless state for a time.
We remember that "the angels which kept not their first estate,
but left their own habitation, he hath reserved in everlasting
chains under darkness unto the judgment of the great day" (Jude
6).

We suppose that "the judgment of the great day" refers to the
judgment of this chapter, Revelation 20:11-15; so fallen angels
will be judged at the same general time as lost men; we suppose
they will go to the same Hell. Why not? Satan is even now
limited, restrained, as God wishes.

Satan was allowed first to bring Job trouble and poverty.
When Satan complained, "Hast not thou made an hedge about
him, and about his house, and about all that he hath on every
side?" God then put Job's possessions in Satan's power but said,
"Only upon himself put not forth thine hand." Then when Job
was still faithful, the Lord said to Satan, "Behold, he is in thine
hand; but save his life" (Job 1:10-12; 2:6).

God limits Satan's activity. Satan asked and was permitted to
sift Peter as wheat (Luke 22:31). We are encouraged to pray daily, ". . .but deliver us from evil," that is, literally "from the evil
one."

Fallen angels, or devils, too, are limited and restrained at God's
will. The legion of devils in the Gadarene demoniac begged
Jesus, "Art thou come hither to torment us before the time?"
(Matt. 8:29), and "they besought him that he would not command them to go out into the deep" (Luke 8:31). So they were
permitted to go into a herd of swine and destroy them. Does not
". . .into the deep" refer to the same bottomless pit where Satan
will be cast for a thousand years? And is not that where fallen
angels, devils are "chained" or kept imprisoned except as God
allows them to work on earth? And those devils knew that at a
future time they would be "tormented," they said, as Satan will
be tormented forever.

We suppose that fallen angels now suffer and in that bottomless pit Satan will suffer, but there he is first to be bound, confined for a thousand years, then confined forever in the lake of fire. If you wish to call "the bottomless pit" different from the lake of fire, they would both be a part of the eternal Hell "prepared for the devil and his angels," we believe. So we might call "the pit" of Old Testament Scripture and "the bottomless pit" of Revelation, Hell, or as states of eternally condemned devils and men.

Satan will be cast alive into Hell at the beginning of the thousand years' reign. "Bottomless pit" is one of the many names for Hell. "A lake of fire burning with brimstone" is another; "outer darkness," another. Satan will not be put to death but bound in Hell for a thousand years. One last test must be had for mankind. Satan is reserved for that, allowed to *"deceive the nations no more, till the thousand years should be fulfilled"* (vs. 3).

The term "the thousand years" is used six times in this chapter and must mean a literal thousand years. The kingdom is mentioned often, as in Isaiah 9:6, 7; 11:1-12; Zechariah 14:9; Matthew 19:28; Luke 1:31-33 and many other Scriptures. But here the time is defined as one thousand years.

VERSES 4—6:

4 And I saw thrones, and they sat upon them, and judgment was given unto them: and *I saw* the souls of them that were beheaded for the witness of Jesus, and for the word of God, and which had not worshipped the beast, neither his image, neither had received *his* mark upon their foreheads, or in their hands; and they lived and reigned with Christ a thousand years.

5 But the rest of the dead lived not again until the thousand years were finished. This *is* the first resurrection.

6 Blessed and holy *is* he that hath part in the first resurrection: on such the second death hath no power, but they shall be priests of God and of Christ, and shall reign with him a thousand years.

Two Resurrections

In verse 4 we are told that those who were beheaded for their witness and the Word died and they lived and reigned with Christ *"a thousand years."* So, the saints converted after the rapture of the church but martyred under the Antichrist in the tribulation time will have a resurrection. This is part of the first resurrection, verse 5 says. So there are two resurrections. One of the saved on whom "the second death hath no power." Blessed are these. But that means there will be another resurrection of the unsaved dead. Note that the following—these all have part in the first resurrection.

1. Christ, "the firstfruits of them that slept" (I Cor. 15:20). But what about Lazarus and others raised from the dead? They were simply made alive again but without glorified bodies, so they died again. But Christ arose with all the glory of a resurrection body, the first of mankind for that.

2. Also in the first resurrection will be others: "Christ the firstfruits; afterward they that are Christ's at his coming" (I Cor. 15:23).

So, at the first phase of Christ's coming, I Thessalonians 4:14-16 tells us:

"For if we believe that Jesus died and rose again, even so them also which sleep in Jesus will God bring with him. For this we say unto you by the word of the Lord, that we which are alive and remain unto the coming of the Lord shall not prevent them which are asleep. For the Lord himself shall descend from heaven with a shout, with the voice of the archangel, and with the trump of God: and the dead in Christ shall rise first."

Then I Corinthians 15:51, 52 says: "Behold, I shew you a mystery; We shall not all sleep, but we shall all be changed, In a moment, in the twinkling of an eye, at the last trump: for the trumpet shall sound, and the dead shall be raised incorruptible, and we shall be changed."

This is part of the first resurrection, that is, the resurrection of saved people as distinguished from the resurrection of the unsaved.

3. But here, at the beginning of the kingdom age, the millennial reign of Christ on earth, we find other Christians saved and martyred and they, too, are said to be part of "the first resurrection." And all these of the first resurrection are to be with Christ

in resurrected bodies. We are expressly told that they are *"the first resurrection"* (vs. 6) and are to be *"priests of God and of Christ, and shall reign with him a thousand years."* But the second resurrection of the unsaved dead is to be a thousand years later, as we will see in verses 11 to 15. The Bible says nothing about a "general resurrection" and a "general judgment."

Once as a young preacher, I prepared a sermon, "The General Resurrection and the General Judgment." It was foolish to do it without a Scripture, a sin I have long ago renounced, but I sought for a text that would mention these terms and discovered there was no such statement in the Bible! There is no general resurrection, no general judgment.

VERSES 7—9:

7 And when the thousand years are expired, Satan shall be loosed out of his prison,
8 And shall go out to deceive the nations which are in the four quarters of the earth, Gog and Magog, to gather them together to battle: the number of whom *is* as the sand of the sea.
9 And they went up on the breadth of the earth, and compassed the camp of the saints about, and the beloved city: and fire came down from God out of heaven, and devoured them.

Satan Loosed: Last Rebellion

In verses 1 and 2 Satan was bound in Hell for a thousand years. We do not think Satan is now in Hell, nor is Satan master in Hell. He is "the prince of the power of the air." He goes about "as a roaring lion. . .seeking whom he may devour" (I Pet. 5:8). He is not now shut up in Hell. He will be for the millennial reign of Christ, then at the close of the millennium Satan will be *"loosed a little season"* (vs. 3), *"loosed out of his prison"* (vs. 7). Why this last test of mankind and how does it end?

We understand that the Gentiles, at the judgment of Matthew 25:31-46, who are invited as saved people to "inherit the kingdom prepared for you from the foundation of the world," will be given glorified bodies, and no rebellion against God can come from these glorified saints. Whence, then, will come those who rebel?

We think little children, unaccountable infants, will come into the kingdom and grow up in natural bodies. Some of them will be saved, some will not be saved, and at that time Isaiah 65:20 says, "There shall be no more thence an infant of days, nor an old man that hath not filled his days: for the child shall die an hundred years old; but the sinner being an hundred years old shall be accursed."

With Satan bound, unsaved people will go on very well in outward righteousness, but the state of the natural man's heart has still the wicked bent described in Romans 3:9-18. So when Satan is loosed and free again to deceive and tempt men, some will become active rebels against God. God will thus prove that even in the perfect environment man is still a fallen creature. Sin is not from bad influence outwardly but by a wicked heart inside, tempted of Satan.

Gog and Magog, ruler and people from the area of Russia, are to lead in this rebellion. They are mentioned in Ezekiel 38. We understand that that country and its ruler would have had part in the war against Israel and God at the time of Armageddon, for "the kings of the earth" were there (19:19) and references in Ezekiel should give that time primarily. But the tradition of atheism and hatred of God in communist Russia is a long-lasting poison. We think the remnant of its teaching will be treasured by wicked men at the close of the age and Satan, released, would bring that back to the minds of succeeding generations of these who rebelled against God. They will rebel against God at the end of the millennium. So a multitude, as the sands of the sea, of the natural men after a thousand years will be led astray.

Jerome and Theodoret identify Gog and Magog with "the Scythian nations, fierce and innumerable, who live beyond the Caucasus and the lake Maeotis, and near the Caspian Sea, and spread out even onward to India, " says Seiss. He also says that the Koran does the same, and represents them as barbarians of the North who are somehow restrained until the last period of the world, when they are to swarm forth toward the South in some great predatory irruption, only to be hurled into Gehenna fire. "It is doubtful whether we can get beyond this by any ethnic or geographic inquiries in the present state of human knowledge. It is also questionable whether this postmillennial Gog and Magog are the same described by Ezekiel (38:1-14)," comments Seiss. "They may be the same, or the one may be the type of the other; but in either case the reference is to peoples lying outside of the most civilized world, among whom the old Devil influence lingers longest. . . ."

Fallen man, even in a perfect environment, is not good but inherently evil, alien from God, and easy prey to Satan's deceit. Then with evil put down again and with no unregenerate, unglorified men left alive, God will be ready to have the final judgment of all the unsaved and will send them to Hell and bring down the Heavenly Jerusalem to a redeemed, made-over earth.

VERSE 10:

10 And the devil that deceived them was cast into the lake of fire and brimstone, where the beast and the false prophet *are*, and shall be tormented day and night for ever and ever.

Satan in Hell Forever

Before this Satan has been "chained," bound in the bottomless pit for a thousand years. Now he is to be "cast into the lake of fire and brimstone," that is, *"where the beast and the false prophet are."* Note: they have been there a thousand years. They are still there, still tormented. So Hell does not mean annihilation. The indication here is that Hell and torment continue forever. It is "everlasting fire" (Matt. 25:41), "eternal fire" (Jude 7), "everlasting punishment" (Matt. 25:46). "And the smoke of their torment ascendeth up for ever and ever: and they have no rest day nor night. . ." (Rev. 14:11).

So Satan is not king in Hell but a wicked one in eternal penitentiary and *"shall be tormented day and night for ever and ever."* Remember, Hell was "prepared for the devil and his angels" (Matt. 25:41). All who follow Satan in rejecting Christ join Satan's eternal punishment.

VERSES 11—15:

11 And I saw a great white throne, and him that sat on it, from whose face the earth and the heaven fled away; and there was found no place for them.

12 And I saw the dead, small and great, stand before God; and the books were opened: and another book was opened, which is *the book* of life: and the dead were judged out of those things which were written in the books, according to their works.

13 And the sea gave up the dead which were in it; and death and hell delivered up the dead which were in them: and they were judged every man according to their works.

14 And death and hell were cast into the lake of fire. This is the second death.

15 And whosoever was not found written in the book of life was cast into the lake of fire.

Several Judgments Mentioned in Scripture

There is no one general judgment, but several judgments are described in the Bible.

1. There is "the judgment seat of Christ." It is to be a judgment of Christians after we have glorified bodies and when we meet Christ. We are not told whether each individual is to be judged and awarded at once when he dies, or at the rapture, though that is inferred.

Second Corinthians 5:9, 10 says: "Wherefore we labour, that, whether present or absent, we may be accepted of him. For we must all appear before the judgment seat of Christ; that every one may receive the things done in his body, according to that he hath done, whether it be good or bad."

We are to be judged and "receive the things done in the body . . .whether it be good or bad." Not the wrath of God but in our own wrongs we must face their results. A loved one unwarned, unwon and then in Hell, will still be in Hell despite all our tears over our failure. We must receive what we have done.

First Corinthians 3:10-15 tells us more explicitly:

"According to the grace of God which is given unto me, as a wise masterbuilder, I have laid the foundation, and another buildeth thereon. But let every man take heed how he buildeth

thereupon. For other foundation can no man lay than that is laid, which is Jesus Christ. Now if any man build upon this foundation gold, silver, precious stones, wood, hay, stubble; Every man's work shall be made manifest: for the day shall declare it, because it shall be revealed by fire; and the fire shall try every man's work of what sort it is. If any man's work abide which he hath built thereupon, he shall receive a reward. If any man's work shall be burned, he shall suffer loss: but he himself shall be saved; yet so as by fire."

I say, there is a judgment seat of Christ for Christians in Heaven. And that judgment does not mean to find whether we are saved. Those whose works abide will receive a reward (they already have salvation), and those whose works are burned will suffer loss, but they themselves "shall be saved; yet so as by fire."

2. *There will be a judgment of Israel.* After the tribulation, every living Jew will be gathered by angels from all over the world. Matthew 24:31 says, "And he shall send his angels with a great sound of a trumpet, and they shall gather together his elect from the four winds, from one end of heaven to the other." Then they will be brought to "the wilderness of the people" and there they will be judged individually and rebels purged out. Ezekiel 20:33-38 says:

"As I live, saith the Lord God, surely with a mighty hand, and with a stretched out arm, and with fury poured out, will I rule over you: And I will bring you out from the people, and will gather you out of the countries wherein ye are scattered, with a mighty hand, and with a stretched out arm, and with fury poured out. And I will bring you into the wilderness of the people, and there will I plead with you face to face. Like as I pleaded with your fathers in the wilderness of the land of Egypt, so will I plead with you, saith the Lord God. And I will cause you to pass under the rod, and I will bring you into the bond of the covenant: And I will purge out from among you the rebels, and them that transgress against me: I will bring them forth out of the country where they sojourn, and they shall not enter into the land of Israel: and ye shall know that I am the Lord."

The remnant of Israel who seek God with all their hearts will be saved (Deut. 30:1-6; Zech. 12:10; 13:1; Rom. 11:26). Oh, what a mighty revival then when they look on Him whom they pierced, every family apart, as one mourneth for his firstborn son! A nation saved in a day, after the rebels are purged out and sent to Hell.

3. There will be a judgment of Gentiles left alive after the battle of Armageddon. Matthew 25:31-46 tells of a judgment "when the Son of man shall come in his glory, and all the holy angels with him, then shall he sit upon the throne of his glory: And before him shall be gathered all nations: and he shall separate them one from another, as a shepherd divideth his sheep from the goats."

This is often called "the judgment of the nations." But that is misleading. The word for nations there is *ethnos* and refers to nations of people. It is the same word as in Matthew 24:14, "And this gospel of the kingdom shall be preached in all the world for a witness unto all nations." The same word is used in Matthew 28:19. In the Great Commission we are to "teach [or disciple] all nations." It is literally a judgment of individuals from all races, the Scripture is saying. A nation does not visit a sick man or give water to the thirsty. It is a judgment of individuals of all nations left alive after the battle of Armageddon. God will have dealt with Israel in a special judgment; now Gentiles left alive will be judged.

After the awful persecution and murder of Christians and God-fearing Jews by the Antichrist, only those who love and trust Christ will take the part of Christians then. So it will be easy to select the saved then. Now it is not so easy. God does not leave it in the hands of individuals to judge who is saved and who is not. "Man looketh on the outward appearance, but the Lord looketh on the heart." But the Lord Jesus will know the saved, and He will be the judge. But He mentions the obvious evidence of salvation here.

This Scripture does not teach salvation by works but the recognition of works from a Christian heart. The Lord Jesus knows every heart and will make no mistake. Only those who are born again by personal faith in Christ the Saviour will appear to Him as Christians.

4. Then there is the great judgment of the unsaved dead discussed here in Revelation 20:11-15.

Great White Throne Judgment

Several questions must be answered about this judgment.

WHO WILL BE JUDGED? Only unsaved people. These are *"the dead, small and great"* (vs. 12), and we have already found that the saved will already have been raised in the "first resurrection" and "on such the second death hath no power" (vs. 6). Now we have the second resurrection, that is, the resurrection of the unsaved dead.

Says Seiss: "The resurrection of the wicked is in no respect identical with that of the saints, except that it will be a recall to some sort of corporeal life. There is a 'resurrection of life,' and there is a 'resurrection of damnation' (John 5:29); and it is impossible that these should be one and the same." Again he says, "Paul tells us expressly that there is an 'order' in it, which brings up some at one time, and others at other times."

"And death and hell delivered up the dead which were in them" (vs. 13), that is, the realm of death deliver the unsaved dead to come to this judgment, the sea gives up the bodies of those drowned in the sea. This is the judgment of only the unsaved dead. Dr. Riley quotes Phillips Brooks saying, "It is difficult for us to imagine that the last man—great and small—will be brought there. The very multitude of them bewilders the mind, and raises the question as to whether some of the smallest will not be overlooked, and some of the greatest of the unregenerate will not be excused. But, God's omniscience will not allow the most insignificant to escape unobserved; and His omnipotence will cause the mightiest to obey the summons."

Will Christians be judged here? No. But Christians will all be present as witnesses. For one thing, it is promised to resurrected Christians, ". . .so shall we ever be with the Lord" (I Thess. 4:17). So we will be there with the Lord. And again after the rapture we will never leave Him.

All Christians must be at the great white throne judgment of the unsaved dead to witness against them. Jesus said, "The men of Nineveh shall rise in judgment with this generation, and shall condemn it: because they repented at the preaching of Jonas; and, behold, a greater than Jonas is here" (Matt. 12:41). The weeping mother will take sides with God against her impenitent son. The preacher who warned will testify against his unbelieving hearers. Thus all mankind will be present at the judgment. The lost will be judged, the saved to witness. But only the unsaved are to be judged here.

The Judge is to be Jesus Christ Himself for "the Father . . .hath committed all judgment unto the Son" (John 5:22).

Basis of Judgment: "Their Works"

"The books were opened" (vs. 12). That is, the records of man's deeds "and the dead were judged out of those things which were written in the books, according to their works." Again, "And they were judged every man according to their works" (vs. 13). Heaven keeps record of all the deeds of men, and of all the thoughts and feelings under which they act. Says Seiss: "Myriads of human beings have lived and died of whom the world knows nothing; but the lives they lived, the deeds they wrought, the thoughts and tempers they indulged, still stand written where the memory of them cannot perish. Yes, O man! O woman! whoever you may be, your biography is written. An unerring hand has recorded every item, with every secret thing . . . ." No mercy here. Nothing is said about forgiveness, about God's grace, about atonement. All these have been scorned; now only righteous judgment applies. People go to Hell because they ought to go. They deserve Hell. God's law is, "For the wages of sin is death; but the gift of God is eternal life through Jesus Christ our Lord" (Rom. 6:23). It is, "Be not deceived; God is not mocked: for whatsoever a man soweth, that shall he also reap" (Gal. 6:7). Proverbs 29:1 says, "He, that being often reproved hardeneth his neck, shall suddenly be destroyed, and that without remedy." Sin must be paid for. Those who reject the sacrifice of Christ for us must pay their own debt for eternal,

never-repented, never-forgiven sin.

Someone asks, "But what if a man never heard the Gospel?" Men do not go to Heaven because they hear the Gospel. They go because they get forgiveness for their sins. And those who do not get forgiveness go to Hell because they deserve to go.

Men will be judged according to their works. That means, then, that judgment will be more severe for some than for others. Hell will be more intolerable for some than for others, depending on their works. All Christ-rejecters go to Hell, but Hell will not be the same for all. All saved people go to Heaven, but some will have more rewards than others, more happiness than others. Since in Hell people suffer "according to their works," God will have the record at hand.

"According to their works" (vs. 12), yes, but in God's sight the sin is not simply in the act but in the heart. "Out of the abundance of the heart the mouth speaketh" (Matt. 12:34). He that hateth his brother is a murderer before he ever pulls the trigger or wields the knife or club (I John 3:15). "Whosoever looketh on a woman to lust after her hath committed adultery with her already in his heart," Jesus said in Matthew 5:28. One who wants to do wickedness or would do it if circumstances allowed, or if he did not fear exposure, is guilty of that sin in the heart. Oh, the sins that the heart intends will be read out of God's record books that awful day!

No wonder Romans 3:22, 23 says, "For there is no difference: For all have sinned, and come short of the glory of God." What a common guilt this race of sinners has!

The legally chaste wife and mother who watches the film or the television telecast of wooing and perhaps adultery of a charming man and dreams how wonderful it would be to have such an experience, God will count with the prostitute or the lewd movie star she envies. The murderer in death row and the woman who hated and condemned to death by abortion her unborn little one, along with the respected and wealthy doctor who gets rich through such murders (even though abortions are made legal and in some cases respectable): all these will be in the same bloody, guilty murderer's row at the judgment.

And secret sins! God's books record, more than the newspaper, more than all the world knows. The secret loves, undetected thefts, crooked financial schemes, the unsolved murders, at the judgment will be exposed as ugly, as hateful, as hellishly wicked as God sees them.

"Another book was opened. . .the book of life" (vs. 12). Why is it here? In it are the names of those born again by faith in Jesus Christ the Saviour, the register of the washed and sanctified through faith in His redeeming blood (See Phil. 4:3; Rev. 3:5; 13:8; 17:8; 20:12, 15; 21:27; 22:19.) "The book of life is opened (vs. 12), which is the register of the saved (13:8; 17:8). It contains the name of not one unsaved person, demonstrating that this is purely the sinner's judgment (vs. 15)," says Dr. Unger.

None of the saved are being judged here, so why the book of life? It is God's loving witness to all that these unsaved could have been saved and would not. It is God's evidence of mercy despised, of invitations scorned, of an atonement for their sins which they refused, preferring their sins.

So, as these lost (all of them) are cast into the lake of fire, they are reminded again of the salvation bought by such sufferings of Christ but refused until too late. Down in Hell the rich man of Luke 16 was told, "Son, remember. . . ." Now the sad tale is told, the end of Christ-rejecting sinners has come, the last unconverted sinner in the world has gone to Hell. "As to eternal fire, no one questions the scientists that fire ever burns within the heart of this earth, and that volcanoes, like Mount Etna, are caused by the fire breaking through where the crust of the earth is thinnest. If one believes the scientists who discover, why not believe the God who created? (Slemming).

Seiss sums up this chapter with these words of warning:

> Ho, ye unbelieving men,—ye dishonest men,—ye profane men,—ye lewd men and women,—ye slaves of lust and appetite,—ye scoffers at the truth of God,—*"How can ye escape the damnation of hell?"* (Matt. 23:33). Ye men of business,—ye whose souls are absorbed with the pursuit of gain,—ye people of wealth without riches toward God,—ye passengers on the voyage of life, without prayer, without church relations, without concern

for your immortal good, your God, or the eternity before you,—hear: *"Hell hath enlarged herself, and opened her mouth without measure, and your glory, and your multitude, and your pomp, and your rejoicing, shall descend into it!"* (Isa. 5:14.) Ye almost Christians, lingering these many years on the margin of the Kingdom, looking in through the gates but never quite ready to enter them, intending but never performing, often wishing but still postponing, hoping but without right to hope,—the appeal is to you: *"How shall ye escape if ye neglect so great salvation?"* (Heb. 2:2-4.)

And if there be any one oblivious or indifferent toward these great matters,—asleep amidst the dashing waves of coming retribution,—the message is to you: *"What meanest thou, O sleeper? Arise, call upon thy God, if so be that God shall think upon thee, that thou perish not!"* (Jonah 1:6). For if any one be not found written in the Book of Life, he must be swallowed up by the Lake of Fire.

Reader, in which book is your name written? Frank M. Davis expressed it this way:

> **Lord, I care not for riches, neither silver nor gold,**
> **I would make sure of Heaven; I would enter the fold.**
> **In the book of Thy kingdom, with its pages so fair,**
> **Tell me, Jesus my Saviour, is my name written there?**

Chapter 21

VERSES 1, 2:

AND I saw a new heaven and a new earth: for the first heaven and the first earth were passed away; and there was no more sea.

2 And I John saw the holy city, new Jerusalem, coming down from God out of heaven, prepared as a bride adorned for her husband.

John Looks Within the Gates and Sees "A New Heaven and a New Earth"

"And I saw a new heaven." J. A. Seiss says about this:

What will that new investment be, to which it is to give place! We cannot describe the meteorology of that new heaven; but it will be a heaven which no more robes itself in angry tempests and menacing blackness; nor ever flashes with the thunderbolts of wrath; nor casts forth plagues of hail; nor rains down fiery judgment; nor gives lurking-place to the Devil and his angels; nor is disfigured with dread portents; nor is subject to commotions breeding terror and disaster to the dwellers under them.

A tremendous gulf of differences stands between this new Heaven and new earth and the former earth and the heavens about it with which we are familiar. When will the change have taken place?

In II Peter 3:7 we are told: "But the heavens and the earth, which are now, by the same word are kept in store, reserved unto fire against the day of judgment and perdition of ungodly men."

The Scripture has just reminded us how the old world, in the flood, "being overflowed with water, perished." The material of the planet did not disappear, but all the surface of it was so changed as to take away every trace of the civilization and life on earth before the flood. So, again there will come a time when this world will be burned over with fire and everything fire can destroy will be destroyed. All the present civilization, the marks of mankind's use and misuse of this earth, will be gone. God will make it into a new earth.

And in that same 3rd chapter of II Peter, verses 12 and 13 say that Christians ought to be in all manner of holy conversation, "Looking for and hasting unto the coming of the day of God, wherein the heavens being on fire shall be dissolved, and the elements shall melt with fervent heat? Nevertheless we, according to his promise, look for new heavens and a new earth, wherein dwelleth righteousness." What an amazing thing that a fire will cause even the planets and the heavens to "be dissolved" when "the elements shall melt with fervent heat"! Ah, but we "look for new heavens and a new earth, wherein dwelleth righteousness."

When will take place this gigantic cataclysm when the earth will be purged by fire, the elements melt with fervent heat? It will happen, II Peter 3:7 says, ". . .reserved unto fire against the day of judgment and perdition of ungodly men." So, while Christ meets all the unsaved, drawn out to face Him before the great white throne set out in illimitable space, the heavens and earth as we see them now will be melted and purged and made new. Then will they be ready for the saints when God comes to make His abode with men and fallen man is redeemed and put back into God's Garden of Eden!

". . .and a new earth." Seiss beautifully describes it this way:

> —an earth which no longer smarts and smokes under the curse of sin,—an earth which needs no more to be torn with hooks and irons to make it yield its fruits,—an earth where thorns and thistles no longer infest the ground, nor serpents hiss among the flowers, nor savage beasts lay in ambush to devour,—an earth whose sod is never cut with graves, whose soil is never moistened with tears or saturated with human blood, whose fields are never blasted with unpropitious seasons, whose atmosphere never gives wings to the seeds of plague and death, whose ways are never lined with funeral processions, or blocked up with armed men on their way to war,—an earth whose hills ever flow with salvation, and whose valleys know only the sweetness of Jehovah's smiles,—an earth from end to end, and from centre to utmost verge, clothed with the eternal blessedness of Paradise Restored!

Unimaginable changes will take place in this new Heaven and earth. "There was no more sea" (vs. 1). And now to this new Heaven and earth comes down "the holy city, new Jerusalem, coming down from God out of heaven."

The church, all the saints of all ages called out to meet Jesus, is sometimes pictured as the bride of Christ (Eph. 5:22-25). But here the bride is that beautiful Holy City. Verses 9 and 10 call the city "the bride, the Lamb's wife."

Dr. Scofield lists here "seven new things" in chapters 21 and 22: (1) A new Heaven, (2) A new earth, (3) New peoples (vss. 1-8). (4) A New Jerusalem (vss. 9-21). (5) A new temple (vs. 22). (6) A new light (vss. 23-27). (7) A new Paradise (22:1-3)."

VERSE 3:

3 And I heard a great voice out of heaven saying, Behold, the tabernacle of God *is* with men, and he will dwell with them, and they shall be his people, and God himself shall be with them, *and be* their God.

God to Make His Home Now Among Men

What a culmination of hope in God's mercy! Now, with the last rebellion put down, with the last unregenerate sinner confined to Hell, God will be able to dwell with men and men, all righteous, all good, redeemed forever!

Inspired Solomon said, "But will God in very deed dwell with men on the earth? behold, heaven and the heaven of heavens cannot contain thee; how much less this house which I have built" (II Chron. 6:18). Here is the desire of God at long last fulfilled. In Eden's Garden God walked and talked daily with Adam, but that fellowship was broken. Sin came in and made all mankind alien, sinful and enemies of God by nature. Mankind went to violence and idolatry "for the imagination of man's heart is only evil continually" (Gen. 8:21), so that the race was wiped out with the flood and only Noah and his family remained.

Then the world again turned to heathen darkness, described in Romans 1, and at Babel God scattered these presumptuous sinners to various languages and races. Then God started over with Abraham and Israel to grow a nation that would serve Him. He came literally in the cloud and fire above the tabernacle. He lived in the Shekinah Glory in the holy of holies. But Israel turned more and more to sin, resulting first in Babylonian captivity, then, after Christ was rejected and crucified, was scattered over all the world, the Temple was destroyed and the Presence of God taken forever from His Temple.

But God was working a plan. Christ came in the flesh to be our Second Adam. He dwelt among men until, with God's foreknowledge and will, He was crucified. But He sent His blessed Holy Spirit to abide in the body of every child of God, beginning the day He arose from the dead (John 20:19-22).

The age goes on, but after our rapture and then Christ's return to reign, there will be a thousand years of peace, with Christ ruling on earth among men. Satan will be bound and sin put down but even so God's dwelling among men is limited by the unsaved who at the first temptation, when Satan is "loosed a little season," will rebel against God, then in a gigantic climax all the wicked are to be judged and sent to Hell. And there is nothing now to hinder and Heaven can come down to earth.

God, a holy God, can now dwell with men in a righteous world, combining Heaven and the new earth as a paradise for God and men. At last the Garden of Eden is to be restored. God's sweet ambition is fulfilled. There is to be no barrier between God and men! We can dwell together in peace and righteousness without the limit sinful men have in communication with God. God will be with us and will be our God!

VERSES 4, 5:

4 And God shall wipe away all tears from their eyes; and there shall be no more death, neither sorrow, nor crying, neither shall there be any more pain: for the former things are passed away.

5 And he that sat upon the throne said, Behold, I make all things new. And he said unto me, Write: for these words are true and faithful.

God Wipes Away All Tears Forever

At first glance one might suppose that immediately on going to Heaven at death or at the rapture and resurrection, all the tears of earth's sorrows would be wiped away. But, no: now the millennium is over and yet here are all the Christians who have been resurrected in glorified bodies and have spent a thousand blessed years with Christ on earth—still they must have tears wiped away.

So glorified saints will have sorrows up to this time, and resurrected eyes will have tear glands! So we may say there will be tears in Heaven up to this time.

Here is a brief outline of my sermon, "Tears in Heaven."

I. Tears in Heaven Over One's Sins and Failures on Earth.

1. *Tears of Shame,* for I John 2:18 says, "And now, little children, abide in him; that, when he shall appear, we may have confidence, and not be ashamed before him at his coming." Some Christians are to be ashamed before Christ at His coming.

2. *Tears of Terror.* "For we must all appear before the judgment seat of Christ; that every one may receive the things done in his body, according to that he hath done, whether it be good or bad. Knowing therefore the terror of the Lord, we persuade men . . ." (II Cor. 5:10, 11a).

Christians must face the result of their sins. One whose loved ones have gone unwarned to Hell will dread to face the Lord Jesus whom they have failed as witnesses. Some will be terrified to face Christ and their works.

3. *Tears of Loss.* First Corinthians 3:10-15 tells of this judgment seat of Christ and how those whose works abide will "receive a reward." (A reward, not salvation—they are already saved.) One whose works are burned "shall suffer loss; but he himself shall be saved; yet so as by fire." Oh, tears of loss after we see our loved ones gone to Hell forever!

II. Tears in Heaven Over Loved Ones on Earth.

1. *In Heaven They Know.* They know when souls are saved (Luke 15:7, 10). Angels go and come continually. All the angels in Heaven knew when Christ was born and came to praise Him. Moses and Elijah knew when to meet Jesus on the Mount of Transfiguration.

2. *Tears in Heaven Over Christians Who Fail on Earth.*

Hebrews 12:1, 2 says,

"Wherefore seeing we also are compassed about with so great a cloud of witnesses, let us lay aside every weight, and the sin which doth so easily beset us, and let us run with patience the race that is set before us, Looking unto Jesus the author and finisher of our faith; who for the joy that was set before him endured the cross, despising the shame, and is set down at the right hand of the throne of God."

Ah, the heavenly grandstand is full, watching our race. They grieve if we fail.

3. *Tears Over Loved Ones on Earth Unsaved.* If the heavenly friends of the Shepherd rejoice over the sheep that are brought home, do they not weep when the sheep is not brought, when the sinner is not saved (Luke 15:7, 10)?

But now we are told that God will wipe away all tears. This is just after Christians will have seen loved ones judged and cast into the lake of fire. What a painful sight! But God will not only wipe away the tears, but we are assured that there will be no more death, no more sorrow, no more pain, no more crying. All things now will be made new. At long last our tears in Heaven are over.

I quote here a beautiful portion from *THE APOCALYPSE,* by J. A. Seiss:

He who dries the tears away is God Himself (vs. 4). Human hands are poor at drying tears. If they succeed in removing one set, others come which they cannot wipe away. Earthly power, however good and kind, cannot go far in the binding up of broken hearts. Only the hand that made the spirit can reach the deep sources of its sorrows, or dry up the streams that issue from them. *"Every tear,"* for they be many;—tears of misfortune and poverty, such as Job and Lazarus wept;—tears of bereaved affection, such as Mary, and Martha, and the widow of Nain shed;—tears of sympathy and mercy, such as Jeremiah and Jesus wept over the sins and calamities of Jerusalem;—tears of persecuted innocence, tears of contrition and penitence for faults and crimes against the goodness and majesty of Heaven;—tears of disappointment and neglect;—tears of yearning for what cannot now be ours;—these, and whatever others ever course the cheeks of mortals, shall then be dried forever.

"And there shall be no more death" (vs. 4). O the reign of death! Whom has it not touched! What circle has it not invaded! What home has it never entered!

> **There is no flock, however watched and tended,**
> **But one dead lamb is there!**
> **There is no fireside howsoe'er defended,**
> **But hath one vacant chair.**

Around our churches lie our graveyards, and all the highways are lined with cemeteries and depositories of the dead. We can scarcely open our eyes without seeing the gloomy hearse, the funeral procession, the undertaker's warehouse, the shop full of mourning goods, or the stonecutter chiselling epitaphs. Every newspaper we pick up has its obituary lists, and every week brings forth its bills of mortality. On the right hand, on the left hand, before us, behind us, around us, beneath us, in all seasons, in all climes, everywhere, is death. We ourselves are only waiting, not knowing what day or hour we shall fall beneath its stroke. . . .

But, the time will be when death itself shall die. . .When the sunlight of the new Genesis dawns upon this stricken world, the grand thanksgiving shall ring out over every zone, from the equator to the poles, that "Death is swallowed up in victory." Never another grave shall then be dug. For "death shall no longer be."

VERSES 6—8:

6 And he said unto me, It is done. I am Alpha and Ō-mĕg-́ă, the beginning and the end. I will give unto him that is athirst of the fountain of the water of life freely.

7 He that overcometh shall inherit all things; and I will be his God, and he shall be my son.

8 But the fearful, and unbelieving, and the abominable, and murderers, and whoremongers, and sorcerers, and idolaters, and all liars, shall have their part in the lake which burneth with fire and brimstone: which is the second death.

Eternal Division Between Saved and Lost

Here are, first, the wonderful promise and offer of salvation again, and, second, the solemn warning of eternal ruin for the impenitent, unconverted sinners. Remember, it is the Lord Jesus speaking still. As He is the Saviour, He is also judge of all, and He describes Himself again like Revelation 1:8, 11, 17; 2:8. The Lord Jesus reminds us of His eternal deity. He is the first and last, the beginning and the end, the Alpha and Omega.

So, again, our Creator-Saviour would not talk about the glory of the New Jerusalem without reminding us that He longs to have all the redeemed ones safe there forever. Note: (1) He said, "I will give"; so salvation is not earned, it is the gift of God, not by works, but by grace. The fountain of water of life is free.

(2) It is for everyone who is "athirst." That means that every person who wants to be saved and wants his sins forgiven, wants a new heart, will have it. "All that the Father giveth me shall come to me; and him that cometh to me I will in no wise cast out" (John 6:37). How simple it is! One is promised, "Draw nigh to God, and he will draw nigh to you" (James 4:8). The heart that sincerely turns to God finds God there waiting. "For whosoever shall call upon the name of the Lord shall be saved" (Rom. 10:13). The dying thief called ignorantly, not knowing how to call, but was saved in an instant (Luke 24:39-43).

"Water of life. . ." (vs. 6). How often that figure is used in Scripture! Like refreshing and life itself to the desert traveler, it is. Here it is not a cup of water but a flowing fountain, an eternal spring.

In Isaiah 12:3 it is pictured as "wells of salvation" (plural) from which the redeemed can draw water of salvation.

In Isaiah 55:1-3 it is "the waters" (plural), free, with no money; includes wine and milk, so one may eat that which is good and that thy "soul delight itself in fatness." And it means, God says, to just "incline your ear, and come unto me: hear, and your soul shall live."

In Psalm 116 the psalmist, delighted that God has "delivered my soul from death, mine eyes from tears, and my feet from falling" (vs. 8), cries out, "What shall I render unto the Lord for all his benefits toward me" (vs. 12). And he answered in the next verse, by inspiration, that he cannot buy, he cannot deserve it, but, "I will take the CUP OF SALVATION, and call upon the name of the Lord."

In John 4:14 Jesus promised the water of life to the woman of Samaria, "But whosoever drinketh of the water that I shall give him shall never thirst; but the water that I shall give him shall be in him a well of water springing up into everlasting life."

Note, not a single drink but a flowing well of water within, "springing up" continually "into everlasting life."

In John 7:37-39 we read:

"In the last day, that great day of the feast, Jesus stood and cried, saying, If any man thirst, let him come unto me, and drink. He that believeth on me, as the scripture hath said, out of his belly shall flow rivers of living water. (But this spake he of the Spirit, which they that believe on him should receive: for the Holy Ghost was not yet given; because that Jesus was not yet glorified.)"

Not only water of life to save one's soul but a fountain of Holy Spirit power flowing out to save and bless all about us! Oh, eternal spring! Oh, water of life, joy, riches, power: never limited, never ceasing! So the Lord Jesus would remind all, "If any man thirst, let him. . .drink."

"He that overcometh" (vs. 7). As in Revelation, chapters 2 and 3, when the term is used as a promise to each of the seven churches, this does not mean an earned salvation. It means rather simply a sweet reminder of things that are coming to the saved who can go through the tribulation and trouble of life. It means light at the end of the tunnel. It means sweet rest and rewards after labor. It means reaping at long last after sowing.

The book of Revelation is a book of plagues. Ah, but Christians, when all is over, we shall "inherit all things" prepared for us! When God tells the blessings of Heaven, He encourages us to be joyful and faithful while we wait for the blessings to come.

Hebrew Christians, facing what seemed to them the unspeakable calamity of the Temple and the city destroyed, the priesthood and sacrifices ended forever, the banishment from the Holy Land, with long generations as a race without a country, as the book of Hebrews warned them, were admonished and we with them, "Cast not away therefore your confidence, which hath great recompence of reward. For ye have need of patience, that, after ye have done the will of God, ye might receive the promise" (Heb. 10:35, 36).

"Inherit ALL THINGS" (vs. 7)! First Corinthians 3:21 tells us, "Therefore let no man glory in men. For all things are your's." We are told that all things are ours; yes, but not yet all inherited. Now Christ reminds us the inheritance will come to us who are the "heirs of salvation." We are saved but have not yet the resurrected bodies, the unlimited fellowship with Christ, the freedom from and limitations of our tainted bodies. But the rest of it all will be ours, thank God, when we inherit our possessions.

But the lost are warned, *"But the fearful, and unbelieving, and the abominable, and murderers, and whoremongers, and sorcerers, and idolaters, and all liars, shall have their part in the lake which burneth with fire and brimstone: which is the second death"* (vs. 8). They will have their part in Hell, the Lord Jesus reminds us. Said Dr. Riley:

> *"But the fearful, and unbelieving. . . ."* When Voltaire was living, he sported his skepticism; it was his boast! When he was dying he was filled with fear; it wrapped his last hours in the blackness of darkness. ". . .*and sorcerers, and idolaters. . .*" Those two terms compass every form of false worship; the magicians of the earth; the so-called Christian Scientist of earth; the spiritualists of earth; the theosophists of earth; what are these but sorcerers; who are these but they that have been deceived by charlatanism, and led away from "the Lamb of God, which taketh away the sin of the world," and from the Spirit whose revelation is perfect, to listen to the rappings of darkness; to be deceived by the priests of Buddha; to be worshiping a principle that has a name but no existence, while denying the Person whose Name is God, and whose character is Love?

Let us have no talk of universal salvation, of a Heaven without a Hell. The eternal separation of saved and lost is clearly stated here as it is many times in the Scripture. Let no foolish softhead forget how awful is sin, how God hates it, how a righteous God, a just God, cannot be righteous and count the impenitent as good as the penitent, the child of Satan as good as the child of God. God cannot be a God of justice and judgment in some parts of the Bible and say here that sin is inconsequential. It is not. It was Satan who said to Adam, "Ye shall not surely die" (Gen. 3:4). And Satan's spokesmen say it yet. But it is a wicked, lying folly. Let no preacher, no witnessing Christian slack up on soul winning and warning and suppose that God's warnings are not sincere and eternally true. So here, near the closing of Revelation, Christ must say it again, as He will in Revelation 22:15, that the unconverted must spend eternity in Hell.

VERSES 9—11:

9 And there came unto me one of the seven angels which had the seven vials full of the seven last plagues, and talked with me, saying, Come hither, I will shew thee the bride, the Lamb's wife.

10 And he carried me away in the spirit to a great and high mountain, and shewed me that great city, the holy Jerusalem, descending out of heaven from God,

11 Having the glory of God: and her light *was* like unto a stone most precious, even like a jasper stone, clear as crystal;

Heavenly Jerusalem, New Capital City of Heaven on Earth

Here the Heavenly City is *"the bride, the Lamb's wife."* In other Scriptures the church, all the saved, is pictured as the bride of Christ. We think the dazzling beauty of the city, the freshness and the joy the Lord Jesus has in it, make it seem like a bride.

It is "new Jerusalem." Then it has relationship to the old Jerusalem. We believe it comes down literally to rest on the earth, taking the place of the old Jerusalem, possibly on the very spot purged by fire so that none but God would know where it should be on this miraculously purged, remade planet.

In II Chronicles 6:6 God said, "But I have chosen Jerusalem, that my name might be there; and have chosen David to be over my people Israel." The former Temple, Solomon's Temple, was destroyed, then rebuilt by Jews after the captivity, then wonderfully rebuilt and restored by Herod the Great. Now the place holds only two moslem mosques, including the beautiful Dome of the Rock.

But is not the place still chosen of God, that God's "name may be there for ever"? And God says, ". . .and mine eyes and mine heart shall be there perpetually" (II Chron. 7:16). I believe this is in some blessed sense a continuation of the old Jerusalem but redeemed and purged and remade and cleansed and glorified.

The land of Palestine is promised to Abraham and his seed "for ever" (Gen. 13:15; Gen. 17:8). We prefer to take that literally. Ecclesiastes 1:4 says, ". . .the earth abideth for ever," not in its accursed, present form but made new. So we think the New Jerusalem will be the capital city of this new paradise of God. Heaven and earth combined, God and man living together.

Will we go and come on the new earth, in the Heavenly City? I suppose so.

The new earth (vs. 1) will have no sea. We must believe that the city of God and the new earth are combined and are as closely related as the old Jerusalem and Palestine were.

Oh, the light of that holy city *"having the glory of God"* (vs. 11) shining like diamonds and precious stones! Who can tell it all until we see it ourselves!

VERSES 12—25:

12 And had a wall great and high, *and* had twelve gates, and at the gates twelve angels, and names written thereon, which are *the names* of the twelve tribes of the children of Israel:

13 On the east three gates; on the north three gates; on the south three gates; and on the west three gates.

14 And the wall of the city had twelve foundations, and in them the names of the twelve apostles of the Lamb.

15 And he that talked with me had a golden reed to measure the city, and the gates thereof, and the wall thereof.

16 And the city lieth foursquare, and the length is as large as the breadth: and he measured the city with the reed, twelve thousand furlongs. The length and the breadth and the height of it are equal.

17 And he measured the wall thereof, an hundred *and* forty *and* four cubits, *according to* the measure of a man, that is, of the angel.

18 And the building of the wall of it was *of* jasper: and the city *was* pure gold, like unto clear glass.

19 And the foundations of the wall of the city *were* garnished with all manner of precious stones. The first foundation *was* jasper; the second, sapphire; the third, a chalcedony; the fourth, an emerald;

20 The fifth, sardonyx; the sixth, sardius; the seventh, chrysolyte; the eighth, beryl; the ninth, a topaz; the tenth, a chrysoprasus; the eleventh, a jacinth; the twelfth, an amethyst.

21 And the twelve gates *were* twelve pearls: every several gate was of one pearl: and the street of the city *was* pure gold, as it were transparent glass.

22 And I saw no temple therein: for the Lord God Almighty and the Lamb are the temple of it.

23 And the city had no need of the sun, neither of the moon, to shine in

it: for the glory of God did lighten it, and the Lamb *is* the light thereof.

24 And the nations of them which are saved shall walk in the light of it: and the kings of the earth do bring their glory and honour into it.

25 And the gates of it shall not be shut at all by day: for there shall be no night there.

Marvelous City Described

1. The twelve gates of the Heavenly Jerusalem are to be named after the twelve tribes. That will have been the case, too, in the kingdom age. The Jerusalem on earth during the kingdom age will have twelve gates also. Ezekiel 48:30-35 tells us:

"And these are the goings out of the city on the north side, four thousand and five hundred measures. And the gates of the city shall be after the names of the tribes of Israel: three gates northward; one gate of Reuben, one gate of Judah, one gate of Levi. And at the east side four thousand and five hundred: and three gates; and one gate of Joseph, one gate of Benjamin, one gate of Dan. And at the south side four thousand and five hundred measures: and three gates; one gate of Simeon, one gate of Issachar, one gate of Zebulun. At the west side four thousand and five hundred, with their three gates; one gate of Gad, one gate of Asher, one gate of Naphtali. It was round about eighteen thousand measures: and the name of the city from that day shall be, The Lord is there."

Evidently God wants to make eternal record of His love for Israel, and that Israel pictured all the people of God, for we who are of the faith of Abraham are the children of Abraham. So twelve gates in the New Jerusalem will be named tribe by tribe for the tribes of Israel, as it will have been in the kingdom age and the great city.

So there are twelve gates with the names of the twelve tribes of Israel on them (vs. 12). God has not thrown away all the beautiful tradition and historical riches of His dealing with Israel. So the name Jerusalem and so the names of the twelve tribes are perpetuated. These gates are three on each of four sides. Each gate is a solid pearl.

T. Dewitt Talmage says the twelve gates, three out of every

direction, means that God wants all the world to come and live in this beautiful city of God.

2. The wall of the city has twelve foundations, with the name of each of the apostles. They are garnished with precious stones (vs. 19).

The wall is 140 cubits high (about 210 feet high). The wall has beauty and spiritual meaning since the gates are never shut. So the wall does not shut out enemies, because it is never night there and the gates are not shut by day. This wall is of beautiful jasper.

3. The city is foursquare, we suppose a cube, 12,000 furlongs or 1,500 miles each way—at the base and that high (vs. 16). The city streets are pure gold (vs. 21).

4. There is no temple to represent God, for He is there visibly and is available and in constant fellowship with His people as is the Lord Jesus Christ (vs. 22).

5. Note these strange things in the new Heaven and the new earth. "No more sea" (vs. 1); "no temple" (vs. 22)—Christ will be the Temple thereof; no sun or moon (vs. 23), since Christ is the light of it. Some have foolishly said there could be no light at the time of creation, before God made the sun. Oh, but God Himself is light and He has light wherever He will. He can have it here with no sun.

This light will light all the new earth, we understand (vs. 24) and kings and the most honored of God's people will bring their glory and honor into the Heavenly City.

6. The gates are never shut. By that we suppose there is to be abundant traffic to and fro flowing from all parts of the new earth into the Holy City and returning.

How Drastically Different Is New Earth and Its Capital From Present Earth

Since there will be no more sun and moon, then the earth will not travel as a planet, in orbit, about the sun. There will be no night there, so it is not turning on an axis to make daylight and nighttime. A new system of coherence and gravity will hold this redeemed planet and the Heavenly Jerusalem together.

On the earth today, if one climbs 29,002-feet-high Mount Everest, he must take extra oxygen to breathe. The gravity of the earth holds the elastic air close condensed down to the earth. But here the golden city will rear 1,500 miles above the surface of the earth and we may be sure there will be abundant air to breathe, for the glorified body will be a perfect body, we suppose, like in the Garden of Eden, and we suppose that the bodily processes of circulation, breathing, digesting food, etc., will be perfect, just as God made them for the Garden of Eden. At any rate, we may be sure that the top of that great golden city will be as habitable and pleasant as the bottom. It may be that the mass of the golden city itself will have the mass attraction of gravity so that it will be surrounded by atmosphere as thick as will the earth below it. God will attend to that matter well.

"And the city had no need of the sun, neither of the moon, to shine in it: for the glory of God did lighten it, and the Lamb is the light thereof" (vs. 23). "Here is your provision for eternal day," says Dr. Riley. "So long as God lives the light of that city cannot fail. Scientists tell us that the moon is growing colder, and will eventually be dead; that the sun itself is likely to go out into darkness as a spark smitten from the anvil; but to the saints these cataclysms are no particular concern, since our God, in whom is no darkness at all, will be still shining on!"

There is to be no more sea. That means that the balance we have now of water, rainfall, evaporation on the surface of the earth is maintained, but it will not be the same in the new earth, with no more sea. Genesis 2:10-14 says:

"And a river went out of Eden to water the garden; and from thence it was parted, and became into four heads. The name of the first is Pison: that is it which compasseth the whole land of Havilah, where there is gold;. . .And the name of the second river is Gihon: the same is it that compasseth the whole land of Ethiopia. And the name of the third river is Hiddekel: that is it which goeth toward the east of Assyria. And the fourth river is Euphrates."

We know that those rivers were not left the same when the

earth was destroyed by the flood, but at least there were rivers and they watered the land. Whether they were simply dissipated as they watered the whole land or whether they flowed into the seas, we do not know. But there are indications that then a perfect, somewhat tropical climate covered the whole earth. As far as we can tell, there were the same plants and animals in the Arctic Circle and Antarctic Circle as in the rest of the world. Great forms of mammoths and other beasts are found frozen in Siberia and Alaska, and coal beds there show that the enormous luxuriant herbage was there as in the rest of the planet. We suppose that the "waters above the earth" (Gen. 1:7) formed somewhat of a canopy that made the moderate climate of the whole world much the same before the flood.

Will it be like that in this new earth? It will have a river, too—the river of the water of life—(Rev. 22:1, 2).

In some wonderful way the new earth and the Heavenly City will be the center of the universe, and God Himself will dwell with men and there will be no need for the sun and the other planets. God who made the whole planetary system self-interrelated and self-sustaining, could He not make this earth alone with the capital city a New Jerusalem, self-sustaining also? God is not the slave but the Master of His own creation. He who made the heavens and earth can make a new Heaven and earth after His own perfect plan. It will not be like the present in many ways. For one thing, there will be no more curse there, so the plants on this new earth and in the Heavenly City will not be weeds, thorns, poison ivy, and will not be accursed. And the animals, whatever are there, will not be the enemies of man. The curse will be passed away.

VERSES 26,27:

26 And they shall bring the glory and honour of the nations into it.

27 And there shall in no wise enter into it any thing that defileth, neither *whatsoever* worketh abomination, or *maketh* a lie: but they which are written in the Lamb's book of life.

A Perfect City and Civilization at Last

All the honor and glory this world ever saw will be brought into the New Jerusalem.

Here is comfort for the saints—no sin, no corruption, no temptation, no defilement. The Christian now may often say with the Apostle Paul, "I find then a law, that, when I would do good, evil is present with me. For I delight in the law of God after the inward man: But I see another law in my members, warring against the law of my mind, and bringing me into captivity to the law of sin which is in my members. O wretched man that I am! who shall deliver me from the body of this death?" (Rom. 7:21-24).

Many a Christian has sung with holy desire

> **Oh, wash me Thou, without, within,**
> **Or purge with fire, if that must be;**
> **No matter how, if only sin**
> **Die out in me, die out in me.**

That holy longing will be fulfilled in the Heavenly City, praise God! For nothing defiling or abominable or unclean will enter that City.

But here is solemn warning for all also. To enter Heaven one must have repented, that is, turned his heart away from sin. We know that no sin can enter Heaven. And we frail mortals who have been born of God, have become the children of God, yet must say, "If we say that we have no sin, we deceive ourselves, and the truth is not in us" (I John 1:8). So there must come and wonderfully there will come a marvelous change.

First Corinthians 15:51, 52 says, "Behold, I shew you a mystery; We shall not all sleep, but we shall all be changed, In a moment, in the twinkling of an eye, at the last trump: for the trumpet shall sound, and the dead shall be raised incorruptible, and we shall be changed." Yes, and Philippians 3:20, 21a says, "For our conversation is in heaven; from whence also we look for the Saviour, the Lord Jesus Christ: Who shall change our vile body, that it may be fashioned like unto his glorious body."

Then here in Heaven are to be only those whose names are

written in the Book of Life, those who have been born of God and now changed into the image of God, and our vile bodies will be made like unto His glorious body.

Chapter 22

AND he shewed me a pure river of water of life, clear as crystal, proceeding out of the throne of God and of the Lamb.

2 In the midst of the street of it, and on either side of the river, *was there* the tree of life, which bare twelve *manner of* fruits, *and* yielded her fruit every month: and the leaves of the tree *were* for the healing of the nations.

3 And there shall be no more curse: but the throne of God and of the Lamb shall be in it; and his servants shall serve him:

The River and the Trees of Life

God had a river in Eden; He will also have a river in the Heavenly City. "One of the gladdest things on earth is water. There is nothing in all the world so precious to the eye and imagination of the inhabitant of the dry, burning and thirsty East, as a plentiful supply of bright, pure, and living water. Paradise itself was not complete without it" (J. A. Seiss).

This water will flow out from the throne of God. We will before have had a picture of that in the kingdom age. Zechariah 14:8 says, "And it shall be in that day, that living waters shall go out from Jerusalem; half of them toward the former sea, and half of them toward the hinder sea: in summer and in winter shall it be." The river of the sanctuary in the kingdom age is described again in Ezekiel 47:1, ". . .and, behold, waters issued out from under the threshold of the house [the Temple] eastward: for the forefront of the house stood toward the east, and the waters came down from under from the right side of the house, at the south side of the altar." The angel measured for Ezekiel and the water grew deeper and deeper. And the 47th chapter, verse 8, tells us those waters went down toward the east country to the desert, into the sea, the Dead Sea, and the waters would be healed. So there would be a multitude of fish in the river and in the Dead Sea, and wherever the water went, they would be healed.

And by the banks of that river "shall grow all trees for meat, whose leaf shall not fade, neither shall the fruit thereof be consumed: it shall bring forth new fruit according to his months, because their waters they issued out of the sanctuary: and the fruit thereof shall be for meat, and the leaf thereof for medicine."

Then in the kingdom age we have a picture of a beautiful life, with the water curing the desert and bringing abundant life wherever it goes. And the waters of the Dead Sea will be healed.

That reminds us that in the new Heaven and the new earth the river of the water of life will be somewhat like that pictured in the kingdom age.

". . .a pure river of water of life." I believe there will be a literal river. But the "water of life" is surely a picture and symbol of salvation. In Revelation 21:6 the Lord promised, "I will give unto him that is athirst of the fountain of the water of life freely." And in this chapter, verse 17b says, "And whosoever will, let him take the water of life freely." In a spiritual sense, one has salvation by partaking of Christ, who is spiritually the Water of Life; but in some physical sense, too, our bodies will be saved, kept and preserved, and this heavenly water of life has something to do with that.

Some have imagined that those who are weary of long years of toilsome service for God in this world will be able to sit down by the river of life, wash and refresh their tired feet in that clear water.

And there will be trees of life bearing twelve manner of fruit, trees that yield their fruit every month, and the leaves are for the healing of the nations (vs. 2).

Again we quote a passage from Seiss' *The Apocalypse:*

These trees, like the River whose sides they line, are first of all for the joy and blessedness of the dwellers in the Holy City; to beautify their eternal home, and to minister to their happiness. They are fruit-bearing trees, yielding their products every month, and each month a new variety.

It is sometimes asked whether the glorified saints are to eat in Heaven? We may safely answer that *they can eat,* although under no need to eat; just as we can enjoy a rose, and yet not suffer from its absence. . . .The Saviour several times refers to eating and drinking in the kingdom of glory. He again and again likens the whole provision of grace to a banquet, a feast. One of the most emphasized scenes of the future, to which this Apocalypse refers, is a *supper,* even the supper of the marriage of the Lamb. And so the implication here is that there will be eating in this Eternal City, the eating of fruits, the eating of the monthly products of the Tree of Life. The inhabitants there drink Life-water, and they eat Life-fruits.

We know that Jesus ate in His resurrected body (Luke 24:41-43), and we shall have bodies like unto His glorious body (Phil. 3:20, 21).

That tree of life was in the Garden of Eden. In some sense it was the antidote for all ills, the cure for all sickness, so it tended toward perfect health continually.

In the Garden of Eden, "out of the ground made the Lord God to grow every tree that is pleasant to the sight, and good for food; the tree of life also in the midst of the garden, and the tree of knowledge of good and evil" (Gen. 2:9). They were not forbidden to eat of the tree of life; in fact, they were told, "Of every tree of the garden thou mayest freely eat: But of the tree of the knowledge of good and evil, thou shalt not eat of it" (16, 17). Ah, but when sin came in, then Adam and Eve were taken out of the Garden of Eden:

"And the Lord God said, Behold, the man is become as one of us, to know good and evil: and now, lest he put forth his hand, and take also of the tree of life, and eat, and live for ever: Therefore the Lord God sent him forth from the garden of Eden, to till the ground from whence he was taken. So he drove out the man; and he placed at the east of the garden of Eden Cherubims, and a flaming sword which turned every way, to keep the way of the tree of life."—Gen. 3:22-24.

If they could eat of the tree of life it would constantly renew their bodies and their health, and now that they are fallen sinners they would live forever in sin. So they must be shut out of the Garden of Eden, away from the tree of life. And the Garden of Eden decayed under a curse on this world and the tree of life itself was removed.

But God is not done with the tree of life. It will be planted

abundantly on each side of the river and in the middle of the
street and there will be abundant fruit, twelve manner of new
fruit every month. And the leaves are for the continual healing
and refreshing and renewing of God's people.

Even now, in spirit, we are told ". . .but though our outward
man perish, yet the inward man is renewed day by day" (II Cor.
4:16). And one sweet day the renewing, the refreshing, the
everlasting life that belong to every born-again soul will be our
possession in body also and life everlasting in a perfect body, like
Christ's glorious body, constantly renewed and healed and made
continually perfect. We will thus "inherit eternal life" in body as
we have now already in spirit.

"And there shall be no more curse" (vs. 3). Plants without
thorns! A ground that smiles to bring forth everything that is
good. And no one will anymore have indigestion, nor upset
stomach, nor infection, nor a cold, nor the constant decay and
erosion that come with old age! Thank God, there will be no
more curse because *"the throne of God and of the Lamb shall be
in it"* (vs. 3).

"And his servants shall serve him" (vs. 3). There will be work
to do, though we do not know all it will be, but it will be wonderful to be well, strong and busy. We will never be tired. There will
be no night needed in which to sleep and rest our weary bodies. It
may be that then everyone may do perfectly what he longed to do
here but was never able to do. Here surely the painter will paint
perfect pictures, the writer will write such psalms and refreshing
philosophy and praises as he could never put in human words
before. And buildings will be so wonderfully built that they will
not rot with age, nor become out of style or inadequate and need
repairs. Thank God, we will serve Him in ways He will know and
that are worth the highest ambitions, the most ardent work and
planning that man can do—but all with joyful hearts, perfect
health and a unity of heart with God! *"His servants shall serve
him."* Praise the Lord!

VERSES 4, 5:

4 And they shall see his face; and his name *shall be* in their foreheads. 5 And there shall be no night there; and they need no candle, neither light of the sun; for the Lord God giveth them light: and they shall reign for ever and ever.

Blessed Association With Jesus

"And they shall see his face" (vs. 4). Now, in our sinful state no man can see God and live (Exod. 33:20). When John saw the resurrected Christ in His glory, he "fell at this feet as dead" (1:17). Oh, "now we see through a glass, darkly; but then face to face" (I Cor. 13:12). Even the truth of God we see so poorly. Our poor clouded minds are too dulled, too worldly, too limited to see truth in its eternal grandeur, all of it without distortion. But we shall see His face and, unashamed, will not hide from His gaze! Sinful Adam ran and hid from God. Now "every one that doeth evil hateth the light, neither cometh to the light, lest his deeds should be reproved" (John 3:20). That is primarily true of lost sinners, but it also somewhat applies to all of us with our human frailty and our conscious unworthiness now.

Dr. R. G. Lee told how, when he was a young man, he spent some time in South America. When he returned, his mother took his face in her hands and demanded, did he stay clean? He looked her in the loving, inquiring eyes boldly and said, "I stayed clean. I never took a drink of liquor. I never touched a woman!" Oh, how sweet when we can look Jesus in the face and know, "Nothing between my soul and the Saviour."

". . .and his name shall be in their foreheads" (vs. 4). What a sweet brand that will be! I can say then, "I belong to Him completely and He proudly owns me as His own." Jesus said, "Whosoever therefore shall be ashamed of me and of my words in this adulterous and sinful generation; of him also shall the Son of man be ashamed, when he cometh in the glory of his Father with the holy angels" (Mark 8:38). But of us who have claimed Him openly, He will not be ashamed. He said, "Whosoever therefore shall confess me before men, him will I confess also before my Father which is in heaven" (Matt. 10:32).

In Hebrews 2:11 God says, "For both he that sanctifieth and

they who are sanctified are all of one: for which cause he is not ashamed to call them brethren."

". . .no night" (vs. 5). On this verse Seiss says: "In the home of the glorified saints there will be no more night. Darkness of all orders, physical, mental, and moral, shall have no place there. As the glory of the Shekinah ever glowed in the Holy of Holies, so shall the Jehovah brightness ever illuminate the heavenly Jerusalem, and all its inhabitants shall themselves be light; for they 'shall shine as the brightness of the firmament, and as the stars forever and ever' (Dan. 12:3)." Jesus is to be our Light. My eyes are a little dim. I must use glasses to read. I do not see as well at 81 as I did in youth. I may drop food, unseen, on my tie; but in the light of Christ's presence we will all see perfectly in that pure light.

". . .and they shall reign for ever and ever." Reign? Yes. "If we suffer, we shall also reign with him" (II Tim. 2:12). In the millennial reign, the apostles are promised they "shall sit upon twelve thrones, judging the twelve tribes of Israel" (Matt. 19:28). Of the twenty-four elders we are told in Revelation 5:9,10: "And they sung a new song, saying, Thou art worthy to take the book, and to open the seals thereof: for thou wast slain, and hast redeemed us to God by thy blood out of every kindred, and tongue, and people, and nation; And hast made us unto our God kings and priests: and we shall reign on the earth."

In the parable of the pounds in Luke 19:12-27, the servant who had gained ten pounds was given to rule over ten cities; and the man who had gained five pounds was to rule over five cities. So now we learn that those who are worthy will reign beyond the millennium in the new earth and the New Jerusalem! We are to judge angels (I Cor. 6:3) and much more, we do not know.

VERSES 6—11:

6 And he said unto me, These sayings *are* faithful and true: and the Lord God of the holy prophets sent his angel to shew unto his servants the things which must shortly be done.

7 Behold, I come quickly: blessed *is* he that keepeth the sayings of the prophecy of this book.

8 And I John saw these things, and heard *them*. And when I had heard and seen, I fell down to worship before the feet of the angel which shewed me these things.

9 Then saith he unto me, See *thou do it* not: for I am thy fellowservant, and of thy brethren the prophets, and of them which keep the sayings of this book: worship God.

10 And he saith unto me, Seal not the sayings of the prophecy of this book: for the time is at hand.

11 He that is unjust, let him be unjust still: and he which is filthy, let him be filthy still: and he that is righteous, let him be righteous still: and he that is holy, let him be holy still.

Brief Summary of Purpose and Trend of This Book

"These sayings. . ." —the whole book of Revelation—*"are faithful and true"* (vs. 6). Then they are to be understood and taken to heart.

A seminary professor, an amillennialist, said, "I do not understand Revelation and no one else does." But he desecrates divine revelation which had a true and understandable message. No one, of course, understands all the infinite wisdom of Scripture, but the main truth is clear to the believing and Spirit-led reader. "Blessed is he that readeth, and they that hear the words of this prophecy, and keep those things which are written therein: for the time is at hand." The sayings are to be understood; so *"blessed is he that keepeth the sayings of the prophecy of this book"* (vs. 7).

". . .the things which must shortly be done" (vs. 6) bear with the next sentence, *"Behold, I come quickly"* (vs. 7). Dr. A. T. Robertson says, "About Christ coming quickly see 2:5, 16; 3:11; 16:15, and already in 1:2f. Once more we must recall that *tachu* and *en tachei* are according to God's time, not ours (II Pet. 3:8)."

The word *"shortly"* as used here is a translation of *en tachei*, which Young's Analytical Concordance describes "with, or in speed." The idea cannot be that these things will take place immediately or within some specified short time. The thing is that they come suddenly and inevitably. All the talk of Christ's coming in the Bible is with the idea that His coming is impending, with no time specified. Christ might come at any time.

In Matthew 24:36 Jesus said, "But of that day and hour knowth no man, no, not the angels of heaven, but my Father only." In Mark 13:32 He said, "But of that day and that hour knoweth no man, no, not the angels which are in heaven, neither the Son, but the Father." Even Christ on earth, in human body, did not know the time of His return. He had laid aside that as part of the marks of deity. He knows now, of course. And in Matthew 25:13 Jesus said, "Watch therefore, for ye know neither the day nor the hour wherein the Son of man cometh." And again Jesus said, "And what I say unto you I say unto all, Watch" (Mark 13:37).

We can see here the transporting joy of John as the main thrust of the revelation is over. How ardently he falls at the feet of the angel! But angels are not to be worshiped. No, he is a fellowservant, one of our brethren who prophesies or tells God's message in power. But angels are really "ministering spirits, sent forth to minister for them who shall be heirs of salvation" (Heb. 1:14). Christians are to "judge angels" (I Cor. 6:3). Worship of angels is forbidden (Col. 2:18).

"Seal not the sayings of the prophecy of this book" (vs. 10). So this book is a "revelation," not a concealment. God gave this revelation to John *"to shew unto his servants things which must shortly come to pass"* (1:1). Let no reader excuse himself from devoted study and meditation to understand this book.

". . .the time is at hand" (vs. 10) means it is impending, not that it will begin immediately but that it could begin at any time. Imminent is the idea.

"He that is unjust, let him be unjust still" (vs. 11). When we have passed the thousand-year-reign of Christ and come to the great white throne judgment, we have passed the time of conversion and forgiveness. Those who pass the time of mercy still unrepentant have crossed the line forever. So the unjust will stay unjust, the filthy will stay filthy, the condemned will stay condemned. The sinner in Hell forever will be wicked still. The filthy will be filthy still.

Says Dr. Ironside about verse 11: "We have set before us the great truth that science itself demonstrates, equally with the Word of God, namely, that character tends to permanence. 'He that is unjust, let him be unjust still: and he that is filthy, let him be filthy still: and he that is righteous, let him be righteous still: and he that is holy, let him be holy still.' It is a divine emphasis upon the solemn truth that as a man is found in that coming day, so shall he remain for all eternity. . . ."

And in Heaven the righteous will be forever righteous, the children of God. Even in this life now some sinners, with full enlightenment, so reject the Lord Jesus and so harden their hearts that that they will never want to be saved and so cross the deadline. They will never repent. But after the millennium, all sinners are forever doomed, forever wicked, forever against God and Christ.

VERSES 12, 13:

12 And, behold, I come quickly; and my reward is with me, to give every man according as his work shall be.

13 I am Alpha and Ō-mĕg′-ă, the beginning and the end, the first and the last.

Rewards at Last

"I come quickly." See also verse 7, so 3:11. Like the phrase "must shortly come to pass" (vs. 1), this does not mean immediately but impending, may come at any moment. So Christians are taught to watch continually for Christ's coming. Mark 13:32-38 says:

"But of that day and that hour knoweth no man, no, not the angels which are in heaven, neither the Son, but the Father. Take ye heed, watch and pray: for ye know not when the time is. For the Son of man is as a man taking a far journey, who left his house, and gave authority to his servants, and to every man his work and commanded the porter to watch. Watch ye therefore: for ye know not when the master of the house cometh, at even, or at midnight, or at the cockcrowing, or in|the morning: Lest coming suddenly he find you sleeping. And what I say unto you I say unto all, Watch."

Matthew 25:13 says, "Watch therefore, for ye know neither the

day nor the hour wherein the Son of man cometh." This obviously refers to the first phase of Christ's coming into the air to
receive His own, like I Thessalonians 4:13-17; I Corinthians
15:51, 52.

". . .*my reward is with me*" (vs. 12). So in the judgment seat
of Christ, His rewarding of Christians as taught in I Corinthians
3:10-15 and II Corinthians 5:9, 10, does not wait for His return to
reign after the tribulation period.

There are many rewards from day to day in serving Christ.
Jesus said, "Verily I say unto you, There is no man that hath left
house, or brethren, or sisters, or father, or mother, or wife, or
children, or lands, for my sake, and the gospel's, But he shall
receive an hundredfold now in this time, houses, and brethren,
and sisters, and mothers, and children, and lands, with persecutions; and in the world to come eternal life" (Mark 10:29, 30).

But far more rewards wait for Christ's coming. "If we suffer,
we shall also reign with him" (II Tim. 2:12). Paul was inspired to
say, "For our conversation is in heaven; from whence also we look
for the Saviour, the Lord Jesus Christ: Who shall change our vile
body, that if may be fashioned like unto his glorious body, according to the working whereby he is able even to subdue all
things unto himself" (Phil. 3:20, 21). So he could well say, "Yea,
and we are found false witnesses of God; because we have
testified of God that he raised up Christ: whom he raised not up,
if so be that the dead rise not" (I Cor. 15:15). Those who love
Christ more and suffer for Him more, may, like Paul, be in a
strait whether to depart and be with Christ "which is far better,"
for "to die is gain" for faithful Christians. Rewards ahead!
". . .In due season we shall reap, if we faint not" (Gal. 6:9).

Again Christ reminds us He is "Alpha and Omega" (vs. 13),
the first and last letters of the Greek alphabet. Christ is all from
A to Z. He is first and last, the beginning and ending. We must
remember He came once as Saviour; He will return as King and
Judge.

VERSES 14, 15:

14 Blessed *are* they that do his commandments, that they may have right to the tree of life, and may enter in through the gates into the city.

15 For without *are* dogs, and sorcerers, and whoremongers, and murderers, and idolaters, and whosoever loveth and maketh a lie.

A Translator's Mistake

Verse 14 is, we think, a bad mistranslation, evidently derived from some gloss added by a zealous copyist to some ancient manuscript. The verse should read, as the American Standard translation has it, "Blessed are they that wash their robes, that they may have the right to come to the tree of life, and may enter in by the gates into the city." No one gets the right to enter Heaven by keeping commandments. Else Nicodemus and Saul of Tarsus we suppose would have been saved, though unconverted. No, "washed in the blood" is the way to be saved. The white garment of Christ's righteousness can be ours only by trusting in Christ who died for us. It is "not by works of righteousness which we have done, but according to his mercy he saved us, by the washing of regeneration, and renewing of the Holy Ghost" (Titus 3:5). "For by grace are ye saved through faith; and that not of yourselves: it is the gift of God: Not of works, lest any man should boast" (Eph. 2:8, 9).

Seiss says on verse 14: "The now better-established reading, to which all consent, literally rendered, is: 'Blessed they that wash their robes, that they may (in that day shall) have the power over the tree of life, and enter by the gates into the city.' " His foot note says:

*See the Codex Sinaiticus, Codex Alexandrinus, the Vulgate, the Ethiopic, and some Armenian copies, Lachmann, Buttmann, Ewald, Thiele, Tregelles, Alford, Wordsworth, and all the great authorities.

Seiss continues: "The meaning is not essentially different; but the true reading cuts out the possibility of a legalistic interpretation, gives to the passage its genuine evangelic flavour, and conforms its imagery to what was previously said in this Book with reference to what brought the great multitude out of the great tribulation (7:14). *Washing,* or cleansing, is the great qualification for Heaven,—'the washing of water by the word' (Eph. 5:26),—'the washing of regeneration' (Titus 3:5),—cleansing by the blood of Jesus Christ (I John 1:7). There is no doing or keeping of commandments that can save us without this (Eph. 2:8, 9). . . ."

We love the King James Version. It has the most beautiful, stately language. It is reverently done. We use the King James Version continually and urge others to use it. We do not recommend any of the paraphrases—Phillips Translation, The Living Bible, Good News for Modern Man, etc. We do not recommend any translation influenced by liberal unbelief like Moffatt's, the Revised Standard Version nor the New English Bible. Some one-man translations are helpful for reference at times but are not adequate to replace the King James or the American Standard Versions. The New American Standard is probably the most accurate of all, though generally we prefer the King James Version.

But verse 14 here is an illustration. The Bible doctrine of inspiration does not mean God guarantees man's translation or exposition or teaching, or man's copying of Scripture. That requires man's careful faith, study and fidelity. Fortunately, in no translation is any Bible doctrine in question. In nearly every case, the differences between good translations are very minor, incidental.

"Without are dogs" (vs. 15). What a list of sinners who miss Heaven! They are called dogs, sorcerers, whoremongers, murderers, idolaters and liars. Remember that I Corinthians 6:9, 10 says a similar thing:

"Know ye not that the unrighteous shall not inherit the kingdom of God? Be not deceived: neither fornicators, nor idolaters, nor adulterers, nor effeminate, nor abusers of themselves with mankind, Nor thieves, nor covetous, nor drunkards, nor revilers, nor extortioners, shall inherit the kingdom of God."

But be sure to note the next verse: "And such were some of you: but ye are washed, but ye are sanctified, but ye are justified in the name of the Lord Jesus, and by the Spirit of our God" (vs.

11). Those who are forgiven, cleansed, saved, are no longer sorcerers, whoremongers, idolaters and liars. Their sins are forgiven, carried as far away as the east is from the west (Ps. 103:12). They are buried in the depths of the sea (Micah 7:19). Those sins are all cast behind God's back (Isa. 38:17). They are "remembered no more" (Heb. 10:17).

> If sin be remembered and cometh to judgment,
> Oh sad the day, God's judgment day.
> But Christ met that judgment for penitent sinners,
> Their sins are all taken away.
>
> Now I am washed whiter than snow, and forgiven.
> How much I gain, eternal gain.
> My sins are all pardoned and cancelled and covered,
> And never remembered again.
>
> No more, no more, remembered no more!
> My sins are all paid for, in Christ's body borne!
> Jesus has died for them, God has forgotten them.
> Who shall condemn when the slate is all clean then?
> No more! no more! remembered no more.
> My sins are remembered no more!

Those outside Heaven are sinners who never turned to Christ for salvation and they remain sinners, unforgiven forever.

VERSES 16, 17:

16 I Jesus have sent mine angel to testify unto you these things in the churches. I am the root and the offspring of David, *and* the bright and morning star.
17 And the Spirit and the bride say, Come. And let him that heareth say, Come. And let him that is athirst come. And whosoever will, let him take the water of life freely.

Jesus Gives Last Invitation in Bible

It is Jesus who gives the invitation: "I Jesus. . . ." Seiss reminds us: "Before he was born, the angel said to Joseph, 'Call his name JESUS, for he shall save his people from their sins' (Matt. 1:21). This name was given him; and this name he still owns in Heaven."

The book of Revelation is what God gave Jesus to have John

write down. John sent the message to the angels (or messengers) of the seven churches in the small province of Asia and what is now Asiatic Turkey. Jesus must press again His place as eternal God. He is the "Root of David," that is, He is the Creator of all things and He is David's God. The Lord Jesus emphasized that in Matthew 22:41-45:

"While the Pharisees were gathered together, Jesus asked them, Saying, What think ye of Christ? whose son is he? They say unto him, The son of David. He saith unto them, How then doth David in spirit call him Lord, saying, The Lord said unto my Lord, Sit thou on my right hand, till I make thine enemies thy footstool? If David then call him Lord, how is he his son?"

The only answer is that Christ is God, eternal Creator of all things.

He is also *"the offspring of David"* (vs. 16). That is, His human body is literally descended from David so that He is "son of David" as well as "Son of God." He is God and Man. He declares here both His deity and humanity.

Here is a sweet invitation. It seems as if Jesus said to John, "I must not close this last book of the Bible and thus close the canon of inspiration without another sweet invitation to sinners." And I imagine it is as if John said, "All right, Lord Jesus, my goose quill pen is ready, my ink of lampblack and olive oil is mixed, my parchment is unrolled." And Jesus gave this, one of the most precious of all God's promises to the unsaved.

"The Spirit. . .says, Come" (vs. 17). The sweet Spirit of God calls sinners to be saved. Oh, how every preacher, every teacher, every soul winner, everyone who witnesses, must remember that the Spirit of God must speak to hearts and use the Word and loving invitation to get people saved.

". . .the bride. . .say, Come" (vs. 17). The bride here is the Heavenly Jerusalem (see 21:2, 9, 10), adorned as a bride, the Scripture says. Ah, who could tell how wonderful is Heaven, the Father's house of many mansions prepared for His own. And the Lord Jesus is saying, "In my Father's house are many mansions: if it were not so, I would have told you." He is saying there is

room for all. You are invited and He is "not willing that any should perish" (II Pet. 3:9). So the Heavenly Jerusalem is waiting to be filled with penitent sinners who come trusting Christ.

"And let him that heareth say, Come" (vs. 17). Every Christian is to tell it. With the joy of salvation is the obligation of telling others. Saving sinners is the dearest thing to the heart of God. It is what Jesus died for. It is the very beat of the Great Commission. Oh, when Jesus said, "All power [authority] is given unto me in heaven and in earth; go ye therefore" (Matt. 28:18, 19), He stated that He had authority over every believer in the world, and He has commanded us to go. In that Great Commission in Matthew the disciples were told when one was saved and baptized he was to be taught "to observe all things whatsoever I have commanded you." Everyone who hears the Gospel has the Great Commission.

Spurgeon spoke once of walking in a busy market place and he heard a man stand up on a box and cry out his testimony for the Lord Jesus. "I ain't got no edication but I want to tell you about my Saviour." Spurgeon said that the man butchered the King's English and in his heart at first there was some thought, Then why doesn't he leave it to other people who have some education to tell it better! But the man continued, "I ain't got no edication but I have heard it and I've a right to tell it!" And Spurgeon said there leaped in his heart the glad word, Yes, if he heard it he ought to tell it. And so ought all of us. "Let him that heareth say, Come."

"And let him that is athirst come" (vs. 17). Oh, here is a call for everyone who is tired of sin, for everyone who wants forgiveness, for everyone who wants peace of heart, for everyone who wants to lose the fear of death, everyone who wants to avoid the slavery of sin and be delivered from the damnation sin brings. Oh, then, whoever is thirsty, come to Jesus and be saved.

The Lord Jesus makes it wonderfully, positively clear, *"And whosoever will, let him take the water of life freely"* (vs. 17).

The Lord is saying that salvation is provided; that you don't have to work for it, that you don't have to beg for it—you simply have to accept it.

We hear silly talk about "easy believism" as if there were some merit in making salvation hard to get! Men speak as if they would like to take part of the credit away from Jesus Christ who paid the whole debt and on the cross cried out, "It is finished." No, God made it easy.

A mother suffers when a child is born but the child does not suffer. Jesus paid a marvelous price, an awful price that equated the torments of the damned in order to save sinners, but the sinner does not have to suffer to be saved, he does not have to weep to be saved; he has only to turn his penitent heart to accept salvation offered. Take the cup and drink it, dear sinner, for it is free!

What is the Scripture saying? "Come, come to Jesus." How often that theme comes up in the Scriptures.

"Come now, and let us reason together, saith the Lord: though your sins be as scarlet, they shall be as white as snow; though they be red like crimson, they shall be as wool."—Isa. 1:18.

"Ho, every one that thirsteth, come ye to the waters, and he that hath no money; come ye, buy, and eat; yea, come, buy wine and milk without money and without price. Wherefore do ye spend money for that which is not bread? and your labour for that which satisfieth not? hearken diligently unto me, and eat ye that which is good, and let your soul delight itself in fatness."—Isa. 55:1, 2.

"All that the Father giveth me shall come to me; and him that cometh to me I will in no wise cast out."—John 6:37.

"Suffer the little children to come unto me, and forbid them not: for of such is the kingdom of God."—Mark 10:14; Luke 18:16.

Believe? Yes; but the heart coming to Jesus—that, itself, is faith. Repent? Yes; but coming to Jesus means turning your heart from sin. That is repentance.

So all one must do is the heart's choice—*"take the water of life freely."* Come! He will never turn you down! Call on the Lord to forgive and save, for He said, "Whosoever shall call upon the name of the Lord shall be saved" (Rom. 10:13).

> Could my tears forever flow,
> Could my zeal no languor know,
> These for sin could not atone;
> Thou must save, and Thou alone:
> In my hand no price I bring,
> Simply to Thy cross I cling.

VERSES 18, 19:

18 For I testify unto every man that heareth the words of the prophecy of this book, If any man shall add unto these things, God shall add unto him the plagues that are written in this book:

19 And if any man shall take away from the words of the book of this prophecy, God shall take away his part out of the book of life, and out of the holy city, and *from* the things which are written in this book.

Awful Plague for Any Who Add to
or Take From Bible

The inspiration and authority of the Scriptures are literally in *"the WORDS of the prophecy"* (vs. 18) and *"the WORDS of the book of this prophecy"* (vs. 19). When the Bible speaks of inspiration it speaks of words literally given, that is, word-for-word inspiration, verbal inspiration. In Matthew 4:4 and Luke 4:4 Jesus said, "It is written, Man shall not live by bread alone, but by every word that proceedeth out of the mouth of God." About the commandments and so about all the Bible, Exodus 20:1 says, "And God spake all these words."

God gave the very *words of Scripture* to Isaiah. Isaiah 51:16 says, "And I have put my words in thy mouth." He said the same thing to Jeremiah (1:9). He said the same thing to Ezekiel (2:7; 3:4, 10). He said the same thing to David (II Sam. 23:2; Acts 4:25). So of all inspired revelation it is said, "Which things also we speak, not in the words which man's wisdom teacheth, but which the Holy Ghost teacheth; comparing spiritual things with spiritual" (I Cor. 2:13). We have Spirit-given matter and thoughts in Spirit-given words. The words are God's words in the original manuscript.

First, there is a plague on all who will add to the Word of God. To them it is stated the plague that shall be added is *"the plagues that are written in this book"* (vs. 18). One may truly be saved and fear he may lose salvation unless he constantly serves God. Spurgeon said that the carnal mind has a tendency to salvation by works. So assurance of salvation may come from the Bible some time after one trusts in Christ. I was saved at the age of nine but did not know for sure until three years later when I saw in the Scriptures, "He that believeth on the Son hath everlasting life" (John 3:16, 18, 36; 5:24; 6:40; 6:47; Acts 10:43; 13:38, 39; 16:31). Salvation is by trusting Christ, but assurance comes by the Word of God. Great sorrow and trouble come from adding works to help pay what Christ has paid fully.

At a Nazarene convention, Dr. Jack Hyles was introduced by an admiring chairman who said, "I believe Dr. Hyles is sanctified and doesn't realize it." Dr. Hyles replied, "I believe the chairman has everlasting life and eternal security and doesn't know it." How much anyone misses who adds to God's Word! He adds plagues and trouble.

There is, I think, clear reference in Revelation, chapters 13 and 17 particularly, to Romanism. Some add prayers to Mary, confession to a priest, saving efficacy to the Mass as a continual, literal sacrifice of Christ's body and blood. The eventual result will be the church of the Antichrist in the tribulation time.

It means destruction to all who depend on priest, church, ceremonies for salvation.

I have no doubt some Catholics, despite all the trappings and false teaching, have some way seen that they can trust Christ and be saved. But we are sure they never have the full peace and joy and growth they should have, plagued by these things added to the truth.

Alas, there are those who add other priests to Jesus, add Mass or ceremonies to salvation, add to their woes and often, perhaps usually, add damnation, with no genuine saving faith.

To Take From Word Means to Miss Salvation

God has offered a place in Heaven, a name to be written in the book of life, but there is no salvation except by the Saviour of the Scriptures on the terms stated in Scripture. To take essentially from the Scriptures means to miss Christ and the atonement, and so miss salvation.

The only Gospel by which people can be saved is stated in I Corinthians 15:3,4, ". . .how that Christ died for our sins according to the scriptures; And that he was buried, and that he rose again the third day according to the scriptures." This saving Gospel is (1) that man is such a sinner he must have a Saviour; (2) it states Christ's atoning death and burial; (3) it states His literal resurrection; (4) that it is on the authority, twice insisted on here, that it be "according to the scriptures." To take out any one of these true essentials destroys the Gospel. Paul said by inspiration: "But though we, or an angel from heaven, preach any other gospel unto you than that which we have preached unto you, let him be accursed. As we said before, so say I now again, If any man preach any other gospel unto you than that ye have received, let him be accursed" (Gal. 1:8,9).

In Mark 8:38 Christ put Himself and the Word of God both essentially in one package: "Whosoever therefore shall be ashamed of me and of my words in this adulterous and sinful generation; of him also shall the Son of man be ashamed, when he cometh in the glory of his Father with the holy angels."

In other words, no inspired Bible means no Saviour; no fallen man, no salvation; no deity of Christ, no salvation; no atoning death, no salvation; no bodily resurrection, no salvation; no infallible Scripture, no salvation.

God's honest preachers, fundamentalists, standing boldly for Christ and the Bible, are sometimes said to be "unbrotherly" to liberals. No unbelieving liberal is a Christian brother. Modernists are said to be so amiable, so uncritical, so pleasant, but they have no Gospel to lose, no Saviour to forsake. I have. Any sound, godly Christian has reason for holy indignation and open denunciation of those who would take the crown of deity from the head of Christ and the atoning blood from God's plan of salvation.

VERSES 20, 21:

20 He which testifieth these things saith, Surely I come quickly. Amen. Even so, come, Lord Jesus.

21 The grace of our Lord Jesus Christ be with you all. Amen.

Last Promise; Last Blessing

At the first, in Revelation 1:7 the theme of the book was given, "Behold, he cometh with clouds; and every eye shall see him, and they also which pierced him: and all kindreds of the earth shall wail because of him. Even so, Amen."

Here it is repeated as it was in 3:11 and 22:7, *"I come quickly."* Jesus reminds the saints at Thyatira, "Hold fast till I come." And let every reader take to heart the warning that Christ will come suddenly, unexpectedly. He may come at any moment. It will be in the twinkling of an eye, so sudden. Blessed are those virgins who have oil in their lamps. Blessed are those who watch continually for His coming and do His will now.

Fiction has painted the picture of a maiden whose lover left her for a voyage to the Holy Land, promising on his return to make her his beloved bride. Many told her that she would never see him again. But she believed his word, and evening by evening she went down to the lonely shore, and kindled there a beacon-light in sight of the roaring waves, to hail and welcome the returning ship which was to bring again her betrothed. And by that watchfire she took her stand each night, praying to the winds to hasten on the sluggish sails, that he who was everything to her might come.

Even so that blessed Lord, who has loved us unto death, has gone away to the mysterious Holy Land of Heaven, promising on His return to make us His happy and eternal Bride. Some say that He has gone forever, and that here we shall never see Him again. But His last word was, *'Yea, I come quickly.'* And on the dark and misty beach sloping out into the eternal sea, each true believer stands by the love-lit fire, looking, waiting, praying, hoping for the fulfillment of His word, in nothing gladder than in His pledge and promise, and calling ever from the soul of sacred love, *'Even so come, Lord Jesus.'* And some of these nights, while the world is busy with its gay frivolities, and laughing at the maiden on the shore, a form shall rise over the surging waves, as once on Galilee, to vindicate forever all this watching and devotion, and bring to the faithful and constant heart a joy, and glory, and triumph which never more shall end.—J. A. Seiss.

We join in the prayer, "Even so, come, Lord Jesus."

We join also in the request, "The grace of our Lord Jesus Christ be with you all." All the saved? Yes. Even if some virgins with oil are asleep and their lamps need trimming? Yes. God's grace be with them, too. With other sheep not of this fold? Yes. With them, too. With some born-again ones who do not abide in Christ, so according to I John 2:28 they will be "ashamed before him at his coming"? Yes. As God loves them we do, too, and we pray God's grace upon them.

May His grace be with them and with all, with Christians whose works mayhap are not abiding—gold, silver, precious stones—but wood, hay and stubble to be burned, as in I Corinthians 3:10-15? Yes. Oh, I seek to love all God's born-again, Christ-loving people. Amen.

Let Us Sing and Rejoice About Heaven

Lord, I care not for riches,
　Neither silver nor gold;
I would make sure of Heaven,
　I would enter the fold;
In the Book of Thy Kingdom,
　With its pages so fair,
Tell me, Jesus, my Saviour,
　Is my name written there?

Lord, my sins they are many,
　Like the sands of the sea,
But Thy blood, O, my Saviour,
　Is sufficient for me;
For Thy promise is written
　In bright letters that glow,
'Tho' your sins be as scarlet,
　I will make them like snow.

Oh, that beautiful city,
　With its mansions of light,
With its glorified beings,
　In pure garments of white;
Where no evil thing cometh
　To despoil what is fair;
Where the angels are watching,
　Is my name written there?-

Is my name written there,
  On the page white and fair?
In the book of Thy Kingdom,
  Is my name written there?

                    —Frank M. Davis.

Ira Stamphill wrote this beautiful song:

I'm satisfied with just a cottage below,
A little silver and a little gold;
But in that city where the ransomed will shine,
I want a gold one that's silver lined.

Tho' often tempted, tormented and tested
And like the prophet my pillow a stone;
And tho' I find here no permanent dwelling,
I know He'll give me a mansion my own.

Don't think me poor or deserted or lonely,
I'm not discouraged, I'm Heaven bound;
I'm just a pilgrim in search of a city,
I want a mansion, a harp and a crown.

I've got a mansion just over the hilltop,
In that bright land where we'll never grow old;
And some day yonder we will never more wander
But walk on streets that are purest gold.